THE SECRETS OF
ANZAC RIDGE

THE SECRETS OF ANZAC RIDGE
IN FLANDERS FIELDS

PATRICIA SKEHAN

hachette
AUSTRALIA

Book subtitle drawn from John McCrae's poem *In Flanders Fields*, published in 1915.

Any copyright holders who have been inadvertently omitted from acknowledgements and credits should contact the publisher and omissions will be rectified in subsequent editions.

hachette
AUSTRALIA

Published in Australia and New Zealand in 2025
by Hachette Australia
(an imprint of Hachette Australia Pty Limited)
Gadigal Country, Level 17, 207 Kent Street, Sydney, NSW 2000
www.hachette.com.au

Hachette Australia acknowledges and pays our respects to the past, present and future Traditional Owners and Custodians of Country throughout Australia and recognises the continuation of cultural, spiritual and educational practices of Aboriginal and Torres Strait Islander peoples. Our head office is located on the lands of the Gadigal people of the Eora Nation.

Copyright © Patricia Joyce Skehan 2025

This book is copyright. Apart from any fair dealing for the purposes of private study, research, criticism or review permitted under the *Copyright Act 1968*, no part may be stored or reproduced by any process without prior written permission. Enquiries should be made to the publisher.

A catalogue record for this book is available from the National Library of Australia

ISBN: 978 0 7336 5156 4 (paperback)

Cover design by Luke Causby / Blue Cork
Cover and internal photographs courtesy of the Australian War Memorial unless otherwise specified
Map by Laurie Whiddon, Map Illustrations
Author photograph courtesy of Westend Photography
Typeset in Adobe Garamond Pro by Kirby Jones
Printed and bound in Australia by McPherson's Printing Group

MIX
Paper | Supporting responsible forestry
FSC® C001695

The paper this book is printed on is certified against the Forest Stewardship Council® Standards. McPherson's Printing Group holds FSC® chain of custody certification SA-COC-005379. FSC® promotes environmentally responsible, socially beneficial and economically viable management of the world's forests.

My mother, Sophie McDonald, always encouraged me to pursue my dreams. She believed in my potential to become a published author and instilled in me the determination to achieve my goals. Her unwavering support has been a guiding light, inspiring me to keep writing and striving for success, no matter the obstacles. Rest in peace, Mum.

CONTENTS

Introduction — 1

Chapter 1	Enlisting	5
Chapter 2	Intelligence Reports	9
Chapter 3	Rendezvous Of The Empire	17
Chapter 4	Farewell To 'Anzac'	22
Chapter 5	Shattered Humanity	27
Chapter 6	Cobblestones For A Bed	35
Chapter 7	Monash Memories	41
Chapter 8	Welcome To Flanders, Boys	51
Chapter 9	Memories Of Steenwerck	56
Chapter 10	Hellfire Corner	67
Chapter 11	Tipperary	75
Chapter 12	News From The 44th	80
Chapter 13	2nd A.C.C.S. Steenwerck	90
Chapter 14	Anzac Ridge	97
Chapter 15	The Anzac Coves	105
Chapter 16	Strong Language	113
Chapter 17	Smoke And Debris	117
Chapter 18	The Old Inns	122
Chapter 19	Mademoiselle From Armentières	126
Chapter 20	Cobbers	132
Chapter 21	Finding Billets	136

Chapter 22	Back For A Rest	143
Chapter 23	Christmas At Steenwerck	147
Chapter 24	The Australian Corps	152
Chapter 25	A Definite Crisis	157
Chapter 26	A Constant Stream Of Bullets	169
Chapter 27	Desperate Times	177
Chapter 28	Corbie On The Somme	181
Chapter 29	Endless Trouble	187
Chapter 30	The Secret Of Circular Quay	196
Chapter 31	Ghosts Of Western Snows	208
Chapter 32	Zero Hour	217
Chapter 33	The Darkest Day	221
Chapter 34	A Military Solomon	230
Chapter 35	The Major's Pet Charger	235
Chapter 36	Behind The Hindenburg Line	245
Chapter 37	Lullaby Of The Guns	256
Chapter 38	Mademoiselle From Amiens	267
Chapter 39	Armistice Day	272
Chapter 40	A Villainous-Looking Lot	277
Chapter 41	Leaving The Battlefield	283
Chapter 42	Always There Are Poppies	285
Chapter 43	Turmoil After The War	290

Epilogue	Time and Eternity	297
Biography of James (Jim) Armitage		301
Timeline of the battles		305
Acknowledgements		309
About the Author		311
Endnotes		313

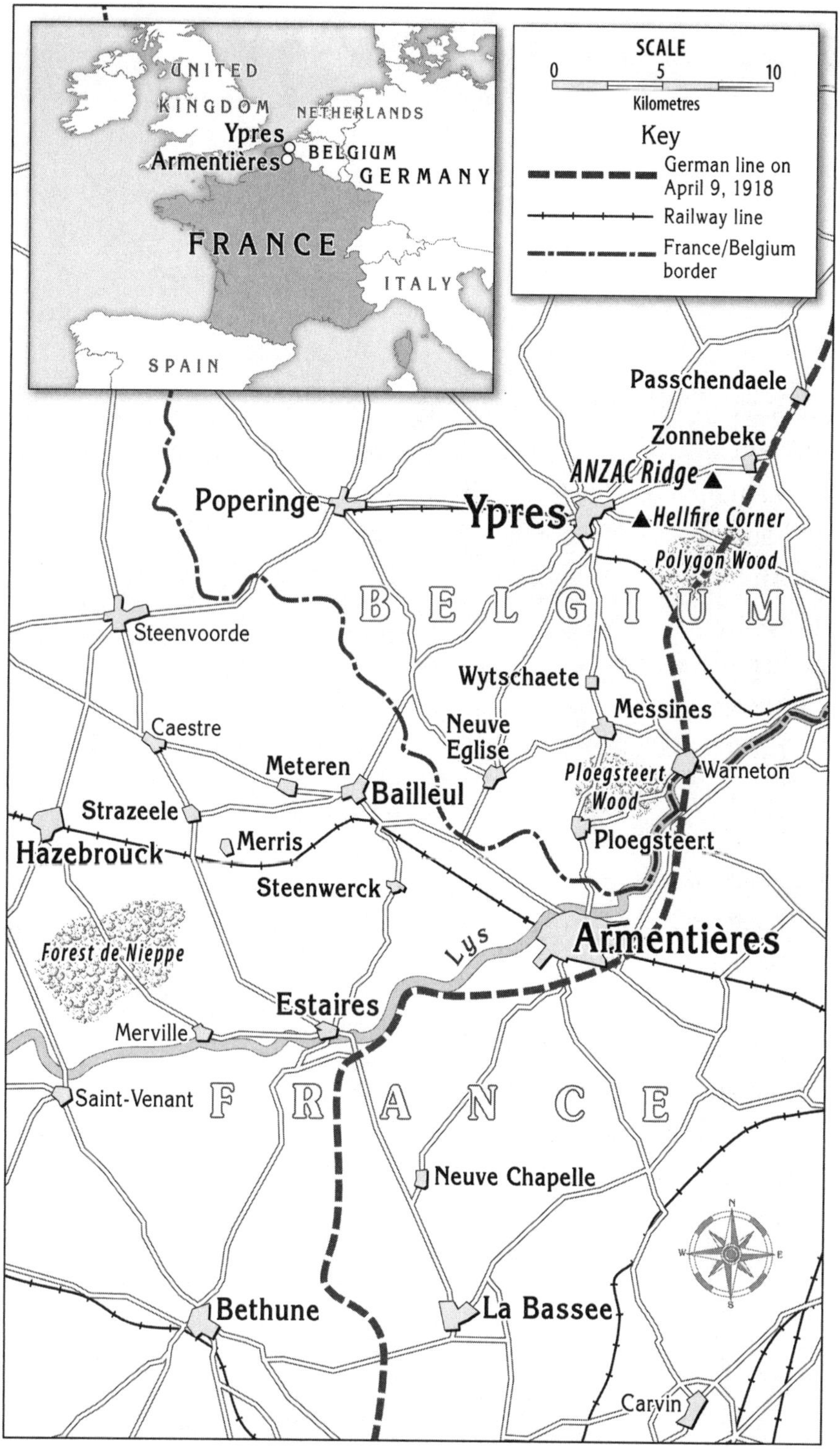

UNITED
KINGDOM
NETHERLANDS
Ypres
Armentières
BELGIUM
GERMANY
FRANCE
ITALY
SPAIN
SCALE
0
5
10
Kilometres
Key
German line on April 9, 1918
Railway line
France/Belgium border
Passchendaele
Zonnebeke
ANZAC Ridge
Poperinge
Ypres
Hellfire Corner
Polygon Wood
BELGIUM
Steenvoorde
Wytschaete
Messines
Caestre
Neuve Eglise
Meteren
Bailleul
Ploegsteert Wood
Warneton
Strazeele
Ploegsteert
Hazebrouck
Merris
Steenwerck
Armentières
Lys
Forest de Nieppe
Estaires
Merville
Saint-Venant
FRANCE
Neuve Chapelle
Bethune
La Bassee
Carvin

INTRODUCTION

WHAT IS TIME?
I asked the golden sun and silver spheres,
Those bright chronometers of days and years.
They answered, 'Time is but a meteor's flare,'
And bade us for eternity prepare.
William Marsden[1]

The Anzac legend is familiar to many, as are the names Anzac Cove and Anzac Ridge. The more well-known Anzac Ridge was at Gallipoli, but most people have never heard of the second Anzac Ridge. This site was located near Steenwerck in Flanders, Belgium. It was at this Anzac Ridge that several important victories were secured for the Allies in World War I: the battles of Passchendaele, Polygon Wood and Hellfire Corner.

During the war, censors strictly forbade the use of place names. Despite this, hundreds of letters from soldiers, doctors and nurses regularly appeared in Australian newspapers during the war years, many mentioning Steenwerck – one harmless name that the censor had not redacted.

I'd never heard of Steenwerck, but this town would prove to be synonymous with secrets. It at first appeared to be just another village in the path of the advancing German army. No references indicated that the location was of any military importance. Soldiers, resting away from the battlefront, even remarked about living a 'charmed life' there. The town had flown under the war radar for years, hiding its secrets in plain sight.

•

As an executive member of the City of Canada Bay Heritage Society, and their Publicity Officer since 1998, I have the privilege of guest-speaking to numerous groups on a range of heritage issues. The topics are mainly inspired by documents and photographs discovered within our extensive archives or have evolved from meeting like-minded people with amazing stories to tell. Our mission is to preserve and publish significant history.

Curiosity always gets the better of me. The thrill of discovering hidden historical gems and connecting the dots of history is so rewarding, especially when such information reveals cryptic clues to secrets of the past.

One day, I discovered references to this second Anzac Ridge in a WWI letter written to a grieving mother whose young son was killed on the ridge after being assigned to the wrong regiment. Further letters, including one from General Sir William Birdwood, revealed events at the height of the Passchendaele conflict. In other documents, soldiers recount their experiences of intense combat at Anzac Ridge.

I stared at my computer screen, puzzled. References to Steenwerck had also appeared in a letter I was transcribing about an earlier flu epidemic in Australia in 1919. In this particular letter, a young woman fleeing war-torn Flanders was anxious after being separated from her mother. All her other family members had died in the conflict. The letter had been sent to a Doctor Percy Davenport. Researching his history revealed little information at the

INTRODUCTION

time, but it was mysterious enough to pique my interest in him, the young woman and the town she was fleeing, Steenwerck, in Flanders.

•

Do you believe in coincidences? I don't. However, I do believe that fate weaves subtle threads into the fabric of our lives in ways that we don't recognise at those particular moments. As one chapter in life's events closes, another opens.

We were in lockdown in 2020 during the Covid-19 pandemic when an associate mentioned that her uncle, James (Jim) Armitage, was in Flanders from May 1918, according to his unpublished war diary. She asked me if I would like to read it.

I was amazed at the insight of Jim's writings, considering he was only eighteen years old when he enlisted. On his nineteenth birthday, Jim and seven mates were assigned to Monash's 3rd Division, 8th Brigade. Briefly leading that 'charmed life' in Flanders, they then headed for infamous battlefields: Messines. Péronne. Amiens. Villers-Bretonneux. Montbrehain.

During the Covid-19 pandemic, I found a purpose in attempting to recover more Anzac stories from history. So many tales remained untold; so many voices remained unheard. I embarked on a thorough journey through the archives.

During my research, I discovered many secrets, including the truth about Monash's *pigeons*, a group of specially trained spies. I then stumbled upon the identity of the Snow Ghost, an Australian commando feared by the Germans, with a high price upon his head.

Who were the Anzac Coves, and what was their mission of mercy? What caused such weird hallucinations in Steenwerck one day, and from whom did Madame Cognac source her endless supply of illicit alcohol?

Jim Armitage wrote of mayhem at the temporary bridge near Steenwerck, erected after dark each night and dubbed 'Circular Quay'; the codename meant to confuse spying eyes or eavesdropping ears.

I read many sources that were vivid, entertaining, heartbreaking and illuminating. Within the setting of the 2nd Australian Casualty Clearing Station at Steenwerck, and with the memories from doctors, nurses, soldiers, patients and stretcher-bearers stationed there, I learned about life on Flanders' battlefields. I discovered the true meaning behind the soldiers' songs 'It's a Long Way to Tipperary' and 'Mademoiselle from Armentières' in thought-provoking articles written by wartime professionals who chronicled the ongoing conflict.

In the war that was supposed to end all wars, there were no real victors. Everyone paid a price, whether they survived or perished. But life went on between the fierce battles, showing the resilience and humour of the Anzac spirit, particularly when the name 'Anzac' was threatened with being abolished.

The unique voices and memories I encountered ultimately became the catalyst for this book. Jim Armitage's diary, as well as the revelations about General Sir John Monash and his unique link to Steenwerck, serve as guiding threads through these experiences. Edited extracts from diary entries, letters and documents form the basis for the narrative. Details of the primary source material can be found in the endnotes.

From Flanders fields, these sources show the fragility of life, the irony of fate, the mental and physical tolls of war and the meaning of mateship.

Beyond the veil of death, Anzac voices reveal their secrets in the distance between time and eternity.

CHAPTER 1

ENLISTING

'Handpicked by the commanding officer for artillery work, we felt superior to the more down-to-earth infantry.'
Jim Armitage[2]

The official army medical file for James (Jim) Armitage describes him as 5ft 10in tall, with blue eyes, brown hair and a dark complexion. Armitage enlisted alongside several classmates from Sydney Grammar School. Jim's close friends and classmates, John Hay Roxburgh and Robert Shute, are mentioned frequently in his diary.

Despite overwhelming odds, Jim and his seven classmates survived the war.

In the following entries, Jim describes his experiences when enlisting.

Jim Armitage's diary[3]

May 1917. *Sydney.* I encountered unexpected events between enlisting in the Australian Imperial Force on 26 May at Victoria Barracks in Sydney, NSW, and disembarking in Le Havre in France on 1 May 1918.

After a few horrifying days and nights billeted at the Showground where we were issued with dungarees, boots made of cast iron I think, and straw to sleep on, and where we were given stew to eat which one wouldn't feed to pigs, I was drafted as a gunner in the Australian Field Artillery camp at Liverpool, NSW.

That experience made me feel homesick when I realised the stark difference between the civilian and army life. After strenuous training, each day I stumbled into my bunk so tired that I passed out, only to be woken in the unearthly hour by trumpets sounding Reveille that would drag us back into the world again.

I survived that first month, feeling fit and alive. With seven other friends who had enlisted together, we were drafted into the 32nd Reinforcements. Handpicked by the commanding officer for artillery work, we felt superior to the more down-to-earth infantry. Our training imparted new skills like map reading, range finding, handling horses, and driving a gun team.

Before we embarked for overseas in November, Colonel Cox-Taylor gave us a frank talk about what we would encounter in combat and how to behave accordingly. Excited and het up, we cheered him wildly. From Central Station to the docks, crowds lined the way as they offered to carry our kitbags.

After boarding His Majesty's Australian Transport Ship *Canberra*, a flotilla of tooting ferries and boats escorted us to The Heads, the entrance to Sydney Harbour. HMAT SS *Canberra* was crammed with reinforcements for The Light Horse, Camel Corps, Engineers, and Infantry. We were squeezed together in suspended hammocks that touched each other, swaying with the ship's movements. When packed away in the morning, there was room for tables, chairs, and a boxing ring. I gained a reputation as a boxer after mentioning that I took lessons. None of my mates would take me on. I stayed away from other troops as I was bluffing and couldn't fight my way out of a paper bag.

At Fremantle we were given six hours' leave. Our party consisted of Phippard, Wilkinson, Street, Brunton and me. We enjoyed an excellent dinner at the Esplanade hotel, our last healthy meal for months.

24 *November.* Took on Western Australian reinforcements. A calm, uneventful voyage, arriving in Colombo on December 5. Port authorities allowed half of our men to disembark and march through town to stretch our legs, but when we reached Barracks Square, we were locked in. That did it! We were perfectly orderly until then. Port authorities certainly didn't understand Australian soldiers, as a considerable number made a bolt for it. We jumped over the walls and took whatever local transport we could find – bikes, rickshaws, and carriages or whatever came along – and headed back into the city.

Because of this perceived mutiny, Port authorities would not allow any more troops to come ashore, which provoked forty men to slide over the side into empty coal barges. They did not get far before the ship's officers made a half-hearted attempt to arrest the absconders. A mass of jostling men blocked the passageways and decks, while our mates at the stern hauled the fugitives back on board.

8 *December.* We sailed from Colombo, joined by the New Zealand troopship *Tafua*, and the British light cruiser HMS *Juneau*, both troopships escorting us to Aden where we parted company.

15 *December.* I contracted measles and was quarantined with thirteen or fourteen other soldiers. The isolation ward had only four bunks. Treated badly with no attention or food, we slept on the open deck. We sailed into a heavy rainstorm, which did not improve our feverish condition. As I lay drenched on my straw palliasse, I decided I'd had enough, found my kit, and went below. Many choose to sleep on deck due to heat and to the imminent threat of torpedoes.

Arriving in Suez on a glorious day without a breath of wind, we were escorted into port by British aeroplanes, silhouetted against the orange and golden glow of a fantastic sunset.

Next morning, we went by ambulance to the Anglo-Egyptian hospital in Suez. After weeks in the rough but comfortable isolation ward, we snuck out the back gate to borrow donkeys and rode at breakneck speed for miles over the desert. We had recovered sufficiently to celebrate Christmas with the Governor, who provided us with a sumptuous feast.

1 *January*, 1918. Ranken* and I re-joined our unit. Given ten day's convalescence leave, we avoided slogging marches and spent most of our time at an aerodrome nearby. 5000 men in camp would be sent to various destinations, reinforcing units: The Light Horse and Camel Corps to Cairo; the Artillery, Engineers, and Infantry to England. At Port Said, we embarked on HMTS *Kashgar*, bound for Naples. We sailed, escorted by two Japanese destroyers.

18 *January*. One destroyer started firing rapidly at some object ahead, while we turned about and made off in the opposite direction with all speed, the second destroyer circling around us. Shortly after that there was a muffled explosion. The Japanese had exploded a mine dropped by a submarine as it submerged.

20 *January*. We arrived off Taranto and were escorted by light Italian gunboats through a minefield into Taranto Harbour, which was crowded with Italian battleships. We wondered why they weren't out escorting convoys through the submarine-infested waters. Taken ashore in barges, we marched to a camp in an olive grove. Next day we entrained for France.

On our arrival at Cherbourg, we had a medical inspection and a welcome hot meal. After dark we embarked on a small cross-channel steamer and were escorted to the nearby coast of England. Next morning, delayed by fog at the wharf, we amused ourselves by watching a variety of brand-new-looking Yanks arriving with their extraordinary equipment. Some officers even carried leather suitcases and umbrellas, looking more like commercial travellers than soldiers. We searched in vain for a bowler hat!

---

*   Arthur Ranken, Jim's fellow soldier and former classmate.

CHAPTER 2

INTELLIGENCE REPORTS

'I hope that in writing about these matters you do not deal too hardly with me for disobeying orders.'
Sir John Monash[4]

'You can't use anything from the Monash diaries,' was the official response from the Australian War Memorial to my request to quote Sir John's wartime words. 'We republished his diaries in 2014; they will not be out of copyright again till 2084.'

'But I won't be alive by then,' I pleaded.

However, Monash's descendants heard about my A.W.M. request. They asked for copies of the chapters that I wanted to use to explain connections between Jim Armitage, that Steenwerck reference, and Sir John's diary entries. Did I dare reveal what I had discovered about Sir John Monash's last hours at Gallipoli? About what he smuggled out of Gallipoli, against strict military orders?

I knew that secrecy and censorship were strictly enforced during wartime, but that familiar phrase 'Do as I say, not as I do' comes to mind when reflecting on how Sir John Monash disobeyed such military orders.

An article published after the war in 1929 would disclose the following facts about the evacuation of Gallipoli in 1915.

The Herald[5]

Strict instructions were issued that no man was to leave behind a scrap of writing, not a letter or a paper that might possibly give any information to the enemy afterwards. Sir John's men were in one of the last batches to leave Gallipoli. They had marched in breathless silence for a mile and a half when Sir John discovered to his horror that he had left his despatch-case, filled with important letters and vital documents, in his dugout!

> 'I hadn't the pluck to explain to them … but I told them to carry on as if I had something to do. Then I went back as hard as I could go to my dugout and recovered the papers. I was quite alone, but I raced back to re-join my men and managed to get to them safely.'

The point of the story is that, for the whole of that dash back and the desperate return, a mile and a half each way, there was actually nothing between Sir John and the Turkish army. The Turks were over yonder in their thousands, while one lonely soldier was here – hurrying back through the night, and then setting off again to rejoin his men. If the Turks had but known!

I asked Sir John if I might publish this story. Here is his characteristic letter in reply:

> 'Regarding that story I told you about the night of the evacuation – by all means, use it if it is of interest to you. I should add that the despatch-case which I went back to find contained not only the whole of the orders for the evacuation – which we had been strictly enjoined to destroy after perusal, but which I wickedly hung on to as an historical souvenir – but also contained the diary letter to my folk at home, which contained a detailed account of

everything that had happened in my part of the Anzac position from the date – some ten days previously – when senior officers first became aware, confidentially, that the evacuation was to take place. It would have been very disastrous if all these documents had fallen into enemy hands.'

•

Monash was the chief of Intelligence Corps in Victoria from 1908 until World War I. When war was declared, Monash was appointed Chief Censor for Australia, a position he held until he became a brigade commander in the Australian Infantry Force (A.I.F).

He left Australia in command of the 4th Infantry Brigade and was at Gallipoli continuously from the landing on 25 April 1915 till the evacuation in the following December. Monash was mentioned three times in dispatches. Monash Valley at Gallipoli bears his name.

General Monash's staff
The Sun[6]
He had the full cooperation of brilliant commanders and staff officers, who served him faithfully and loyally, as they had previously served General Sir William R. Birdwood, Commander of A.I.F. at Gallipoli.

Before battle, he regularly assembled all his staff, and together thrashed out every detail of proposed operations. By this method, every man knew not only what was expected of him, but also what everyone else was to do. Once settled, the battleplan was never tinkered with, for early experience had shown that such tinkering invariably produced confusion and delay. The result of this policy was clarity of understanding and decisive early action.

By this method confidence was established right from headquarters to the front line.

In referring to the bulk of his permanent officers of the A.I.F., Monash had nothing but praise. He was particularly impressed with Lieutenant-General Sir C. B. B. White, whom he described as an ideal staff officer of brilliant mentality.

General Blamey was mentioned as an ideal helper, while divisional commanders Generals Hobbs and Rosenthal were in the technical professions. They were formerly architects, and he an engineer. All were gunners in the earlier stages of their military careers.

The only professional divisional commander was General MacLagan who, before the war, was Director of Training at Duntroon.

•

The above article went on to discuss the psychology of the Australian soldier with regard to his sporting instinct.[7] A field commander had to correctly judge the kind of appeal to make to the men at contrasting times, the same appeal not always being the right one. The right appeal to make was determined by passing events, the state of the men themselves, the state of the enemy and the situation generally. As the article states, 'One appeal that never failed was the honour and prestige of the Army, a stronger appeal than any wishy-washy stuff about fighting for liberty, the oppressor's destruction, or anything of that sort.'[8]

Intelligence staff

The following sources reveal the intelligence network that Monash had gathered around him within his division.

The Sun[9]

Major Stewart Hunn was chief of the Intelligence Staff. It was not the actual work which he did himself – which was valuable – so much as his organisation of the intelligence service throughout the corps. There were two or three German speakers in every battalion, obtained from amongst the Australians, many of whom could speak fluent German. He commented that one Australian sergeant-major drilled the German prisoners in German almost as well as their own German sergeant-major.

The Richmond River Herald[10]

The Intelligence Service also organised a system of a dozen men from each battalion, specially trained to watch for smoke and dust, aeroplanes, gunfire, the movements of troops, movements on the central railways and roads, anything that gave correct inferences from their observations to read the signs of the times. These men were trained and then let loose in their units to gain actual experience in this work.

One particular man, perched up in a tree, might not glean much information himself, but by piecing together information obtained from men at different posts, valuable information was secured. That a new division was going out, or an attack threatened, was deduced by the enemy either wiring himself in if he did not intend to attack; or pulling up his barb-wire, which generally indicated an impending assault.

G.H.Q. kept a small gang of trained spies, never more than half-a-dozen, referred to as the *pigeons*. They were men who looked like Germans. Whenever a battle was anticipated, these soldiers grew their beards for three or four days, and donned Boche uniforms. Speaking German fluently, they were fully coached in what troops were in front of them, they knew of passing events, and read the latest captured German newspapers.

When prisoners were put into a yard with one of our apparently despondent chaps, they would get into conversation and in this way obtain much valuable information.

•

Monash's qualities

The next source shows the foresight of Monash when interacting with other generals, the way he encouraged his junior officers to use their initiative, and his free-thinking attitude to handling his troops.

The Sun[11]

Doubtless the German High Command, before making General Monash's acquaintance in battle, regarded him with contempt; just now they are frantically busy trying to prevent him taking a slice of the Hindenburg Line.

General Monash, like all good generals, is pre-eminently positive, and the whole quality of his attitude of mind shows a confidence to succeed in any task. His military inspiration is for a pertinacious offensive. Hence the Australians in France have been fighting without respite for 24 months and as a result have wrested from the Huns over 100 villages and 200 square miles of French territory. You can motor rapidly for two hours due east of Amiens and not reach the limits of the Australian captures since April.

General Monash attributes his success to the devotion and skill of junior officers, most of whom were commissioned in France. Although the general consensus at that time was that a democratic army and wholesale promotions would deprive us of officer caste and be a dreadful thing, he found the exact opposite. It was a true and successful system. By opening the way to ambition, it stimulated ambition, and he reaped the advantages of having the best men in the right jobs. Many junior officers would prove to be dazzling successes, as shown by the honours won.

There was a good deal of scepticism concerning discipline in the Australian army. Some thought that in excessive freedom there was too much of the spirit of civil life, and too little of the machine-like character.

'Now, see those men out there,' General Monash once said, pointed to a struggling corps in the field nearby, 'They are not saluting me. Their general is passing, but they carry on. We don't make too much of these symbols of discipline; what we want is not signs but discipline itself. One of the supreme final tests of discipline is that every man at the appointed time and place will be resolutely ready to do his job.'

General Monash and his staff were full of admiration for the Australians re-bridging the Somme Canal and swamps beyond. They swiftly built pontoons across the deep water, constructing a wide bridge capable of handling guns and lorries of great weight; this work being completed within 48 hours, under continuous fire.

Questioned about German morale, General Monash thought that they were a long way from the end, but the Hun was beaten. If the weather proved favourable he expected that the enemy would be out of France by Christmas but couldn't say the same about Belgium.

He was asked, 'You don't regard the Hindenburg Line as too formidable?'

'No,' replied General Monash. 'It will be taken in due course.'

Ducked my bloody head

An amusing article showed General Birdwood's sense of humour.

Don Dorrigo Gazette[12]

Meanwhile, General Birdwood told an English colonel of the old British ramrod type, just how difficult it was to make the Australians understand that they must salute their officers. 'In fact,' he said, 'they rarely take any notice of us, and show no reverence for officers.'

The colonel was righteously indignant and muttered something about 'teach the beggars a lesson if he had them.'

General Birdwood smiled and went on to relate this story. He was going the rounds of the trenches when he came upon a big Queenslander doing sentry duty who, beyond a casual glance, took no notice of the general. Presently, however, he saw a shell coming, and yelled, 'Duck your bloody head, Birdie.'

'And what did you do?' gasped the horrified colonel, evidently expecting to hear of a court-martial.

'Do?' responded the general with a twinkle in his eye. 'Why, I did as I was told. I ducked my bloody head.'

CHAPTER 3

RENDEZVOUS OF THE EMPIRE

'I was afraid that Gallipoli had swallowed up all the Australians, but one evening I found this little Flanders town crowded with brown-faced men, wearing that well-known sombrero with the rising-sun badge.'
Dr Joseph Dawson[13]

The unnamed refugee

This is the letter I mentioned earlier containing an appeal for support from a young woman fleeing war-torn Flanders, who was anxious after being separated from her mother. All her other family members had died in the conflict. The letter had been sent to Doctor Percy Davenport, a soldier recuperating at home in Singleton, NSW. He had returned to Australia from Steenwerck in Flanders.

In the following extracts, the unnamed letter-writer explains her plight during the Fourth Battle of Ypres, when Steenwerck was in the direct firing line of the German advance.

April 1918. You will have seen in the papers that we have been compelled to leave Steenwerck ... Our flight has been terrible. We could bring nothing with us and have had to leave everything behind. I assure you it was awful. I am now here in Normandy not far from Jersey. Life is very calm and quiet compared with what we have just passed through and seen. There are many things I wish I could tell you, but it is impossible, the censor not permitting any mention of such matters ...

Just before leaving Steenwerck I saw the Major who had just returned from Italy. I have written to him also to tell him that I am a refugee, safe but heartbroken ...

I hope that you have quite recovered and that your wife is well. I do so hope that you will write to me and sometimes think of the happy times passed at Steenwerck with the officers of the 2nd Australian Division ...

Unsigned

What could Doctor Davenport have done? After convalescing, he had become the Medical Officer at the Walker Emergency Hospital in Concord West, in Sydney, NSW. The 2nd Australian Casualty Clearing Station (A.C.C.S.) situated at Steenwerck no longer existed. Surviving staff had returned to their pre-war hospitals or homes.

The doctors at Steenwerck

I went back in time in my research which disclosed that Doctor Davenport served at the 2nd Australian Casualty Clearing Station. Finding its location was in Steenwerck also revealed information about a colleague, Surgeon-Doctor Joseph Dawson.

Dawson's writings from 1915 detailed being in charge of the officers' section of the Casualty Clearing Station. His words brought Steenwerck's setting to light in very dramatic terms.

Surgeon-Captain Joseph Dawson, *The Register*[14]

30 December 1915. French Belgium is usually a wonderful place, but now it is dismal, dull, wet, and cold. The countryside is desolate and in many places so devastated. The mud is beyond speech, the towns are depressing and unlighted. Further up, amid ruined villages, the troops are billeted in filthy outhouses or are hanging onto trenches full of mud and water, which threaten to cave in under the disintegrating influence of almost incessant rain.

Sometimes in unbiased, detached ways, one wonders why sane, intelligent soldiers should be floundering around in Flemish mud, instead of enjoying the warmth and comfort of their own civilization. But, after all, it is a wonderful place – the meeting place of Imperial Britain.

While seeking food at the local railway station, I met a doctor friend from Singapore, breakfasting on rolls and coffee. He was looking for a brigade of Royal Field Artillery to which he had been attached as a Medical Officer.

In a little teashop, where G.H.Q. (general headquarters) reside, I encountered a young graduate in medicine from Sydney, with whom I had travelled on a mailboat. He was the Medical Officer to a battalion of Scottish Fusiliers. I later heard that he was killed within the month by a trench mortar.

That day, being near headquarters, I sought the Red Cross Society's storeman to beg extra comforts and equipment for our new Officers' Hospital. I found to my surprise, that it was Mr. Ken Rumford, whom I last saw performing with his wife at the Adelaide Exhibition Building. Ken is a well-known singer, giving concerts for the Red Cross. He's now taking an active role using his own motorcar to transport the wounded from the frontlines to our base hospital.

When the Officers' Clearing Station was first opened, two patients, who lay in adjoining beds, recognised one another. They had last met in a Peruvian jungle.

A wounded subaltern of the Rifle Brigade proved to be a lad I had known years ago in Brighton, as a schoolboy. The veterinary surgeon of my old Territorial Brigade of Gunners, a doctor from York where I used to live, and also a man who was at school with me, both of them arrived in the same week.

An Officer of the Line, who received a Military Cross while he was in our hospital, was an erstwhile Fourth Mate on the P. & O. liner, the SS *Mongolia*.*

A flying visit to a neighbouring town enabled me to meet, on the same afternoon, a brother-in-law I had not seen for three or four years, and a well-known cricketing padre, whom I had encountered previously.

Now scarcely a day passes that I do not admit to my care someone I have met somewhere in this or the southern hemisphere.

I was afraid that Gallipoli had swallowed up all the Australians, but one evening I found this little Flanders town crowded with brown-faced men, wearing that well-known sombrero with the rising-sun badge. As these Diggers marched down the street, elderly peasants paused to gaze after them and muttered in awed tones, 'Ah! Les Australiennes [sic].'

They were the No. 1 Australian Divisional Supply Column, acting as Supply to the No. X Division of Kitchener's Army ...

Dreary, dirty Flanders is indeed the rendezvous of Empire. The 'legions that never were listed' are gathered here from the Five [sic] Continents and the Seven Seas.

•

A morass of mud

The following extracts highlight the difficulty faced when supplying the troops, often under constant fire, and the dangers faced by the stretcher-bearers.

---

*   Sunk June 1917.

The Argus[15]
The Supply Corps attached to the Anzacs do wonders getting up food and ammunition in view of the counter-attacks, though recent repeated blows have so weakened the enemy that they may well be content to sit still and nurse their wounds.

Stretcher-bearers worked throughout the night. At one time it was necessary to call for volunteers to man the stretchers. Several New Zealanders responded but were then shot by German snipers, and four more men were wounded within minutes. The New Zealanders effectively initiated stern retaliatory measures, and by midday all the wounded were brought in …

A review of the present British line shows that Australians are in the forefront, their greatest advance being the Anzac centre about two-thirds of a mile along the top of the ridge, near the railway towards Passchendaele village. Substantial numbers of our most gallant soldiers have given their blood for this place, going through hell in efforts to take it.

Newcastle Morning Herald[16]
Our Ops. Commander thanked the Red Cross society for helping us in Australia (before leaving), in Egypt, and for the last six months in France. We have the honour to be one of the most advanced clearing stations well up near the front and have a complete electric lighting plant. The army is now equipping all the others.

Colonel Stacy, founder and first commanding officer of this field hospital since the unit was formed in Melbourne, remained at Trois Arbres until the Germans broke through the line in the last months of the war. Patients had to be hastily evacuated by motor lorries. The staff made their escape on foot. From this time up to the signing of the Armistice the hospital was continually moving, owing to the enemy's advance.

CHAPTER 4

FAREWELL TO 'ANZAC'

'I don't care a damn for your loyal service
when you think I am right; when I really want it
most is when you think I am wrong.'
Sir John Monash[17]

An email arrived from Sir John Monash's relatives, forwarded by the Australian War Memorial. With a sense of anticipation, I carefully read the contents. They granted me permission to delve into Monash's diaries, a treasure trove of historical secrets, and to print the related chapters. Among the revelations, one stood out: Monash's unexpected connection to the infamous bushranger Ned Kelly. The diaries painted a vivid picture of their encounters, each entry more astonishing than the last.

But perhaps the most shocking discovery was the government's plan to abolish the name 'Anzac'. The very thought left me astounded, a stark reminder of how history's tides can shift in the most unexpected ways. At that time, the diggers had no conception of the significance that the Anzac name would eventually bear.

The following interview with General Monash covers his reaction to the proposed abolition of the name 'Anzac' and reveals surprising highlights from his career.

Reporter Norman Campbell, interview for the *Daily Mercury*[18]

Once I asked General Monash that very question, 'What was the proudest moment of your career?'

Monash knit [sic] his brows for a moment in his characteristic way and said, 'I've had two proud moments which I recall. One was when I called a council of war just before we broke the Hindenburg Line; the other was when I had a yarn with Ned Kelly.'

Of course, I asked for details as to both events.

'I was a school kid at Jerilderie,' explained Sir John, 'when Ned Kelly and his gang took possession of the township and held it for three days. That was in February 1879. Like all the other youngsters in the place, I was keen to get a glimpse of the famous outlaw. So I went round in the morning, rather early, to the hotel which Ned had made his headquarters, and saw him come out of the place and squat on the veranda's edge to have a smoke. He beckoned me over, and asked my name and so forth, and then he gave me a short lecture. I can assure you, a Sunday school superintendent couldn't have given me sounder advice as to human conduct.

"The council of war I called on the Western Front on the occasion I have mentioned was a ticklish business. I wasn't afraid that I couldn't convince my Australian generals that I was right, but several British generals were also present. Each one of these was a professional soldier. Each had been born into the cast-iron traditions of the British Army. Each subconsciously felt some disdain for my views – I, a mere citizen soldier. Well, I had to convince these men that my plan was the best possible in the circumstances, and not only that, but send them away from that council enthusiastic about it, and eager to carry it out. I did it. That, I think, was really the proudest moment of my life.'

Sir John spoke with concern about the threatened abolition of the name ANZAC. 'This event long foreshadowed, and prompted by the Commonwealth Government, has at last come to pass. The Commander-in-Chief (Sir Douglas Haig) decided about ten days ago that all Australians should go into one corp. So the name Anzac[19] disappears. 2nd Anzac as a corps name disappears, and 1st Anzac becomes the Australian Corps. The Chief is obdurate that the corps shall contain only four divisions. At the same time, our reinforcements have fallen off so badly, it became a question as to which one of the five divisions would have to go. Mine was the youngest in the field, but universally regarded as the best of the five.

'Therefore it was no surprise to me when I learned the Fourth Division was to go. They are not going actually to break it up, in case conscription goes through, and later we may be able to build it up again. But the Fourth Division (MacLagan) goes away to the base and will be used as a recruiting ground for the other four divisions.

'I find myself once more in command of the same sector of front which I captured in June and July, with my headquarters at the old place at Steenwerck, and the 5th Division is on my left, 1 and 2 being in reserve. These latter two will relieve 3 and 5 in about a month's time.'

Lieutenant Stewart Hansen

Lieutenant Stewart Hansen was aide-de-camp to Monash. He died of wounds in France on his 23rd birthday in February 1917. Hansen's entry showcases the troubled feelings of Anzac soldiers when they heard about the proposed abolition of the term 'Anzac'.

Williamstown Advertiser[20]

Under General Monash our battalion strength has been enormously increased during the last month owing to the influx of reinforcements, but changes of immense proportions are to take place during this week.

The most sorrowful part about the whole business is that the original Anzacs are to be no more. The 4th brigade will be detached from New Zealanders. There is weeping and gnashing of teeth in consequence as we have trained, fought, and suffered together for upwards of twelve months.

To celebrate the farewell the New Zealanders gave a farewell concert and smoke night. The New Zealand general felt it so keenly that, on attempting to speak, he broke down.

General Monash also felt the parting. He gave an eloquent speech of farewell, which caused rousing cheers. Our friends, the Māori, headed by their Despatch Rider, then danced a farewell *hacka* [haka] in full warrior dress and paint, the D. R. prefacing the performance with a short speech in excellent English. Afterwards the officers were entertained. We arrived in camp at midnight.

Anzac, a name sacrosanct

The contention around the term 'Anzac' is further discussed in the following article.

Casterton News[21]

July 1916. An appeal is being made to manufacturers and to other traders in Great Britain to abstain from use of the word Anzac as a trade description in order to avoid wounding the feelings of Australian and New Zealanders, to whom the name is very dear.

Australians and New Zealanders alike have special interest in the name coined by them out of the initial letters of the Australian-New Zealand Army Corps. Both were included in operations on Gallipoli, with camps or bases on the small bay they christened Anzac Cove. The place so named has been made sacred through its baptism with the blood of Australians and New Zealanders, and the graves therein where fallen Anzacs sleep the sleep of death.

The hope is that Australian and New Zealand Parliaments, in conformity to the general sentiment of the people they represent and the feelings of the Anzacs who survive, will make it an offence to use the words *Anzac* and *Anzacs* in any other way than in association with the place, men and events to which they were originally applied, and with the special significance originally attached to them through the glory won for themselves and for their respective comrades by the splendid gallantry of the soldiers who will live in history as the Anzacs.

Tramp! Tramp! Tramp!

Despite the soldiers' 'splendid gallantry', the reality was often different after the war. This following piece recalls a post-war march taking place in 1922.

Evening News[22]

There comes to you from the distance the sound of a band, and a measured, steady tramping of men. It carries strangely through the City air. There is in it life, spirit, and vigour. It gives you a sense of alertness. You step smartly along. Tramp! Tramp! Tramp!

There was in that measured sound a note of challenging. A note of invincibility. The band played gloriously. The crowd cheered madly in its pride of these men swinging gallantly along – in those days. The soul, the spirit of marching. Triumph and power were in it – in those days.

In these days a bedraggled khaki figure, supported on crutches, stands on the corner – the spirit of marching now dead to him. He did not see that destiny ahead in the years gone by.

The little box he rattled was empty. One sleeve of his tunic just as empty. 'Spare a penny for the band?' – 'All Diggers!' The City crowd passes him by.

CHAPTER 5

SHATTERED HUMANITY

'The appreciation we receive from the lads makes our work worthwhile.'
Sister Mary Jane Derrer[23]

A nurse in France

Sister Mary Derrer nursed thousands of wounded soldiers back to health and strength when they met with disaster.

'The 60th, over the top...'[24]

'The air was thick with bullets...'[25]

'Hundreds mown down in the flicker of an eyelid...'[26]

'Cut in two...'[27]

'A sniper – my – brother...'[28]

'Keep under the parapet...'[29]

Sister Derrer heard these snatches as she treated the maimed soldiers who had appeared in their hundreds. Many more, beyond human aid, had been left behind in the wire entanglements where they fell.

The 2nd Australian Casualty Clearing Station was three miles from Ploegsteert Wood, Messines. This station, nearest to the trenches, comprised a collection of huts and tents in the vicinity of which shells continuously fell, but the doctors and the nurses stuck to their posts. For courage under fire, four Australian nurses, including Sister Derrer, were awarded the Military Medal.

Isolated within the danger zone, a continuous stream of casualties arrived from the trenches; some staying for weeks, others to pass on. During the Messines fighting, the strain upon the hospital and its workers was tremendous; thousands of cases handled, foe as well as friendly.

Mary Derrer was interviewed in a long article published in the *Daily Mercury* (Mackay) on 18 December 1917.[30] She had returned to her hometown in Queensland after two and a half years on active service. In the interview, Sister Derrer supplied interesting facts relating to her war experiences.

Further extracts showcase the harrowing experiences of nurses as they risked their lives near the battlefront, as well as the high respect they were shown by soldiers.

Daily Mercury[31]

Reticent when asked about the details of her nursing experiences, Sister referred instead to a letter received from a soldier, one of scores sent to them from time to time, eloquent of the attention that men get from their nurses. 'This,' added the Sister, 'is one of hundreds of similar appreciations we nurses receive from the lads, and it makes our work worth while.'

> Just a note to say good-bye, and to thank you for your goodness to me. You saved my life when we all thought it had petered out, and you have looked after me scrupulously ever since. Sister, I do not even know your name, but I love you. And yet, not you exactly, but rather an incarnation of all the nurses who have tended me since this war began.
>
> A wonderful woman, 'A lady with a lamp!'

I cannot thank you enough, but there is a little girl down under who would like to, and who will in her heart when she hears about you. Now, what shall I call you when I tell my people down yonder about you? My Steenwerck – no, that's no good – my Australian sister. What could be nicer?

And they will respect and honour you as if they had seen and known you personally. I was never too good at saluting officers, but I would go out of my way to salute a nurse.

With this I salute you.

In the big Messines stunt, more than 1,000 men were attended at No. 2 A.C.C.S. in 20 hours. The staff at this station varied from 24 to 15, according to the work in the lines. So far as the nurses were concerned there was no time for idleness, Sister being of the opinion that these outstations were understaffed. 'But then,' she added, 'our work is nothing to what the boys are doing in the trenches.'

So close to the lines, the clearing station was subjected at times to a shower of missiles from British shrapnel sent up by anti-aircraft guns to chase German aviators off forbidden ground. 'The apostles of Kultur' obtained a direct hit on the hospital, resulting in five men being killed, two shockingly mangled, twenty others wounded.

One bomb fell within one hundred yards of Sister Derrer. The missiles flew everywhere. Pandemonium reigned amongst the patients but the nurses on duty, three in number, including Sister Derrer, together with the doctors, calmed the fears of the inmates, and the wounded were soon having their injuries attended to. This work was done in the dark because of their electric installation being damaged.

Sister Derrer secured the Military Medal, and received a letter from General Birdwood, in which he stated:

I write to tell you how very pleased I am to see that you have been awarded the Military Medal in recognition of your fine conduct during the bombing of your hospital on the night of the 22nd of July last.

The courage and presence of mind which you displayed were admirable and have thoroughly earned you this decoration, upon which I send you my heartiest congratulations.

With my kind regards,

W. Birdwood.

Sister Derrer was requested to attend Buckingham Palace to be presented with the decoration but, about to leave for Australia, she was unable to go.

Queensland Times[32]

The nights were terrible but beautiful, the sky and earth being irradiated with star shells and searchlights, making the place as light as day.

When off duty the Australian nurses sat outside their small, collapsible tents listening to the guns booming and watching the play of lights towards Armentieres and the Somme.

The Daily Mail[33]

One form of entertainment the nurses had was watching aerial encounters. A Lieutenant in the Australian Flying Corps flew for the exceptional period of 127 hours over one week, during which he brought down two German planes. One day this Lieutenant found himself surrounded by a swarm of German fighters. His machine was nearly shot to pieces, with the propeller knocked off and the under-carriage smashed. While knocked unconscious for a short period, his machine dropped 6,000 feet. He awoke, conscious of impending death, but managed to regain control. Gliding down inside the British lines, he crashed into a shell hole. Only slightly injured, he had a remarkable escape from death.

Probably the most picturesque, though awe-inspiring, scene witnessed by Sister Derrer was the reflection and noise of intense bombardments from the *heavies*, which continued sometimes right up till midnight, and lit up the surrounding country for miles.

For a time, she could not sleep on account of the terrific din, but soon accustomed herself to it. One trouble was the night alarms of bombs and gas attacks, which necessitated them hopping out of bed and seeking shelter in an uninviting dug-out.

'Eight or nine months of this,' added Sister Derrer, 'makes one fed up with sunny France but, after my holiday, I will be glad to get back amongst the soldiers again.'

Death of a major-general

Major-General 'Pompey' Elliott was a famous and well-revered leader among the troops. Soldiers and civilians alike followed his adventurous career.

Being used to the glory and the adrenaline of living dangerously, his death by suicide after the war's end seemed so tragic.

Smith's Weekly[34]

The secret of the nature of Major-General 'Pompey' Elliott's death was closely-guarded. The great soldier appeared to have died from natural causes, as the result of a haemorrhage.

As a fact, his was a Coroner's case, and therefore as open to the public, if they had known where and how to inquire, as an inquest on the humblest citizen of the land … Pompey Elliott is, in a sense, a possession of the Australian people, and there was no reason why the circumstances of his passing should have been withheld.

Certainly there was no moral stigma in the fact of a man holding an office of trust and jealously anxious to safeguard his professional honour, when the reputation of solicitors was being assailed from all quarters, taking the short road out of life during a mental lapse, in which he was under the delusion that the affairs of his clients had suffered shipwreck.

It was more to 'Pompey' Elliott's credit that his fine sense of honour should have been so wounded that he preferred death to the suggestion even of having badly advised clients into making investments at Canberra, that graveyard of political hopes.

One may picture the intensity of the suffering that drove him into making three separate attempts to end an existence that had become insupportable. When, in his agony, he could cry out, 'I am done, I am useless. I have nothing to live for,' and to beseech his nurse, 'Why cannot you give me something to make me sleep forever?' the pitch of his mental tortures may be realised ...

General Elliott took his own life by severing an artery and vein above his elbow.

'Knew you not Pompey?'

Three hundred thousand Australians knew Pompey in the days of his conquests and glory. Not one of them knew the Pompey of bitterer days, when lonely and despairing, unbalanced, perhaps by some legacy of his campaigns, he found himself driven to the act which closed so tragically a famous fighting career.

Wounded souls

Philip Gibbs, a renowned war correspondent, penned numerous articles during the war. His vivid descriptions capture the essence of the old inns and estaminets that the soldiers frequented daily when away from the battlefield. Many archive stories were set in these evocative locales. I was fascinated to read his first-hand accounts of wartime life, based on real events, documenting this cast of intriguing characters.

Recreating these settings from half a world away would be a daunting task. However, Gibbs' words breathe life into these events, transporting readers to the heart of the action.

The Telegraph[35]

Worst of all sights on a battlefield, or in a casualty clearing station, were men stricken with shell-shock, shaking with a kind of ague, pitiable. High explosive forces, the tremendous concussion of gunfire, the frightfulness of modern war, had suddenly snapped something. They were wounded souls. Not all of them have recovered.

Not all of them were conscious of mental illness until after the war – perhaps several years afterwards. They were "nervy." Their friends and relatives wondered at their quietude, or their ill-temper, or their restlessness and indecision. They had no sympathy from people eager to help the crippled ex-Servicemen or the blind soldiers and sailors.

These others showed no wounds. It was only in their minds that they suffered, until some of them committed suicide and others [were] sent into pauper asylums.

And others still – thousands of them – fell into a hopeless condition of neurasthenia, unable to earn their own livelihood, afraid of the world and themselves, with few friends to understand their misery or give a helping hand.

The worst cases of shell-shock received some kind of pension. Other cases, to whom mental distress came gradually, were not entitled to any pension, or made no claim for one. They were among the "heroes" of the war. They had done their duty with the best of them; but now, in the time of forgetfulness, they were forgotten, and the busy, joyous, selfish world passed them by, not guessing at the tragedy of these wounded souls, these nervous wrecks, these sad-eyed, stammering wan-looking fellows who wept sometimes in their lonely rooms and dared not apply for jobs which they knew they could not hold, even if luck gave them a chance ...

Tragedies, pitiable beyond all words, because they have been suffered in loneliness, in the agony of long-waking nights, with secret fears hidden even from wives and mothers, who knew these men when they were gay lads, before the war.

Wartime atrocities

Atrocities witnessed by the men were documented in many German soldiers' diaries and would be seared into the memories of our troops. Acts of savage cruelty, of unspeakable inhumanities, could never be described to one's families and friends.

Mr Alexander Powell, war correspondent of the *New York World*, wrote the words below on 12 March 1915:

> In one case, a man and his son were dragged out of their house and bayoneted in the presence of mother and daughter as revenge for the killing of an Uhlan, who was really shot by a Belgian soldier. [36]

Powell also recalled:

> I counted twenty bayonet wounds on the face and neck of the father. I helped to bury the victims. A fleeing woman carrying a baby was overtaken and the baby shot ... [I] entered a cottage and saw a girl, still alive, with both hands and feet cut off. [37]

CHAPTER 6

COBBLESTONES FOR A BED

'The billeting arrangements had been bungled, and all hands simply lay down on the cobble stones of Steenwerck and cursed the cold and wet and the staff until daybreak.'
Captain Cyril Longmore[38]

Captain Cyril Longmore

Captain Cyril Longmore (1887–1964) was a military historian, journalist, soldier and author of four books, one of which was titled *Eggs-a-Cook! The story of the 44th*. He moved to Western Australia in 1905 and later became editor of the *Western Mail*, a Perth newspaper. In his writings, he demonstrates the vagaries of warfare while living under typical battalion conditions.

The Australian[39]

November 1916. The Armentieres Sector. The 44th Battalion disembarked at [Le] Havre, and after orders, counter-orders, and much confusion, it was ordered to 'San Vic' rest camp, the route being up a gentle rise. This gentle rise (one in five) kept its uniformity of slope all the way around a corkscrew road. When the exhausted troops had done five miles of it, they understood the necessity for having a rest camp at the top of a hill!

The English officer in charge of the camp had received no instructions to prepare for the battalion. He therefore would not issue tents, blankets, or rations.

This meant that the first night in France was remembered as one of icy misery, with bitter winds howling across the top of the hill, and the slush and mud underfoot giving a foretaste of the major influence it was to have over the men's lives during the next two years.

Next morning orders came through that the battalion would arrive at the rest camp, so red tape was satisfied, blankets, tents and rations were issued. Everyone made themselves as comfortable during the next two days as was possible under the wintry conditions.

Instructions then came through that the battalion was to move to the forward area.

Marching down the hill to the station, the battalion entrained – 40 men (with all their equipment and three days' rations) to each horse truck. The memories of the next two days and nights in that train linger yet. The cold was so intense that the crowded condition of this affair proved to be a blessing in disguise.

Our first billets in nearby Bailleul were reached at midnight and the troops tumbled into the mud of the railway yard. Two companies were lucky and found motor buses detailed to take them to their billets. The other two companies marched along slippery cobbled roads to Steenwerck, which was reached about 4 am.

The billeting arrangements had been bungled, and all hands simply lay down on the cobble stones of Steenwerck and cursed the cold and the wet and the staff until daybreak.

Then, after much delay, each company was detailed to its billet – some fair, some bad. A and B Companies were in glass hot-houses with many panes of glass missing, and with only places here and there where no rain could get in.

In A Company's hot-house the engineers had placed some pontoons. As these pontoons occupied the only dry places, efforts were made to shift them in order to make the space they occupied available for the diggers.

It was days before authority could be obtained. The fuss and the care which the department concerned took of those pontoons made the diggers think that pontoons must be playing a prominent part in winning the war. Those hot-houses were cold billets. As B Company's wag remarked, 'The Lord help us if we're ever billeted in a refrigerator.'

By this time, the 9th and 10th Brigades of the 3rd Division were actually in the line. The 11th was in reserve to the other two, and occupied its time by parades, working parties, visits to the trenches by officers and N.C.O.'s, watching aeroplanes – and last but not least, learning French from the Mademoiselles of Armentieres and Steenwerck.

This state of affairs lasted for three weeks, then the 11th Brigade took over the front line. The sister battalion of the 44th was the 42nd, the latter occupying the Epinette portion of the Armentieres sector on December 22, 1916.

The 44th then moved from Steenwerck to billets in Armentieres, and from this time active service actually commenced. With several working parties sent to the frontline trenches every night, fatigue parties and carrying parties, their time was fully occupied.

On December 29, the 44th relieved the 42nd and took over the front line for the first time, moving in for its tour of duty via Lunatic Lane, one communication trench leading from the ruined lunatic asylum at Armentieres to the reserve trenches. The battalion was now in its tenth month of existence as a complete unit, and members had begun to think that they would never see Fritz in his native state. For the next 22 months they were destined to see more than was necessary for the worst gluttons for punishment in the battalion.

The sector occupied was flat country dotted with shell holes, and here and there a ruined farm. Trenches were mostly breastworks built of sandbags with the floor duck-boarded for convenience of movement. The communication trenches were A-framed and rivetted, but the dug-out accommodation generally was poor, simply amounting to improvised shelters from the weather.

None of them would stop a direct hit from even the smallest shell. Water was up to the knees in the duck-boarded trenches in many places, whilst off the duckboards mud reigned supreme. It was almost impossible to drain the water off on account of the extreme flatness of the locality.

Western Mail[40]
The 3rd Division had been in the line for about a month – new troops full of vim – and they succeeded in stirring Fritz up until he retaliated with similar vim. Unfortunately for the diggers, the infantry seemed to be the main target for the artillery of both contestants. If the Australian artillery fired at Fritz's front line he retaliated, not at the offending artillery, but at the inoffensive infantry in the front line opposite the sector of his own line which was being bombarded. If the Australian trench mortars opened up, so did his. Again the footsloggers suffered. It can be imagined, then, with what interest the infantry received the news each day that there would be a *shoot* at a certain time, and the suspense with which they awaited it, and the inevitable retaliation.

Fritz in this sector was well supplied with *Minnies*, a trench mortar shell which popped from his line, and could be seen going straight up, its flight followed with the naked eye until it came to earth, and, after a pause, burst. It was most interesting to watch – when not directed at the part of the line occupied by the watcher. Then, of course, it was murder! These minnies created a *windy* feeling. No dug-out in the line would stop the appalling explosion they made. The tremendous destruction to earthworks and trenches made them probably the most feared projectile the infantry had to face.

The first battle casualties of the battalion were caused by a minnie which burst on 'B' Company's parapet on December 30, 1916, killing instantly three lads of that company.

A coincidence about these first casualties was the names of the men killed: Anderson, Barker, and Cameron. A grim alphabetical beginning!

No-Man's land

Longmore also wrote about trench routine in No-Man's land, that vague stretch of ever-moving, contested ground between the battling forces.

Western Mail[41]

The battalion commenced at once the trench routine practised in peace training and kept it up with minor alterations right through the piece. With the nightfall a patrol would steal out into No-Man's land and perform a set task, such as 'examine enemy wire at such-and-such a point,' or 'examine ditch at so-and-so.' This patrol remained out for two hours, and when it returned another would go out, and this procedure was carried out through all the hours of darkness.

The result of this was that the men got very confident in their patrol work, and by denying Fritz the right to patrol freely, kept command of No-Man's land. Patrol duty was certainly risky work, but it suited the Australian temperament, and consequently, there was never any lack of volunteers to carry it out. To the patrolling activity and efficiency of the Australian Corps generally can a fair share of its success be attributed.

Front line troops were issued with two kinds of flares, one white and the other red. The white flare was used in case anything suspicious was seen over the parapet, and the red – the SOS – signal was only to be used in order to bring down the Australian artillery on the enemy front line in case of an attack. These flares were poor old things, and they were very seldom used.

The German flare, on the other hand, was very bright and hung in the air for quite an appreciable time. He used all the colours of the rainbow and kept them going from dusk until dawn. When it is realised that one of his flares would light up an area of hundreds of square yards as brightly almost as daylight, it can be imagined that the task of the patrols was not too pleasant. If a patrol was moving when a flare was fired, its members would stand fast, only inclining the head slightly towards Fritz, and remain motionless until the flare had died down. The German relied on his flares for some protection against surprise attack, and the Australians relied on the consistency and the initiative of their patrols.

This is not authentic – but the story goes that one night a sentry directed the attention of the officer of the watch to some suspicious object in front of the 44th's wire. The officer had two Verey light (flare) pistols, one with a red and the other containing a white light. Said he, 'Watch while I put up a bright light,' pointing one pistol up and in the direction of the suspicious-looking object and holding the other at arm's length behind him. Bang! In his excitement he pulled both triggers. The white light hit the parapet a foot in front of his pistol and the red one took the toecap off his batman's boot and the now unmistakable 44th patrol out in front shouted out that they were a_____ windy lot of _____!

CHAPTER 7

MONASH MEMORIES

'I hate the business of war and soldiering with a loathing that I cannot describe, the awful horror of it, the waste, the destruction and the inefficiency.'
Sir John Monash[42]

The Diary of General Sir John Monash

Many books, including the extract by Captain Cyril Longmore in the previous chapter, chronicled the Anzac legends over the past century. However, discovering Steenwerck's significance to General Sir John Monash added a new dimension to these narratives. Delving deeper into the archives, I unearthed captivating insights into the personalities from various brigades who passed through the town en route to different battlefields. Monash's letters and diaries, published in later years, further unravel the intriguing mystery of Steenwerck.

Monash diaries and letters, as published in *Courier Mail*[43]

9 December 1916. I am installed in full command of nearly 5 per cent of the whole of the British line, with jurisdiction over an enormous area, including two large towns, a dozen smaller villages and hundreds of hamlets, with control over the civilian population as well.

My headquarters are in a chateau in the town of Steenwerck. The chateau is modern and well-equipped with electric light, hot water service, and large grounds with stables and garages attached. The owner is a Captain in the French army, and his family still occupy a part of the house. The headquarters is well within the sound of our guns, but out of reach of any danger except aeroplane bombs. The Boche[*] is very quiet and undemonstrative.

On both sides of me are British divisions. The Third Division is fully coming up to expectations and has settled into its work most smoothly.

The latest event of interest was the visit today of the Commander-in-Chief, Sir Douglas Haig. I turned out the whole of my reserve brigade and detachments from all the other units of the division, and Sir Douglas rode around with me and had a look at them. He looked grey and old. On parting he put his arm around my shoulder as I rode beside him, and with much feeling and warmth, he said, 'You have a very fine division. I wish you all sorts of luck, old man.'

Baths in beer vats

Describing life around the lines near shell-shattered Armentières, in a letter to his wife, General Monash remarked on his railhead for war supplies, comparing it to Melbourne's goods yards, which he had designed before the war. *'Steenwerck is at any hour of the day a far busier sight than the Spencer Street goods yards. Traffic on some roads is more congested than Flemington Road on a Cup day.'*[44]

Monash continues below.

---

[*]   German force.

Monash diaries and letters, as published in *The Herald*[45]

I have two divisional baths; one at Steenwerck, one at Pont de Nieppe, a suburb of the large town. In these I wash 2,000 men daily with hot water in great brewery tubs. Each man hands in his old underclothes and gets in exchange a complete clean outfit. I employ over 200 girls in the laundries washing and ironing the soiled clothes. It is quite a show, but how they live and work all day in steam so thick that they can't see 6ft in front of them, I don't know.

It's a fine sight to see the boys splashing about in the great beer vats. They come out looking nice and pink. I have a medical officer in charge of each bath, with a small staff to help him. My pioneers work the boilers, as firemen and stokers.

3 March 1917. It is no secret that the British attack on the Somme last year was begun a month earlier than General Sir Douglas Haig wished. It was originally intended to postpone the advance until sufficient of His Majesty's Land Ships [tanks] were in commission to make the onslaught decisive. But happenings at Verdun, with the imminent risk of losing the fortress, compelled prompt action, so the Somme offensive was launched.

Haig was instructed to relieve the French at the cost of letting the enemy see these tanks before there were enough of them at the front to waddle to the Rhine. The monsters proved their worth, but instead of half a dozen there should have been a thousand. By letting them be seen in action on the Somme the Allies gave the foe six months in which to imitate them for the following spring.

To make up for the shortage of real tanks the men were encouraged to fabricate dummy ones. As soon as the word went round, engineers and pioneers vied with each other in rapid tank manufacture. Dumps and stores were clandestinely robbed of hessian, paint, wire, nails and battens, and some weird monstrosities were produced. The best and most plausible of them were selected and actually used on the day of the battle. Before dawn, four men dragged out each dummy into a position from which it was bound to be seen by the enemy, and there abandoned it. There is little doubt that this ruse contributed its share to the day's astonishing success.

Now Britain has a host of tanks, and Allied commanders are eager to put them into action. Every month's mud and snow are a gift to the foe, whose arsenals are working day and night at other forts on wheels and weapons to combat them. As soon as frosts harden the sticky, muddy ground, or if the spring is mild, the Allies will leap to the attack. If their calculations are right and the foe have not found an efficient reply to the new engine of war, the coming campaign should be decisive. British ingenuity conceived the idea of over-running trenches, rendering dug-outs and subterranean strongholds of no avail by building land Dreadnaughts.

16 March 1917. With reference to the statement made that I might take up military work as a profession after the war, I hate the business of war and soldiering with a loathing that I cannot describe, the awful horror of it, the waste, the destruction, and the inefficiency.

Many a time I could have wished that wounds or sickness, or a breakdown of health would have enabled me to retire honourably from the field of action like so many other senior officers. My only consolation has been the sense of faithfully doing my duty to my country, which has placed a grave responsibility on me and my division, who trust and follow me. I owe something to the 20,000 men whose lives and honour are placed in my hands to do with as I will. My duty once done, and honourably discharged, I shall, with a sigh of relief, turn my back, once and for all, on the possibility of ever again having to go through such an awful time. I might never see my home again. I wonder, can you realise the deep yearning I feel for a few months' peace and quiet life within the portals of my own home. To be re-joined to it and to you and Bert [Bertha, his daughter] is my constant daily longing. The extinction of that hope would make my present life of turmoil, strife and horror almost unbearable.

15 May 1917. I will send you a photograph of two young lady friends of mine, the twin daughters of my late landlady at Croix du Bac. They came to tea yesterday at Steenwerck and presented me with the photograph. Although they look different in it, yet in real life it is quite impossible to distinguish them.

The other day one of them was ill. One of my doctors brought along some pills and made the other twin take them by mistake. They often swop names and deceive their own mother. Their father was killed at Verdun.

You should see their little piece of acting. Their only excursion into English: Says one in a loud voice, "Dosson, my hat and stick." (Dawson, my batman.)

Says the other, saluting: "Yes, General. Here is it!"

20 June 1917. When the enemy commenced to shell the town of Nieppe I took up all the motor cars, motor lorries and waggons I could lay my hands on. In one day and night we managed to get away over 1,400 old people, invalids and children, and put out several large fires in the local factories. My men worked with a will, as they always do. The Mayor was very grateful.

26 June 1917. The British and Australian soldiers in this part of the world have not taken long to Anglicise local names. So firmly has the habit of mis-pronunciation seized on everybody that even the French interpreters and the civil population are regularly adopting the new pronunciation.

If you wish to ask your way you must, in order to make yourself understood, adopt the current modern pronunciation. Thus, Gris Pot becomes Grease Pot, Ploegsteert is Plug Street,

L'hallobeau is known only as Hullabaloo, Ypres is referred to as Wipers, Sailly is naturally Sally, Hooge is recognisable as Huge, Steenje is called Stingy, Fournes becomes Furnace. And Steenkweert [sic] is, of course, Stink-wort. Houplines could not be other than Hoop Lines, Rolanderie* is known as Roland's Dairy, Erquinghem is pronounced as Erkingham, Armentieres is Airman-tears. Wytschaete is referred to as Witchety, Poperinge is Pop Ring, and Bailleul is Bally Oo.

10 September 1917. We are in the Blequin area, with headquarters at Chateau Hervarre. Being so near the coast (40 minutes by motor), I took the opportunity of making several trips to interesting military depots and schools at various points.

Thus, at Wimereux, just north of Boulogne, there is the camouflage factory and school. Do you know that the word *camouflage* means disguise or concealment; the art is directed to making things look different from what they really are!

A harmless looking, half-shattered tree is really an observation post, made of iron, and covered outside with bark and branches, but hollow inside, furnished with ladders, telescopes, and a perch for the observer, who peeps through a strip of painted gauze. A gun pit is made to look like a haystack or a heap of farm manure. A telegraph pole is actually a concealed periscope; an old rusty petrol tin, lying derelict on the parapet, is really a sniper's peephole; a harmless grassy slope is a machine-gun emplacement.

Protection has to be arranged against observation from the air as well as from the ground. The factory employs hundreds of Chinese and French women who make enormous quantities of camouflage articles of all kinds, to the order of front-line divisions.

Much of the painting and modelling is done by real artists and sculptors, some of whom have pictures in this year's Academy.

---

* A farm.

I saw several of them painting sheets of iron to look like brick walls, and canvas sheets to look like a sandbag parapet, also modelling soldiers' heads out of papier-mâché, for use in drawing the fire of enemy snipers.

January 1918. A plane belonging to an Australian squadron attached to my division brought down a German machine, then mysteriously disappeared. Two days later it was found 100 miles away, safely landed, but with both the pilot and observer killed. For hours the plane flew in ever-widening circles until, with its petrol supply exhausted, it glided undamaged to earth. Even more extraordinary was a notice received from Germany advising that the two pilots had been buried there with military honours.

Of all the places I have lived
Monash letter, *The Newcastle Sun*[46]

April 1918. The 1st Australian Division was sent hastily back to Flanders, and stopped the Boche advance west of Bailleul. This division arrived just in time to save my good friend the Baroness de la Grange's chateau at La Motte.

I had a letter from Jeanne Plouvier (late of Steenwerck) in which she tells me that she and her mother had just ten minutes in which to clear out, in the clothes they stood up in, and they had to go the first 35 miles on foot under shellfire. Of all the places I have lived in, the Plouviers' house at Steenwerck was the most comfortable and the people most hospitable and helpful. We had there beautiful hot baths.

•

Jeanne Plouvier … at last I had the identity of that young refugee! Now that I knew her family name, it was easier to track references in the Monash diaries, when Sir John Monash described events at the Plouvier house. He also mentioned receiving Jeanne's letter in a message to his wife dated 2 May 1918, barely three weeks after Jeanne Plouvier and her mother fled Steenwerck during the bombing. Monash referring to having hot baths led me to discover the following snippets about the lack of bathing facilities on the battlefields.

•

Intimate attire
Lieutenant H. Williams in *Sydney Mail*[47]

When the civilian population fled Villers-Bretonneux they took with them as much as they could carry or pack into small carts. In spite of frequent shelling, troops in the early days of the occupation of this sector used to wander into town and inspect the houses. In many of these madames and mam'selles had left behind intimate articles of attire.

Some of the troops, who had been strangers to a bath and a change of underclothing for many weeks, promptly discarded their verminous undergarments and decked themselves out in feminine finery. A few of these men, garbed underneath their uniform in the daintiest of lingerie, became casualties. Great was the astonishment and amusement of nurses in clearing stations upon undressing them.

A nice hot bath
Western Mail [48]

No sooner had the diggers settled down to enjoy their spell when Sergeant "Massa" Johnson,* B Company, pratted his frame in No. 8 Platoon's quarters. Visions of fatigues made him unpopular. He was assailed with advice to go away and lose himself.

---

*   Bombardier Roy Johnson, 8th Australian Field Artillery Battery.

'Is Day* here?' he asked. 'I've got a good job, and I want him for my second wave. We've got to take over the divisional baths. We'll probably get the military medal for it.'

When Johnson and Day arrived at the baths, the Divisional Laundry Sergeant was anxious to hand over. Pointing, he said, 'Socks, towels, underpants. Give a clean change to every man and get his dirty clothes in exchange. I'll be back tonight and give you more clean clothes for the dirties. Sign here. S'long!'

Day was appointed receiver-general and took his post alongside a big window with a wide ledge opening into the bathroom. The roster had been arranged for thirty men every twenty minutes. The first team arrived, undressed, enjoyed a hot bath, dried themselves, and came to the window for their change. Their dirties consisted of ladies' stockings, silk knickers, and flimsy undervests – rainbow colours which even a month's wear had hardly dimmed. The 4th Brigade had been in the line around Villers-Bretonneux for a long time, and their chatty, (lice-riddled) army issues had been swopped for the fancy stuff in the battered town.

Day called Johnson across. He looked at the feminine fripperies and laughed. He said, 'No, only military issues exchanged.' Then bedlam broke loose. After a heated argument, Johnson finally agreed to the exchanges, so the bathing went on swimmingly. The silk and woollen underwear made a gorgeous heap of colours, and the pile grew alarmingly.

Johnson went away and drowned his sorrows in an estaminet (inn). He came back looking worried. 'Watch me and that Laundry Sergeant fight the best of twenty rounds for the championship of Muddy Picardy this evening,' he said. He made

---

*   Sergeant Edwin Day, 8th Australian Field Artillery Battery.
    M.M. Gallipoli.

another trip to the estaminet then came back and laughed at the growing colour scheme.

At 4 o'clock the Laundry Sergeant returned, bustling in through the front door. When he saw the rainbow he turned the colour of dirty fat, swallowed his Adam's apple, and aged ten years. Then he went for Johnson. He said that all of the shortages would be charged in his pay-book; the war would have to last another twenty years before it would again be in credit.

'They had nothing else to give me, and by the look and smell of them, those ladies' undies wanted changing badly.' After the first shock, Johnson stood up manfully to the onslaught of the Laundry Sergeant's wrath. It was necessary that he should. He had been in charge of the divisional baths for one day, and was 300 flannels, 600 underpants, and a million socks short in his accounts. Several officers were brought into the argument, and then a merry squabble proceeded.

When Sergeant Johnston [sic] was finally allowed to depart, he was told that 'the issue is still in doubt.' There was never any doubt about the issue. The clean undergarments of the 4th Brigade testified to that. But Johnson heard no more about it.

CHAPTER 8

WELCOME TO FLANDERS, BOYS

'It is providence how a man got away without being blown into eternity.'
Thomas Arthur Johns, 3rd Australian Field Artillery[49]

Jim Armitage shortened the name of Vauxin to Vaux at times, but the town of Vaux is 409 kilometres south from Steenwerck. For clarity, I kept the full name of Vauxin, 10 kilometres from Steenwerck, in the following edited extracts. Here, Jim describes the conditions in London and then Flanders.

Jim Armitage's diary[50]

January 1918. *England.* Arrived at camp for months of endless marching. An outbreak of mumps confined 24 of us to isolation for another month in the Australian Military hospital at Sutton Veny.

The orderly did his best to keep us in check but these men from various nations were the liveliest crowd I have ever met. We gave the orderly such a terrible time by staging furious pillow fights, using the beds as barricades. These affairs often ended in bloodshed. We were docked £1 to cover the cost of the destroyed bed-linen.

On leave in London, I attended all the theatres and lived a luxurious life, making my headquarters in the Notting Hill area.

30 *April*. The draft assembled at 9 am. Our entire kit, besides our bandolier, water bottle, gas mask and mess tin, consisted of one waterproof ground sheet, one blanket, one spare pair of socks, one change of underclothes and our small haversack with a few personal knick-knacks.

We embarked at Portsmouth on a cross-channel boat together with other English troops and a great many Americans. The crossing was rough, and we had a miserable trip, landing at Le Havre on 1st May. Marched 8 kilometres to the Australian General Base Depot. This base is rough, and we were billeted 15 to a tent.

The next day we were issued with steel helmets and marched to the great gas schools in the hills outside Le Havre. By the time that we finally got there, we were nearly dead with the unaccustomed weight of the steel helmets but had to go through more long and tedious gas drills, which we considered unnecessary after all our gas drills in England.

4 *May*. We left camp and started our long march up the line. Bob Shute, John Roxburgh, and I had been drafted into 3rd Division. Phippard went to 5th Division. We got to Liercourt on the 5th of May, my nineteenth birthday. We marched eleven kilometres to Longpre, where we entrained for St. Leger. From there we marched about 5 kilometres to some billets of wet straw laid down in old cowsheds (my birthday night). That night we were flooded out and moved to drier quarters. 'Welcome to Flanders, boys,' said the billeting sergeant.

8 *May*. This morning we took to the open road in the direction of Vauxin. The weather was frightfully hot, and our heavy kits nearly broke our backs. After walking all day we had covered a distance of 25 kilometres, finally reaching Vauxin. This rest camp was right alongside a large aerodrome. A wonderful sight to see 50 to 60 planes rising into the air at sunset and to go through all

kinds of manoeuvres. Next morning, we marched to Divisional Headquarters, situated in woods outside Abbeville, only a couple of kilometres behind Amiens. From this camp we saw anti-aircraft shells bursting around our fighters and German planes. That night, camped in the woods, we had our first experience of German night bombing.

10 *May*. We arrived at 3rd D.A.C. Headquarters at Pontnoyelles. Allocated to different batteries; Roxburgh, Shute, and I went to the 30th Battery in the 8th Brigade, 3rd Division.

A new Commanding Officer took charge of the battery the day we moved. Major D. B. Walker is a Sydney man, who won a Military Cross in the March retreat. We discovered that our new Major was a very fine chap!

That same evening, we went up to battery waggon lines which are just outside what was once Pontnoyelles, about 6 kilometres behind the line. From the way the section sergeants argued over us, we concluded reinforcements were badly needed, strengthened by 3 bodies neatly sewn up in their blankets, packed inside the tent waiting for removal.

One reinforcement was Flannagan, a rather delicate, young boy. Battery Sergeant Major McMurray, said jokingly, 'I don't want to scare you, but it's rather a coincidence. A namesake of yours came to the battery a fortnight ago. He was killed a couple of days later!'

It turned out to be Flannagan's brother. The poor lad was shattered, the S.M. horrified at what he had said. The incident made the rest of us realise we had arrived at the war!

•

Jim mentioned Major D.B. Walker arriving to take over command of their battery on 10 May 1918. Jeanne Plouvier's letter stated seeing 'the Major' before she fled Steenwerck in April 1918. Could D.B. Walker be the same Major?

Further research concerning Major Dallas Bradlaugh Walker disclosed the following comments from the archives.

Major Walker had been stationed at Spy Farm, the code name for Mouquet Farm and the scene of a disastrous battle, before being reassigned to Jim's division after the March retreat. Although Jim said that the Major was 'a Sydney man', the Major served in the New Zealand Medical Corps.

Major Dallas Bradlaugh Walker
Macleay Chronicle[51]

16 March 1918. Things are getting a bit more lively here. Every night, there is a big raid on in this sector, and the guns are blazing away like one o'clock. Fritz made a couple of biggish attacks on us a couple of nights ago but got it very much in the neck, as he always will in this part of the line. He has two chances of getting through, his own and Buckley's.

It's a sight for the gods to see our guns going at night – they light up the whole of the sky incessantly – and the noise!

There is a difference of opinion here as to whether Fritz will attack this Spring or not, but there is no difference of opinion as to what is going to happen to him if he does. Whichever side attacks is going to have a terrible time and there must be terrific loss.

Our air service is an absolute treat. Fritz has got the 'wind up' completely. Every day it is the same old story; a dozen or twenty of his planes down to two or three of ours. You rarely see one of his over our way, while ours spend the whole day over his territory spotting guns, dumps, etc., and dropping bombs. One of his planes came over the line the other day and took observations.

Everyone wondered why our anti-aircraft guns were so silent. After a while he set out to go home, and there were four streaks of lightning from the clouds above him as he crashed to mother earth, a smouldering mass.

We have a little plane which is like the proverbial *greased lightning* and can run rings around Fritz. You can believe all you hear about our being top dogs in the air. We are, easily.

All the same, I cannot help thinking that all this business is going to last a long time yet, 18 months or two years at the least. The Hun is not going to give up Alsace-Lorraine till he has to – and that is not yet.

My present headquarters, rather a famous place, is called Spy Farm. It was the scene of heavy fighting recently and was Lord Kitchener's headquarters while he was in France. It is surrounded by trenches and barb-wire entanglements on an immense scale.

I go to Paris for a week's rest in 10 days time. Am seeing a bit of the world – but guess New Zealand or Australia would be as welcome as anywhere.

CHAPTER 9

MEMORIES OF STEENWERCK

'About three or four miles further we passed through Steenwerck, a fine big place, full of life. It was hard to believe it was situated in the war zone.'
Bombardier Walter Parry[52]

From hundreds of stories about Steenwerck in the National Library of Australia's Trove archives, I selected the following cameos to showcase various aspects of the town of Steenwerck. The writers range from those who just passed through to those who inhabited it. From long-lost loves to charming spies, helping hands to hallucinations, these stories prove that this hidden gem of a town was indeed a popular and vibrant place.

Soldier of fate
Smith's Weekly[53]
Every Digger who was fortunate enough to be parked in the 2nd Australian Casualty Clearing Station at Steenwerck appreciated and admired the nurses there. Paddy Noonan went several steps further and lost his heart to one of the sisters, a breezy Irish girl.

With knowing smiles, she repelled his advances for a time, but on the day that he was to be cleared for Boulogne, she came to his bed and slipped an envelope into his hand. It was a promise of marriage should they ever meet again. Paddy's temperature soared.

His plans to effect the meeting, however, had a setback when he was invalided home in 1916. He went to New Zealand to recuperate, re-enlisting there in August 1918.

Reaching England early in November, he was impatiently awaiting a draft for France when the Armistice was signed. Paddy, heartbroken, was a sick man when he boarded the NZ troopship *Tahiti* at Liverpool, bound for home.

A week out, he became a cot case and went into hospital. The nurse detailed to attend him proved to be the girl of his dreams. She had Paddy on his feet before the vessel cleared the Panama Canal. And now? They are working a farm of their own in Taranaki, N.Z., with two little Paddies and a Colleen as 'hands.'

Cogwheel
Smith's Weekly[54]

Olympus, the Brass Hat* in charge of our detachment, picked the worst winter's night in France to shift us from Strazeele to Steenwerck.

Through the misty night we travelled for hours and hours and hours, while many times commenting on the sameness of the French villages through which we were passing.

Towards dawn, something clicked in the brain of Harry Fitzgerald Harlock,† who had seen to it that officers and men were fortified with a double issue of service rum. As a result I left the sheltering bulk of big Dick Clintock at the rear of the column and

---

* Slang word for main officer.
† Lieutenant Harry Harlock, 4th Battalion.

reported to our leader. 'I have got an idea there is someone just ahead of us, Cogwheel! Canter along and find out where the hell we are, and how far off is Steenwerck?' he ordered.

About 100 yards ahead were the vague outlines of horsemen. I caught up and started to address the rearmost man of the column, when my horse plunged forward and ranged up alongside big Dick, in exactly the same position that we had occupied for what seemed the last sixteen miles. We had been following ourselves round and around the same village, Sailly-sur-la-Lys, a few miles from Steenwerck.

Several days later, after the Messines battle, we pulled out of the line to rest. We were feeling tired, dirty, hungry, and lousy, but a good sleep and a hot meal put some new life into us.

Food on the frontline

Life went on in the estaminets, which were small French inns or cafes often located in the front rooms of existing homes. Soldiers and their officers, tired of bully-beef rations, would come here for a decent breakfast or dinner, which usually consisted of eggs and chips.

Most estaminets were safe havens, although a few would prove to be sites where all was not as it seemed. Eyes spied the regimental badges that told of battalions passing through. Ears overheard important military information, usually mentioned in passing within general conversations – information for which the enemy paid handsomely.

Although walls bore posters warning 'Loose lips sink ships' or the terser 'Shut Up!' there was many a slip, particularly when the bock, vin rouge or cognac flowed freely in the evenings after a long, wearying battle. In one little inn, all was not what it seemed, when the nearby bombing school tested the secret trench mortars being developed.

Western Mail[55]

Nearby was a little estaminet, the name of which slips my memory. Three sisters ran this inn, the chief attraction being one charming, vivacious sister with more than ordinary intelligence. She was known far and wide by the sobriquet 'Scotty,' on account of her perfect mimicry of a braw Scots laddie all the way 'frae Glesca', ye ken!'

Guard soldiers and military police of three allied countries patrolled this estaminet, which practically adjoined the area bombing school, where trench mortars (a close secret when we arrived in France), and other forms of bomb-throwing were the subject of instruction to regimental officers and N.C.O.'s. Consequently men from hundreds of different units passed in and out of the estaminet where Scotty entertained all and sundry with her wit and charm.

I happened to be at the bombing school when a friend invited me to come and meet Scotty while he replenished his store of tobacco, of which he had a varied assortment.

Scotty was all that she was reported to be. In reply to one of her sallies I quoted the old tag, *'Varium et mutabile semper femina.'* (Woman is always a fickle and changeable being.) She immediately turned to me, saying in French that she knew a lot of men to whom the tag could apply.

I asked how she understood Latin, especially with my vile accent. She replied that she had attended a convent in Ypres, 'avant la guerre.' I paid no further heed to her but went on chatting with my friend whom I had met after a long separation.

Later, when she came along with coffee and cognac, I had an idea. Thanking her, I muttered in German (with which I was slightly acquainted), 'Danke schoen!' (Thanks, very much).

Immediately she was startled and turned a scared face to me. Then she recovered herself and was brighter and more Scottish than ever.

My friend pooh-poohed the idea that she was more than she seemed, but I felt determined to investigate further when suddenly recalled 'at the tout' to my battalion.

That night we entrained for Albert and the Somme. I forgot about Scotty and her strategic possie for the acquiring of information, but since I have often wondered just how much news Fritz got from this part of the world.

The King's Regulations
Inverell Times[56]

Charlie North was one of the many Anzac soldiers billeted in Steenwerck. Behind what in pre-war days had been a large convent, there was a pump at the end of a closed-in alley way. That spot, with its water supply and shelter from the elements, soon became the troops favourite rendezvous for washing and shaving.

Facing the alley way were two small cottages, still occupied. As there were no gutters or means of sanitation, the water thrown on the cobbled roadway by the soldiers soon became objectionable to the occupiers of the cottages.

One afternoon, over several cups of café-au-lait, Madame brought the matter to Charlie's attention, asking if he could do anything to stop the men from using the pump as a washing centre. Anxious to oblige, Charlie asked for pen, paper, and tacks. In a few moments, he had tacked up in a conspicuous position over the pump the following notice: *No washing allowed here. By order.*

When the next mob appeared, that notice caught their eye. After a word or two among themselves, they departed. The news spread, and within 12 hours the spot was deserted.

The following day, while sitting at Madame's window, Charlie noticed the Operations Commander, accompanied by the adjutant and the usual retinue of orderlies, approach the pump.

After a grave inspection of the warning, they turned solemnly about and moved away.

No doubt inquiries would be made to ascertain who had put up the notice. When it was discovered that a mere private had done it without any authority, there would certainly be some charge preferred against the perpetrator under that elastic code known as the King's Regulations.

Swearing Madame to secrecy, Charlie hurried back to his billet to await developments. When on parade next morning, the following was read out as part of the orders of the day: 'Owing to orders from Headquarters, troops are forbidden to use the pump in the small alleyway at the back of the convent for washing or any other purposes.'

Smith's Weekly [57]

Marie's joint near the village square was the most popular estaminet for our mob. How we used to make the old piano work overtime!

Here, too, the troops entertained those hearty New Zealanders. One evening we aroused the wrath of the Assistant Provost Marshall, and his band of satellites, through encouraging a prolonged exhibition of the haka, the Maori War dance by those wonderful Kiwi Islanders.

Although Steenwerck was only about four miles behind the front line, the village seemed to bear a charmed life. Up until the last time we were billeted there in 1917, no shells had landed nearer than the railhead, half a mile away.

We used to listen with awe to the heavies passing overhead to Bailleul and Hazebrouck, both many miles further back, and thanked our lucky stars that they were not 'drop-shorts.'

I often wondered what the secret of the immunity of this little village was, seeing that within its environs were Divisional Headquarters, Artillery H.Q., hospitals, army theatre, etc.

The village square was the park for several different companies of Heavy Motor Transport. What a target the church spire must have appeared to Jerry! It was visible for miles.

Do any of the boys remember when the village of Steenwerck went crazy, when it listed to starboard and just as quickly took another list to port?

I distinctly remember the church tower being at an angle of 45 degrees while the road took the form of a huge sea serpent, quite green, with cobblestones assuming the shape of scales on the monster's back. Think what would have happened if the authorities hadn't removed four enormous barrels of high-powered XXXX beer, which had been inadvertently delivered to our canteen, instead of the customary low-powered Bock.

Prohibition in the war

Tensions rose when alcoholic drinks were banned in the war zone, as seen in the following extracts.

Northern Star [58]

Paris. 2 June 1918. A decree was issued today by the French army authorities categorically forbidding the selling or consumption of alcoholic drinks in the war zone. Violations of the order will be strictly punished.

Smith's Weekly [59]

Madame Cognac of Steenwerck, whose little house stood back off the road which led to the railway station, did a roaring trade after hours. Officially there were no spirits to be had anywhere. Their sale was prohibited in all estaminets.

She charged half a franc for a thimbleful – or was it an egg-cup? All drinks came out of the one bottle which, of course, had to be replenished countless times during the late night and early morning. We wondered where she had the bulk of it planted. When admission had been gained, the inside of her cottage was a revelation. There we stood, shoulder to shoulder, all down the hallway, in the parlour, her bedroom and kitchen, waiting patiently in the gloom for Madame Cognac and her bottle. Her apron pocket bulged with our half-francs.*

Silence was the order; none spoke above a whisper. Those who did were dealt with, and never came there again. Although at times we doubted the quality of her cognac, it warmed us up and we needed warming in those days.

•

Discrepancies between the quantity of soda siphon bulbs ordered by one officers' mess and the amount realistically used were not realised until a stocktake after the war.

Likewise, another mess reported the mysterious disappearance of bottles of brandy. However, a memo cautioned to not jump to conclusions based solely on 'circumstantial evidence', but where did Madame Cognac get her supplies? And from whom?

•

41st Battalion at Messines

The following piece describes the importance of secrecy in the use of key words in communications, as described by a signaller. Although this section seems innocuous, if somewhat cryptic, it would eventually lead me toward solving one of the major mysteries of the story, the fate of Jeanne Plouvier.

---

*   Madame Cognac often ducked into the other bedroom to check on her sick child.

***Tweed Daily*[60]**

13 June 1917. The battalion rested and reorganised at Neuve Eglise for a few days, then moved back to Blanche Maison, a stone's throw from Steenwerck, where the battalion was billeted in the surrounding farmhouses. Great attention was given to specialist training; Lewis gun, bombs, signalling and scouting. An instance of doggedness was shown when an officer, accompanied by a signaller, met a West Australian carrying a Lewis gun. The gunner was scarcely able to drag the gun. The officer suggested that the signaller relieve him of the burden. The gunner declined, saying he'd carried the 'blinking thing in and would carry the blighter out again.'

I might tell you a signaller is granted lots of privileges. He wears a blue bar, and it takes him anywhere. 'Our work is entirely secret and very important for sending messages, according to weather and circumstances. As long as we adhere to secrecy the enemy cannot find our key words, but one slip may mean a whole battalion's lives.' …

21 June. The rest spell ended. At 4 am the battalion moved past Steenwerck station, with its huge dump of engineering material, to Hillside Camp. At sundown we wended our way through the streets of Neuve Eglise, the back-wash of the big offensive, to historic Messines Ridge. Before Messines was reached, guides from the battalion which the 41st relieved, met us in the fading light and took us over the hill.

•

The Battle of Messines: 7–14 June 1917

The Battle of Messines in June 1917 was a significant engagement on the Western Front. The British Second Army, led by General Sir Herbert Plumer, launched an attack near the village of Messines in West Flanders, Belgium.

One of the most remarkable aspects of this battle was the use of underground mines. British forces spent months tunnelling under the German lines, placing nineteen mines filled with around one million pounds of high explosives. When detonated, these mines created one of the largest non-nuclear explosions in history, which could be heard as far away as London. This devastating blast destroyed German defences.

The battle was a tactical success for the British, capturing the strategically important Messines Ridge. This victory was crucial as it set the stage for the subsequent Battle of Passchendaele.

British troops secured the ridge with support from tanks, cavalry and aircraft. The infantry encountered minimal resistance, with many German soldiers staggering across the battlefield in a state of confusion. Over 7,000 prisoners were captured that morning.

Preparation for the battle began a year earlier, involving the excavation of mines beneath the ridge. These mines were strategically placed under the German lines by tunnelling companies from General Plumer's Second Army.

The battle served as a prelude to the much larger Third Battle of Ypres, for which the preliminary bombardment would begin on 11 July 1917.

When the Anzacs reached Messines, they saw where tons of mines had ripped the hillside apart, killing more than 10,000 German soldiers. These detonations were considered the largest man-made battlefield explosion until the atomic bomb.

War correspondent Philip Gibbs witnessed the Battle of Messines, which took place from 7 to 14 June.

Philip Gibbs, *Kyneton Guardian*[61]

Our mother earth is strewn with the bodies of German soldiers. They lie, grey wet lumps of death, over a great stretch of ground, many of them half buried by their comrades or by high explosives.

Most of them are stark above the soil, with their eye-sockets to the sky.

No morbid vision of an absinthe-maddened dream of Hell could be more fearful than what I stared at standing there, with the rain beating on me across the battlefield, the roar of guns on every side, and the long, rushing whistles of heavy shells in flight overhead. The place was a shambles of German troops. They had machine-gun emplacements here, and deep dug-outs under the cover of earth banks …

The secret of the German retreat is here on this ground. To save themselves from such a shambles they were falling back to new lines, where they hoped to be safer from our massed artillery. Over this ground the young manhood of Germany spent itself, but it was not worthless ground on which they suffered agonies. They fought desperately, and came on again and again, but the massed counter-attacks were swept to pieces by our fire.

Our guns found them and poured fire upon them. All this garrison had been killed and cut to pieces either before or after death. Their bodies, or fragments, lay in every shape and shapelessness of death, in puddles of broken trenches, or on the edge of deep ponds in shell craters. The water was vivid green about them, or red as blood, with the colour of high explosive gases. Mask-like faces, with holes for eyes, seemed to stare back at me as I stared at them, not with any curiosity in this sight of death, for it is not new to me. I was counting their numbers, and reckoning the sum of these things who, a little time ago, were living men.

After the disaster at Messines, one German boy, who looked not more than fifteen years of age – a child – was found lying in a shell hole by the side of a dead man who had been shot through the temple. He was a gibbering idiot through fear. Not the only one.

CHAPTER 10

HELLFIRE CORNER

'If Fate is with us, who can be against us?'
John A. Williamson[62]

Skirmishes at Hellfire Corner

During World War I, Hellfire Corner was a significant landmark in the Ypres Salient battlefields and was fought over throughout the war.

Private John Alexander Williamson was a soldier in the 48th Battalion and would later author the book *They Simply Fade Away*. He enlisted on 25 May 1916 and returned to Australia 30 June 1918. This following extract from his *Western Mail* article captures the perilous conditions at Hellfire Corner, a busy intersection for troops. Many skirmishes occurred there between 1915 and 1918.

Western Mail[63]

September 1917. 48th Battalion. Cross-roads, outskirts of Ypres. At a comfort funds stall we took the opportunity of resting and making any small purchases that were possible. Before resuming our journey, our leader made a rearrangement of our formation, thus putting B Company section in the lead – a seemingly unimportant move, yet one big with fate for us all, as the event was soon to demonstrate. Presently we negotiated that dreaded bend in the road. A battered signpost, drunkenly leaning, tells us we have reached Hellfire Corner, a spot known to every soldier, either by repute or unenviable experience.

Hellfire Corner did not belie its name or its reputation – it was red hot. Shells were falling everywhere in quick succession. We could make no speed, as roads were fearfully impeded by traffic both to and from the line.

Comes the shell we could scarcely hope to escape, drops with a roar and a flash at the rear of our line, and almost the entire 'D' section is out of action. All is confusion. About half of our number are lying in the road dead or wounded; the remainder dazed and wobbly with shellshock. A circumstance which lightened the blow a little was that a dressing station stood right alongside – an indication of the number of casualties at this spot. The A.M.C. lads soon had our unfortunate comrades under attention.

To speak the truth, before Hellfire Corner I had been, inwardly at least, shaky and tense in every fibre. Suddenly, through the din, there flashed to my consciousness, like the words of a spoken command, 'If fate is with us, who can be against us?' Instantly, as the psychologist would say, I was made whole. Peace slid into my soul.

So, presuming High Fate to be an ally, I was, at any rate, miraculously transformed and entirely at ease thereafter. So much for the power of thought!

Even in the midst of such preoccupations, I could not help being struck with the vivid and abrupt contrast in appearance presented by the landscape. On our right still grew trees, bushes and grass in their natural state, green and refreshing, a balm to the senses.

The other side was fringed by a high camouflage screen, ripped and frayed into irregular patterns by shell-fire and other agencies. Through those gaps, as if peering into some uneasy future, we snatched fleeting glimpses of the terrain which broadly constituted the firing line. Melancholy pictures of ashen-grey or black desolation, of ruin and confusion, as far as the eye could range. The tumultuous and cataclysmic forces of nature, fire, flood, earthquake, tornado, acting in concert, could hardly produce a nearer presentment of primal chaos.

Our next step was to re-join the battalion, which had taken up its position in the support trenches at Polygon Wood on Anzac Ridge – a wood in name only, for hardly a stick or a stump of the original plantation remained. The lads in the trench didn't welcome our daylight over-the-top entry, some of them calling out at our approach, 'Don't bleeding well come in here, you blanky, blank dopes! You'll draw the crabs!'

Painful experience had shown the men that seldom did any daytime movements escape the attention of the enemy or his guns. However, Fritz did not flatter us with undue attention. Once in the muddy trench confines we late-comers made a concerted and gritty attack on our rations; gritty for the reason that every shell burst, even comfortably distant, brought down on us a shower of Flanders earth from the parapet.

My recollections of this stunt are somewhat blurred and indistinct, but certain unrelated incidents and impressions remain. Necessity restricted our activities for the most part to the covering darkness of night, these being concerned chiefly in the conveyance of necessities to the front line, and in burying the dead.

Even the night did not always serve to screen us from the enemy. The latter made lavish use of star shells which produced a ghastly, yet effective, counterfeit of daylight, illumining No-Man's land like another, but throngless, Broadway.

In the daytime we stagnated in our muddy ditches where, as if in some gigantic game of patience, we awaited whatever hand Fritz and Fate had to deal.

Never a day passed without a stir or a scrap at some part of the front; sometimes in the early morning presaging a hop-over, sometimes in the evening as a night-cap, sometimes even during the night telling of a raid or merely a false alarm.

At such times, the big guns made their presence known in no ambiguous manner; they spoke with no uncertain voice; they crashed into the heavens with a rending, rolling roar, just like the thunder of a thousand storm-tossed breakers pounding on a rock-bound shore. At the rending of the heavens, the earth quaked and shook, and the very air trembled. A barrage, provided it was directed from our lines, was a sheer delight to hear; it thrilled as would some grand organ or a mighty orchestra in a frenzy of sound. It inspired us with confidence, with a feeling of power irresistible, and with a sense of satisfaction that our torturers were being served as they so persistently served us.

This sense of exhilaration was not untempered. Indeed it carried a scorpion sting in its tail; the thought of retaliation, for never did Fritz fail to give measure for measure.

The fact that we had been assigned the duty of burying the dead gave some indication of the recent slaughter in this quarter. We required no verbal instruction as to the necessity for this action; it was borne on us in another and no less forcible manner. The stench of decaying flesh had pervaded and polluted the very air we breathed, hanging over all like a foul miasma, especially so as the weather was dank and mouldy. In this respect, Hellfire was certainly the worst *corner* in my experience.

At length, our spell of duty ended. We marched away from this doubly unwholesome area under cover of darkness. As we passed down the trench each man shook a skeletal hand that somehow protruded out of the trench-wall, and with varied expressions and, no doubt, mixed feelings, bade its erst-while owner good-bye.

The Scone Advocate[64]

'Do you remember,' says one who went back later, 'how the limbers used to gallop across Hellfire Corner? I was there today. They've built a farm on it. How the drivers used to grit their teeth and go hell for leather, and then pull up and say, "Hell!" and look surprised to be alive. Do you remember, eh?'

Polygon Wood

The nearby woodland area, known as Polygon Wood, was totally destroyed during the war. Australian soldiers were heavily involved in the fighting that took place at Polygon Wood during the Third Battle of Ypres, which lasted from 31 July to November 1917.

The Sydney Morning Herald[65]

In 1917, Australian soldiers added fresh laurels to their already magnificent reputation by the part they played in the Third Battle of Ypres. The attack on September 20 was when so many of our men fought death – marking the great struggle for Polygon Wood. At dawn, in a wet mist, following upon drenching rain all night, the heroic British line swept forward in the knee-deep mud and slush.

The Australians, on Plumer's* right, cleared as their first task Glencorse Wood and the Nun's Wood. By 10 am they had taken Polygon Veld, at the north-western corner of Polygon Wood. At midday they secured the whole western half of the wood up to the racecourse, thus reaching their final objectives.

The ground over which this terrific battle was fought had been fought over so many times that it was nothing but a sea of mud, littered with the debris of battle, and foul with an indescribable

---

* Field-Marshall Herbert Plumer, British army (1857–1932). Messines Ridge offensive, 7 June 1917.

stench. Wood? There was none; only the shattered and blackened stumps of a few poor sticks of trees remained; and of the racecourse only the earth foundation of what was once a grandstand stood as a landmark.

Polygon Wood to those who saw it as it was then will ever recur as the background of a nightmare experience. And yet it must still remain a hallowed ground for Australia, for it was there so many of her gallant sons died for national liberty and honour.

The Sydney Morning Herald[66]

Few struggles in the campaign were more desperate or carried out on a more gruesome battlefield. The maze of quagmires, splintered woods, ruined husks of pill-boxes, water-filled shell holes, and foul creeks which made up the land on both sides of the Menin Road, was a sight which, to the recollection of most men, must seem like a fevered nightmare.

It was the classic soil on which, during the first battle of Ypres, the 1st and 2nd Divisions had stayed the German rush for the Channel. Then it had been a broken but still recognisable and featured countryside. Now the elements blended with each other to make of it a limbo outside mortal experience, almost beyond human imagining. Only on some of the tortured hills of Verdun could a parallel be found.

Then came another great attack six days later, when the Australians carried the remainder of Polygon Wood and assisted the sorely-tried British division on their right. Ypres, it has been said, was to Britain what Verdun was to France, *'the hallowed soil which called forth the highest virtue of her people.'*

The role of the *Smith's Weekly* newspaper

Smith's Weekly (1919–1951) gave voice to soldiers by publishing their wartime adventures. The newspaper was founded by prominent financier Sir James Joynton Smith, a former Lord Mayor of Sydney. Journalist Clyde Packer, father of Sir Frank Packer, was another founder.

Mainly targeting the male ex-servicemen's market, *Smith's Weekly* published sensational stories, satire and controversial opinions, mixed with sports and finance news. Also included were short stories, cartoons and caricatures as main features.

In the 1920s, one attraction was the Unofficial History of the A.I.F. feature, which published regular material by soldiers. These works helped to preserve the notion of the 'digger' as an easy-going identity who disrespected authority. Tracing individual writers was often difficult. In trying to attribute the following story, I found five soldiers with the surname 'Brown' in the 55th Battalion.

Corporal Brown, *Smith's Weekly*[67]

Our battalion (55th) held the line across the nearby Anzac Ridge just after the Polygon Wood stunt. Three of us from 'B' company, Dick Hall, Dick Bishop, and myself (none of us 21 years of age), were detailed to slip across from the trench we were occupying to pick up spare tins (mostly kerosene) from a pill-box about fifty yards away.

The tins were for tea, soup, and any other liquid refreshments the ration parties could get through from a dump half a mile in the rear.

Fritz was having his usual busy day at our expense, heaving over anything in the Krupps line from Daisy-cutters to High Explosives.

As we toed it from the trench to the pill-box (young Hall in the centre), a whiz-bang burst right on us. When the smoke and mud cleared, Dickie Bishop had reached the pill-box. I was gazing at the still form of Dickie Hall. Young Hall had stopped the full issue!

Hickson, of our Company, and I wrapped poor Dick in a blanket and started to dig his last resting place a few yards from where he fell. All the while we were engaged at our melancholy task a German Taube was cruising directly above us at less than a thousand feet. The pilot was probably the fellow who had signalled our movements to his very accurate artillery.

He was still there when we finished, in spite of savage bursts of machine-gun fire from our lines. At a signal from Hickson and I, half a dozen of our lads hopped out of the trench shelter and stood bare-headed with us, while someone read a short service as a last mark of respect and tribute to the memory of one of the most popular youngsters in the battalion.

What a target we made for the pilot of that Taube! But nothing happened until we clapped on our steel helmets and sprinted for the shelter of the trench again.

Then Fritz moved. He zoomed down and sprayed that trench with machine-gun fire until we thought it rained lead. After he'd gone, his artillery kept us on the jump for more than an hour. But that Fritz was a chivalrous gentleman in the presence of the dead.

CHAPTER 11

TIPPERARY

'Then, wonder of wonders, they turned to "Tipperary". Did we sing? Ah! It was months since we had let ourselves go like that. Right from the heart the old song came that night.'
Reverend Corporal Stutley[68]

During my research on the 6th Field Artillery Brigade I came across many references to the troops singing as they marched to, or staggered from, the battlefields. Most popular among soldiers of numerous nationalities was one song titled 'It's a Long Way to Tipperary', often shortened to just 'Tipperary'.

Reverend Corporal Stutley was attached to the 6th Field Artillery Brigade on 9 September 1915, according to army records.

I found Reverend Corporal Stutley's explanation of the song's popularity a fascinating insight and an emotional experience for him, and also for me.

Reverend Corporal S. J. Stutley, *Australian Christian Commonwealth Magazine*[69]

Today one seldom hears 'Tipperary' sung in France, at any rate by the British Tommy. The first time I heard it sung in France was at Le Havre. It was afternoon, and French children were trooping home from school. There was little sound from them until they came around a bend in the road and caught sight of the new soldiers, the first division of the Australian Field Artillery to arrive in France.

They were silent for a moment, then as a token of warmest welcome to the big, bronzed fellows from Egypt, with their picturesque chapeaux, they broke into the greatest of all the soldiers' songs.

'C'est un long chemin jusqu'a Tipperary, c'est un long chemin aller.' Their voices rose clear and confident, as first in French and then in English they sang it.

The Australians along the roadway stopped, listening wonderingly at the strange words, but when the English version commenced, they sang it with deep-throated notes that were only silenced by the shrill cries of the same youngsters demanding souvenirs, with shouts of 'Vive l'Australie! Vivent les Australiens!'

The next time I heard it was in one of those tiny villages that lies scattered just behind Armentieres, where 'Tipperary' was known to the peasantry only by name or by repute. The song of the English they used to call it; but of the words and their significance they knew little or nothing.

It was at an estaminet, one of those wayside cottages which since the coming of Tommy, at any rate, are always to be found with an open door and cosy hearth. There is champagne at 5 francs, or ever-present vin rouge and vin blanc at 1½ francs per bottle, and the sharp, home-made beer of France at 1 penny per glass nearly always on sale – and eggs, always eggs. As I entered, I heard 'Tipperary'. Someone had started singing it in French, breaking off halfway to tackle his plate of eggs.

Madame, a refugee from Lille, looked up after tending to the stove and demanded with sudden interest, 'This Teeperaree, is it far? Is it that you live there also, you Australians? I know that it is home of the English, but why do you call it your home?'

I hastened to explain to her that not only the English and the Australians, but the Irish and the Scottish, the Canadians and the South Africans all sang it.

'Then it is more than a little village in Ireland!' said she. 'It is your chez-vous, n'est-ce-pas? The home of each one, as well as the big family hearth of all the soldiers of the L'empire Brittanique.'

'Yes,' I assured her, 'something like that.'

'But my Teeperaree, it is at Lille,' she sighed. She told us of the little cottage outside of the town, with its roof of mossy tiles, of lilac drooping from the eaves, and the pretty hedge of hawthorn and brier rose that encircled the garden.*

She asked again, 'Is it very, very far to Teeperaree, M'sieu?'

In reply we drank to the big push that we were expecting day by day. As we rose to go, we smiled and said, 'Not far now, Madame.'

Down by the Somme I heard it again. Our division had just come out from the inferno of Sausage Valley to the sweet quiet behind the line. Though bone weary, the lads still managed to mutter it as they struggled back to their billets.

I heard it yet again at a concert, one of those rare joys in a soldier's life on active service. It was our second night behind the line. We had just left our part of Pozieres in the hands of another division. I shall not easily forget that night.

We had the whole gamut of American ragtime played by the orchestra. There was no score, but the pianist played with a frenzy of joy. The violinist (some unwilling quartermaster had guarded his instrument for him after many bribes) ripped through piece after piece with a gaiety that caught us all. We forgot the heaving trenches, the deafening *crump* of bursting shells, all the indescribable nightmares of first-line life. That tired, strained look

---

* Lille was occupied by the Germans at the time.

about the eyes and mouths gave way to the old light and smile. The old recklessness returned.

Then, wonder of wonders, they turned to 'Tipperary'. Did we sing? Ah! It was months since we had let ourselves go like that. Right from the heart the old song came that night.

Quietness fell on us as the last notes died away on seeing a dispatch-bearer rushing through the door. He delivered his missive and departed. The colonel rose, the scrap of paper still clasped firmly in his hand. 'Comrades,' he shouted. 'Ridge taken; all counter-attacks on Pozieres repulsed with heavy loss.'

We had helped to take Pozieres and to hold it, and our comrades had come in, and they held it. That was enough. We did not cheer for a moment, for the grim picture that we had forgotten for the while came back with stunning force. Then we cheered and cheered.

Later, coming along a narrow strip of road, I seemed to see familiar figures and they were hurrying as though to meet someone. Then I knew where I really was – Somewhere in Tipperary. Yes, I know it was only a dream.

We are still on the road to Tipperary. It has had a lot of queer turnings lately. Some of them seemed to go in quite the wrong direction, but they turned out, at last, to be quite all right. And though we never sing it now, and though we grumble more even than we used to, yet we say to ourselves, 'It's a long, long way to Tipperary'.

I stretched out that night on my greatcoat under a cherry tree in a tiny orchard, just dozing off to sleep. The good news and the songs I had heard seemed to mingle together, a bit here and a bit there, but all part of the one theme.

A long, exhausting fight, but Pozieres has begun another path for me. 'It's a long, long way to Tipperary, but we're not downhearted yet.' Following right on as though it, too, was part of the whole,

'The ridge is taken. The ridge, the ridge is taken. Pozieres holds, it still holds.'

•

Though severely wounded in battle, Reverend Stutley drafted a book on the importance of that song for the soldiers, which he successfully published on his return to Australia in July 1917.

CHAPTER 12

NEWS FROM THE 44th

'We should no more dream of pitting Australian armies against German, than of pitting Tasmanian sculpture against French.'
G. K. Chesterton[70]

The top brass

The 44th Battalion had a long history within Steenwerck. They formed part of the 3rd Division under the command of General Monash, who commented on just how proud he was of how that division was shaping up. A variety of stories follow, some showing how inflexible some of the top brass could be. Following orders was an absolute within the Army, even when it led to ridiculous situations, as we will soon see.

Captain Cyril Longmore, *The Australian*[71]

September 1917. The 44th Battalion was badly battered in the Messines fighting. Old Bill's thousand were a shadow of the lusty fighting force which left Fremantle a short year before. Many faces were missing from the depleted ranks but, in their passing, they established glorious precedents which set a high standard for new arrivals and which, to their credit, the reinforcements never lowered …

Colonel William Mansbridge was posted to staff duties in England. The sense of loss to the battalion in parting with Old Bill, the individual who had guided it until fully maturing as a fighting unit, was great indeed.

After a few days rest, the battalion marched to Nieppe, occupying the Armentieres sector, where our Officers' billet was conveniently cross-sectioned by the Huns.

Here two new factors appeared. The first was the sudden, definite recognition of sport in the necessary training of a soldier for active service. This meant that mornings consisted of the ordinary military training, but afternoons were given over entirely to sports of all kinds. As the weather was decent, and with no other distractions, the sporting events were entered into with all the vim and vigour that characterised the Digger. This resulted, after the first fortnight, in an appreciable decrease in the number on sick parade.

The second factor was the introduction of organised bombing raids on a large scale over the areas occupied behind the line. Almost every night squadrons of combatants did their best to make sleep impossible. The sentry's three sharp whistle blasts (for lights out) were promptly obeyed.

The intensity of air organisation could be seen by the infantryman. Lines of observation balloons; aeroplanes, both scouting and fighting, and anti-aircraft guns on motor lorries, were much in evidence. By night the bombing planes, with dozens of searchlights criss-crossing the heavens, seeking to get the intruders inside their rays, and the thunder of the anti-aircraft gun's barrage on some located plane – these, with the extra windy feeling which all felt when bombs were falling from space, left no doubt as to the part the Air Force was playing in this war.

Bombers created more fear at night than the actual damage which they caused deserved. On rare occasions when one was brought down, by a lucky Archie hit or by tracer bullets from British fighting planes, there was genuine, and excusable, exultation at the sight of the blazing bomber falling to earth. Generally, its bombs burst on impact.

On August 20, the battalion left the battle sphere for the back areas to reorganise, refit, and train for further big work which lay ahead.

Entraining at Steenwerck station, after the usual discomforts of a troop train, the battalion detrained at Wizernes station. A fourteen-kilometre march brought us to Merck St. Lievin, the prettiest little village that it was ever the 44th's good luck to strike in France. Merck was situated in a deep valley, through which a river flowed, with fruit trees and crops surrounding it. There was a general air of prosperity, and no signs of war excepting for the absence of menfolk. Merck gave promise of a very enjoyable time.

The village people have had no troops billeted for two years and were inclined to look sideways at Australians, in consequence of which much rumour had credited them. However, the Digger soon fixed that. Within two days he was part and parcel of Merck, playing with the kiddies and helping with farm work, as if he had been there for years.

As bad luck would have it, the battalion was only allowed one week at Merck, because at this stage the necessity for its use as an artillery area was recognised. Preparations were in hand for another big attack. Morning and afternoon found all hands fitting themselves for various jobs. Sport was still a crucial factor and helped to build the stamina of troops up to a very high standard. If ever stamina was needed, it would be needed in the next stunt, as the 44th found to its cost.

25 September. The campaign began. Three stiff marches led the battalion to Poperinge, where they camped in tents outside of town.

For the first time during this war, five Australian Divisions were in the same area. Two were already in the thick of fighting in front of Ypres, and the other three were soon to be thrown into it, literally 'up to the neck.'

Poperinge was the railhead for British troops fighting in the Ypres salient. As fighting on the Western Front was now practically confined to this sector, it became a target for aerial bombing raids on a tremendous scale.

The difference in sound of British and German planes was marked. The former's engines made a level purr, while the latter buzzed loud and soft alternately. German bombers carried five big bombs, each about 3 feet 6 inches long and a foot in diameter. The windy feeling was felt by everyone, although not everyone would admit it.

With all hands sound asleep in a tent, comes the unmistakeable buzz of the Bosche plane. Boom! one. Boom! two (nearer); Boom! three (still closer but half a mile away yet). Not a sound or a move from the 'sleepers'. Boom! four (seemingly in the next field). A slight but uneasy stir. Boom! the fifth and last. A simultaneous and deep sigh of relief from everyone, a general turning over, wriggling and twisting. The occupants settle down once more to their interrupted slumber. Slumber, too, that might have been their last if their luck had varied ever so little.

2 October. A portion of the nucleus (a percentage of all ranks kept out of fights so that, no matter how heavy the losses, the battalion would have some old hands to graft the reinforcements onto) was sent up to do a cable-bury. They travelled in buses, no sooner alighting when a Fritz aeroplane dropped bombs and killed or wounded about twenty men.

At 10 pm the following night the battalion commenced its approach march and moved in single file to its assembly position on Hill 40 near Zonnebeke, across five miles of shell-torn ground.

The Zonnebeke was ordinarily a small creek, but shell-fire had chopped and churned it up, forming an impassable liquid morass about 150 yards across.

When the head of the column (and 700 men in single file on a dark night forms 'some' column) reached the Zonnebeke, it was found that the duckboard bridge over it had been shot away.

There was nothing for it but to sit the battalion in their damp tracks while the guide found another crossing. After an hour's search in darkness and mud, another bridge was found closer to the railway line. By 2 am the battalion was assembled in its allotted position.

Owing to the lack of opportunities for reconnaissance, it was necessary that the battalion be led by one guide. As A.I.F. men are aware, the job of suiting the pace at the head of the column to the requirements of men towards its rear was no easy one. However, the pace set was no more than one mile per hour. Touch was thus maintained and without any disorganisation, and with only a few casualties by shell-fire, the assembly was completed.

The Australian attack was timed to start at 6 am, and their barrage was to come down a few minutes before that. During the preceding hours, the Aussie guns were quiet but, as it happened, Fritz had decided to attack Australian positions on the same morning (October). He was ten minutes too late, as his attack was timed to commence at 6.10 am. His troops, among whom were the famous Iron Division, noted as never having lost a trench or failed to take its objective, assembled at the same time as the Australians. When both completed their arrangements there were, unknown to each other, two bodies of assault troops lying in some places within fifty yards, awaiting the dawn to have at each other's throats.

The German barrage started. From that time the troops endured an ever-increasing storm of high explosive shells, literally showering the area in which the Diggers crouched in shell holes with no possible cover, awaiting the arrival of the one which must sooner or later fall into their particular shell hole.

Casualties in the 44th were numerous. 'D' Company lost fifty per cent of its strength and the other companies also suffered heavily. In addition, the usual Flanders drizzle drenched everyone to the skin. Under such circumstances the wetting was of minor importance. It was another of those proverbial straws which, however, never broke the Diggers' backs. Only those who endured it can imagine what the suspense was like.

Suddenly a flash of fire behind, a thunderous deafening roar in front, giving notice that Australian guns were hitting back. As the barrage went forward the infantry, eager for action, followed it closely. Dead, wounded, and dazed Germans met the view everywhere.

The enemy attack was completely disrupted. Five minutes after the barrage, his attacking troops were either casualties or on their way back as prisoners of war. However, isolated concrete dug-outs, protected from shell-fire and manned by staunch machine gunners, held out. Each caused many casualties before they were wiped out but did not hold up the general advance.

The spectacle then was lines of casual Australians following the barrage with rifles slung over their shoulders, smoking cigarettes, or souvenired cigars.

Captain Tom Bone,[*] a popular officer, was killed by a shell on the Ridge. In addition to being a brave and efficient soldier, Tom had a beautiful voice. His singing at the various camp concerts had been keenly appreciated by all who heard him.

---

[*] Captain Thomas Bone, 44th Australian Infantry Battalion, killed 5 October 1917.

Western Mail[72]

Then my company was camped at Jesus Farm, in the muddiest field in Flanders, about three kilometres (five by road) from Steenwerck. Orders were received that the battalion was to parade at Steenwerck for review by the Divisional Commander.

Greatcoats and ground sheets were to be carried in their packs.

The eventful day arrived. As the company assembled on its own parade ground before the march to the village, it started to drizzle. The officers were perturbed. Quite a lot of debate took place as to whether the Orders should be carried out to the letter, or whether the circumstances would permit an alteration. As a runner, I was dispatched to battalion headquarters to find out whether the order still held. In the meantime, the company would march, greatcoats in pack. I remember floundering across that Flanders fallow, each step gathering more of France on my boots, while the drizzle gradually worked up to a steady rain.

I arrived at headquarters and delivered my message. More perturbed officers! Oh, yes! The order distinctly said, 'Greatcoats in pack.' Ten minutes elapsed before I heard a voice say, 'Send the runner along to brigade headquarters to find out.'

Off I went again, this time only a few hundred yards. Another wait. More perturbation.

I heard voices in the Holy of Holies at Brigade discussing the matter. 'You had better see the Brigade Major.' Then the Brigade Major's voice boomed, 'Countermand the order at once. Send a message that greatcoats will be worn.'

Through pouring rain, off I went again. As I reached the outskirts of the village, I met the company, every man wet to the skin. The company halted. I delivered my latest order to the Ops. Officer. 'Remove your packs and put on your greatcoats.'

The troops did so and continued the march. At last, we arrived at the parade ground with everyone wearing greatcoats. Hell!

The sun came out. Believe it or not, the sun shone for the whole of that review, while the troops 'steamed.'

The Mount Magnet recruits

Many of the 44th's recruits came from Mount Magnet, the longest surviving gold-mining town in Western Australia.

They insisted the 44th was the reason why the term 'digger' was applied to men of the A.I.F., they having been diggers before the war. Brigadier-General Cannan eulogised their famed digging prowess in the trenches, claiming its members had dug more trenches than the other three battalions, 41st–43rd, combined. The 42nd battalion challenge that claim.

One miner recalled some lively memories of those billets at Steenwerck, including the time that they occupied some very dodgy glass hot-houses that certainly did not live up to that name.

Although the building had been a plant nursery, doors were missing, most of the glass windows were broken, and the place was terribly draughty, wet and uncomfortable. Despite these freezing conditions, when the soldiers set fire to some timber supports for warmth, officialdom made them pay damages.

One soldier's most memorable story concerned a young boy named Nobby, who turned up in camp one day. Here the soldier will tell you in his own words.

Western Mail[73]

Early one morning a boy about twelve years of age came in and shouted, with a Cockney accent, 'Nobby is 'ere and all ahbart it.' He had a basket under each arm filled with hot buns, cakes, cigarettes, and picture postcards. He did good business. The next day he brought his mother and later introduced an old man as his dad.

Nobby seemed to like the Aussies. It was amusing to see him teaching French to about thirty Diggers, all firing questions at once.

He spoke French, German, Belgian and English fluently. He told us the colours of all the troops who had camped there before us, where they went to and where we were going. He was right, too.

Nobby was a bright, good-looking boy, with Anglo-Saxon features, blue eyes, fair skin, broad shoulders, and a thick neck. He claimed to be French, but he did not resemble any French type that I saw. Indeed, he looked a typical German. His English was perfect and the way he imitated the Cockney was good enough for me to appreciate. I came originally from South-East London and could speak that familiar dialect quite well. He told me he learned it from London regiments that had camped there before us.

Months later, I went over to Steenwerck. During my visit, I made inquiries about Nobby. He had been a terrible brigand, my informant told me. Nobby, his *father,* and his *mother,* were caught red-handed supplying information to the enemy. They were convicted and shot. The boys were so sorry for Nobby, the general opinion being that the British would have found his youth an extenuating circumstance. He obviously hadn't thought that scheme up on his own.

The sniping contest

Captain Longmore resumed his story of life in the trenches, when peeping over the parapets almost cost one lieutenant his life during a sniping contest, and described the necessity for filling out a casualty report.

Western Mail[74]

One misty morning Fritz was very daring. In spite of the fact that the trenches, at one part of the front, were 25 or 30 yards apart, a sniping contest was taking place at anything from 30 to 200 yards distance. Just as one of the 44th boys signalled a "bull", Lieutenant Alf Guy, with his pal Sergeant-Major Dick Cornish of

A Company, with more daring than good judgement, looked over the top to investigate.

The two tin hats at this short distance formed a target which even the worst shot in the whole German army could hardly fail to score on, and without any sound, the little lieutenant fell to the bottom of the trench, a shot passing through his tin hat and the left side of his head.

Cornish immediately reported the casualty to the next officer in charge of the line and an inspection revealed the sad fact that Alf was apparently out for keeps. Laying him aside and attending at the moment to the more important business of getting even, the sniping continued.

Sergeant Bert May[*] immediately evened the score by knocking a Fritz's cap (together with a goodly part of his skull) a decent three feet in the air. There was no doubt about this German going west. When matters quietened down a little, they took another look at Lieutenant Guy, chiefly with the object of collecting his few personal belongings to send home, and of performing a hasty trench burial. Before those arrangements were complete, however, Alf showed unmistakable signs of life, and cancelling the order for the burial and amending the casualty report, the officer in charge had him taken to the safe precincts of the advanced dressing station, situated about 300 yards from the front line, where the doctor pronounced that the lucky young officer had a fighting chance.

Removed to the security of the clearing station at Steenwerck, Alf slowly strengthened his slippery grip on life. His strong constitution, coupled with the unremitting care and attention bestowed on him by doctors and nurses of the Medical Corps, enabled him to recover and eventually return to Western Australia.

---

*   Sergeant George Albert May, 41st Battalion. Carpenter, enlisted 31 May 1915.

CHAPTER 13

2nd A.C.C.S. STEENWERCK

'You can see by the graveyards where a casualty clearing station has been. You come to think of the Casualty Clearing Station as the place where the boys go to die.'
Keith Murdoch[75]

The soldier Keith Murdoch

Long before he established the Murdoch media empire, Keith Murdoch was an Australian war correspondent. He arrived at the 2nd Australian Casualty Clearing Station in Steenwerck due to a minor foot injury. Murdoch had previously written to Prime Minister Andrew Fisher about his war experiences: *'It is of bigger things I write to you. I shall talk as if you were by my side, as in the good days.'*[76]

Unlike his earlier letter on gross mismanagement at Gallipoli, he was full of praise for staff at the Steenwerck station.

Here, soldiers were triaged upon arrival, their fate decided within moments. Some were whisked away for surgery, others given a quiet corner in which to draw their final breaths. The lucky ones, if such a term could be used, were stabilised and prepared for transport to more permanent medical facilities. Murdoch's insights into the condition of his fellow sufferers reveal for me an up-close-and-personal account of life and death near the battlefields.

The Herald[77]

December 1917. Here, the mortally wounded are brought if they have not breathed their last on the long stretcher-journey or at the main dressing station. Here, the sorely stricken have their fight for life, sinking to utter weakness, lying for nights and days in pain, refusing death to the last. There is an inescapable atmosphere of tragedy. It is a place where brave men sometimes moan and cry, where the sounds of the night are sounds of distress and death, where youth looks aged, strong men are weak; where flesh wounds are stitched, where the surgeons are constantly working.

Yet the sense of tragedy does not sink deep nor brood in the Casualty Clearing Station. Of all the places on the battlefields, it is the one place where Australian mothers would get most comfort and feel most proud, for there is a genuine kinship over casualties.

It comes partly from skill, partly from physical stamina, but mostly from that fine asset of the digger – indomitable, invincible, indefatigable spirit. Those men defy their material wounds. In their weakness they are more masterful than ever. They are not going to allow torn flesh and smashed bones to beat them.

This Casualty Clearing Station to which I was sent, with a mere damaged ankle, lies white and quiet on the rim of a peaceful farming village. Steenwerck is outside all shelled zones. You feel again on the edge of a forgotten land of women and children. There are the rolling sounds of guns in the distance. On the ground beside the colonel's tent is a large cross of red and white stones, a petition to enemy aeroplanes – often not heeded.

Such noises and sights have become second nature, and do not affect the pleasure of being among homes without shell marks, and with pleasant-faced women and children who come, agog with curiosity, to peep into the wards.

The dozen large marques stand in lines three deep, edged by duck-boarded paths. A group of assorted huts shows the centre of the Administrative area. There preside the staff registrar, commanding officer, dentist, barber, dispenser, carpenter, and x-ray operator. Equally mixed in are specialists and tradesmen, permanent Army Medical Corps men, recruits from infantry units, and the all-important orderlies.

Kilted infantrymen carry the stretchers from the motor-ambulance to the receiving tent. Long-serving Royal Army Medical Corps non-commissioned officers register the new patient and label him for a bed. Another willing group advances him along the duckboards.

The Casualty Clearing Station gets its staff from the highways and byways of the army. Somehow the kind-hearted and good-natured gravitate to it; un-armed men who will work their skin off scrubbing the floor of a sick room or unmurmuringly bend their backs to the stretchers for long days and nights during times of fighting.

These are busy periods. The ambulances roll up along the roads with load after load. They go slowly. Even the best of roads is rough to wounded men. Every jolt means a sharp pang. Ask any five seriously wounded men what moments were worst – four at least will tell of the ambulance. That is why the receiving tent shows so many taut faces. During these minutes of waiting for stretchers on the ground, the pain of the ambulance drive is still wearying them.

Their wounds as yet bear only make-shift dressings. Blood is oozing out again, vitality is low. At the aid post far up the line, where the battalion doctor has given first aid, the man has been labelled. From post to post and from station to station, hands have fingered the stout envelope tied to the tunic, and eyes have read the diagnosis.

Here, in the receiving tent, a new paper is slipped in. The envelope never leaves the wounded soldier until he is discharged.

It goes with him to the ward where it is first tied to his bed, then onto him – with more papers added by now – to indicate a hospital at the coast or a trip to Blighty.

You feel that you are taken hold of in the receiving tent by a strange army machine which will pass you through process after process until you are either dead or presentably cured.

It pursues its purpose as remorselessly and inevitably as that other machine which, having put its man into uniform, passes him on and on through every form of training until he is a fit soldier in the line.

Lying in the ward, you get closer to the young Australian's soul than you have ever thought possible. I felt like a spy listening to brave men's most sacred secrets. Yet these lads' ravings showed such pure and good things that I propose to tell of them. As veils dropped from their minds and the clouds of unconsciousness lifted, there were revealed jewels of thought and motive.

Brave lads, single-minded and simple-hearted. On my right, a young country boy from Portland, Victoria, a harbour engineer; here on my left, a Sydney University under-graduate, unchanged by all this fighting. Down the ward there, the mere boy who raves so much is a Riverina farmer's son, with a picture of his mother seemingly burning in his brain.

When they speak unconsciously, they are always either at home among their dear ones, or on the battlefield amongst their brave comrades.

Could any fact of the Australian Imperial Force be more piquant? Could anything be at once more comforting and hopeful to a nation that asks but two things of its young men; that they should be true to their homes, and be strong fighters for their nation's cause?

Here, in the sincere confessional of the hospital ward, was proof that none can doubt.

I lay for two days and nights among many desperately hurt men. Not once did I hear a word that would not console a mother or gratify a patriot. Released from consciousness, the young fighter's mind sped straight for his mother. 'Mother! Oh, Mother!' cries this Riverina lad. He talks at times gaily to her; at other times he tells her of the pain.

Other men do the same. It is always the parents, sisters, and brothers. Or it is a critical moment of the battle in which, as they speak their inmost thoughts, they discuss difficulties, exhort and command and console their men, tell of their anxieties and what they want to do.

Their words speak of a deep and simple earnestness. 'They're there — and there. Those bullets — it's the machine-gun near the wood. It's straight for it, men. I don't see any other way. Now men, it's straight for it!'

They are always the words of youngsters without personal fear, with earnest desire to do their duty with love for and faith in their platoons, with the responsibility of lives in their hands and leadership in a battle.

The Sisters, members of the great British nursing staff, whose most forward posts are at the Casualty Clearing Stations, make the ward a place of singular comfort and brightness. They look pretty in uniform, with their badges and medals. The degree of vitality in wounded men may be gauged by the interest in their nurses.

This Day Sister has arranged her ward so that *chest* cases are ranged on one side, *head* cases are at the top and mere breakages and flesh hurts are in a bottom row. Playful jealousy is part of the day's amusements, and the Major across the way, who has his arm black with morphia given to ease a jagged leg wound, is accused of impossible caresses.

Opposite is a Tasmanian Colonel, who moved up with his headquarters when shrapnel struck the lot. Every chest case is serious; it gives more chance of cure than the *abdominals*, but it takes a longer course. The Colonel has never lost his smile. He has that character of Tasmanian calm upon him – unchanging, unswerving, smiling. Twice they drew pints of fluid from his chest, but though he grew pale, he kept smiling.

His young officers come to see him, serving as his eyes, and he hears of how his battalion has won through. His only fear is that he will be away for the next stunt. He dictates a letter to his Brigadier beseeching that, by hook or by crook, he be sent for in time. A gallant and trusty Colonel, he will suffer this war for 20 years if needs be.

But none of them doubt ultimate victory or their own capacity to see more heavy fighting. You should hear this quiet, red-headed Upper Hunter boy tell how Chuignes was taken. You can hear the bullets pinging and thwacking and see our gallant lines charging forward. They fear neither death nor defeat. The one matters little; the other cannot touch them.

Great London surgeons come to dress their wounds, shaking heads and voicing opinions. Smart young British general practitioners walk the wards and venture on diagnoses. Now and then men on stretchers are taken to the operating theatre for examination under anaesthetic. Skilled orderlies move about, fixing bandages or noting a change in pulse rate.

These are normal events which pass unnoticed, but the rumour that a hospital train is to go to Boulogne tonight creates a stir. Nearly everyone wants to go. The Colonel fidgets with his *Peggy* bag, a glaring calico contrivance – a recent Red Cross gift, in which he keeps his prized shaving apparatus and a few French coins. The Major swears that he is fit for travel.

The Trench Fever cases assert they are much better, so orderlies pack them on stretchers, and they are repacked upon comfy beds in the fine broad train. They are another step nearer to Blighty. It is sometimes worthwhile to hide a lot of pain.

Fully ninety per cent of the ward will soon be gone. Others come. What of the remaining ten per cent? Some cannot be moved for many days.

And others? Well, the middle-aged one-star lieutenant, who got the oxygen all last night, died this morning.

And the Riverina boy? The screen is around his bed. They are moving him, also, to the mortuary.

CHAPTER 14

ANZAC RIDGE

'He has passed away in a worthy cause for liberty and righteousness.'
Lieutenant Albert Parker, 60th Battalion[78]

I regret to inform you

During the war, the greatest dread of those left at home was to receive a telegram or letter mentioning three specific words.

The phrase 'died of wounds' conveyed to the sorrowful partners or parents the enormity of their loss, yet it offered no detailed explanation of what had actually happened to their loved one.

Following such terse notification, the families usually received a more formal letter, either handwritten by the soldier's commanding officer and giving some accurate information about the individual's demise during the heat of battle, or a typewritten letter from the Red Cross who handled enquires for more information on the location of their gravesite. Such letters documented the war's horror and heartbreak.

Of more use to those families were letters or even visits from fellow soldiers, who were able to give more precise, heartfelt stories about the soldier's last moments. Many such letters are still preserved in our national archives.

General Sir William Birdwood, published in *The Gosford Times*[79]

A.I.F. Headquarters, France.
Dear Mr. Woodbury,
It has taken me some little time to answer your letter regarding your boy, who was killed in action on 14th of April last, as on making inquiries in the 2nd Machine Gun Company, which you mentioned in your letter, I found he was unknown in that unit.

I had therefore to write to our Records Office at the Base and ascertained that he was serving with the 5th Company of the 2nd Machine Gun Battalion.

Since writing to me, you will, I hope, have received a letter which was written you by his section officer, giving you the details available. The battalion was then in the line east of Amiens, and while your son was near the village of Boves, returning from the line after delivering rations, he was killed by an enemy shell. He was buried in the cemetery at Boves, and the battalion chaplain officiated at the grave.

I feel for you very deeply in your sad loss. I well know that it is irreparable, but trust that it will afford you some comfort to know your boy was prepared to make the supreme sacrifice fighting gallantly for our noble cause of right and liberty. I had hoped I might be able to find out the unit of your other boy when making inquiries in the 2nd Machine Gun Battalion, but no one there could give me this information. I hope you have the best of news about him. You may well be proud of both your boys. I am very glad indeed that the gallantry and devotion to duty displayed by your son, Harold, was recognised by the award of the

Military Medal, which I always think is such a fine decoration for a boy to gain.

With my kind regards, and again my deep sympathy with you in your great sacrifice.

Yours sincerely,

Wm. Birdwood.

Albert Parker, published in the *Horsham Times* [80]

January 1918.

My dear Mrs. Knight,

On behalf of the officers, N.C.O's. and men of A Company, 60th Battalion, I wish to express our deepest sympathy with you in the loss of your boy (218-1), Private A. C. Knight.

On the morning of October 10, we were on Anzac Ridge, and an enemy shell burst on the trench where your son was standing. He was buried. When we were able to dig him out there was no movement, but he was taken immediately to the dressing station.

The doctor stated that he had passed away. He was buried by the medical officer. It was his first time in the line, yet he was very brave, and never flinched from duty. We have lost a faithful comrade and feel keenly your loss. He has passed away in a worthy cause for liberty and righteousness. Each man of us is willing to give life itself if need be for those in the homeland. He has gone to his reward for work well done.

With deepest sympathy, your representative in the A.I.F.,

Albert Parker, Lieutenant.

On Anzac Ridge

The tragedy of war was further documented in the following entry about sustaining a wound amid the death of one's comrades.

Mildura Cultivator[81]

Gunner P. Ken Clark spent only four days with the 101st Battery on Anzac Ridge but saw more of real red war in that short time than in all his previous experience. The crash of shells and the noise of gunfire was so incessant that there was scarcely a minute of the day or night when the earth did not vibrate owing to the concussion.

'Picture a dark night, with jets of flame continually shooting upward to your rear; white and coloured flares and Verey lights bursting and illuminating the skyline to your right, left and front; bright flashes from bursting shells adding to the Guy Fawkes display here and there. And the drums of your ears which are filled with cotton wadding almost bursting as the ground vibrates beneath your feet. The air is rent by an endless succession of bangs, booms, cracks, crashes and thumps. Picture all this and you will have some idea of what it was to be on Anzac Ridge when a night strafe was on.'

Ken was wounded in the thigh (in three places) by fragments from an explosive shell, which mortally wounded three of his comrades. Companions immediately applied a field dressing, and stretcher-bearers bore him away. Ken's opinion of the stretcher-bearers is that they are 'the bravest of the brave,' and there are few of them who have not earned the V.C. several times over. All day and all night they carry on, risking death at almost every step, so that their wounded comrades might get through to safety.

A solemn funeral

Major-General Holmes, an Australian officer prominent in the Battle of Messines, was killed on 2 July, while escorting several dignitaries over ground captured during the battle, when a high explosive German shell struck his car.[82]

Daily Herald[83]

General Holmes was buried at Steenwerck beside the Australian clearing station. There was a large assemblage of British, Australian, and New Zealand officers and men. The coffin-bearers were General Wisdom, Colonels Dowse, Watson and Heritage, and Majors Fraser and Lyons. The gathering included Generals Birdwood, White, Godley, Russell and many British generals.

A gallant endeavour
Private J. H. Shearer, *Brisbane Courier*[84]

Messines. August 1917. Rain ceased at dawn, leaving heavy cloud cover, but visibility was fair. The enemy artillery was active at night in the central and southern portions of the battle front, especially on the Broodseinde Ridge, Anzac Ridge, and Roulers railway, putting down considerable quantities of gas shells between 4 and 4.30 am. When the barrage began the enemy machine gunners answered with a terrible rattle.

In a gallant endeavour to bring in a wounded comrade, a sterling bearer, Lionel Tyson, made the last sacrifice. Men of his calibre are rarely met. Conscientious to a degree, and full of human sympathy, his memory will long be cherished by many in the regiment.

Busy night removing wounded to dressing station. Major Mundell was injured by rifle bullets and died shortly after arrival at the casualty station.

Rested in dug-outs all day and made preparations to move up to relieve troops in the front line. Left under cover of darkness and travelled three miles through rain and mud, across country and long winding saps. The effect of our bombardment was ghastly. It had ploughed the country with shell craters, torn fields of barbed wire to twisted shreds, and broken trenches to shapeless ditches. The town of Messines was now heaps of ruins being lashed by explosives.

In the darkness we had taken a wrong turn. It was almost dawn before we arrived at an enemy cement pill-box, which was to be our home for the period of our stay while holding the line. To strike a match would give the position away and draw fire, so we crawled into roughly constructed bunks and briefly rested.

At dawn, through a small window in the concrete wall, we saw our shells reducing the buildings to dust in the village of Warneton. It was well-known that an old sugar refinery sheltered (German) machine guns and this huge structure soon tottered and fell across the cobbled street. Aeroplanes flew low over our outpost positions, and we could detect the features of both pilot and observer. All day we kept under cover. Heavy shelling round the blockhouse, and two direct hits shattered a corner.

Marched in the early morning to the ruined city of Ypres and were soon billeted in the shattered ramparts on the canal bank. The world-famed Cloth Hall and Cathedral lay in ruins.

On the hillside a forest of white crosses marked the resting-place of comrades who had made the last sacrifice in the cause of justice and righteousness. A feeling to avenge on the morrow the sacrifices of these martyred slain came over us. Instructions as to form of attack, timetable of barrage and study of aeroplane photos of the scene of the morrow's operations were given in minute detail. Shells were falling amongst the ruins of the city throughout the day. Our guns bustled along either bank of the canal and other commanding positions. At dark, our battalions fell in on parade, and the eight kilometres march to the scene of attack was commenced. At midnight, a halt was made for two hours to allow the waning moon to set over the distant hills. Enemy planes overhead dropped bombs and artillery signals.

Shells from guns of huge calibre tore up the swampy marshes behind and in front of us. The enemy front line was plainly visible by the brilliant flares from a hundred pistols. The muddy roads were strewn with wreckage from transport lorries. Red Cross cars passed towards the clearing station laden with their suffering human freight.

On we passed through winding saps, over duckboards which bridged the reeking marsh. A shell burst with a deafening roar; word was passed back for stretcher bearers. Our officers ordered a halt and along the crest of the ridge, amidst columns of mist and smoke, we lay in shell holes, waiting for our artillery barrage to open.

Before dawn, at the moment set down, the messengers of death went screaming overhead. For 20 minutes we lay before the order to advance came along the line of waiting troops. The flash of steel rang out, and the first wave moved on amidst the smoke and darkness, under cover of one of the finest artillery barrages of the war. The S.O.S. signals went up along a two-mile front of the enemy. A counter barrage was launched on our supports and advancing troops. Anzac Ridge and Polygon Wood were won. Three of our squad were wounded, some officers and men being disabled.

Strong calls were made upon the men to carry out the work of consolidating the ground so dearly bought. Working hard all day and a greater part of the night, we were carrying in the wounded across the marshes under shell-fire. Privates Marshall and Moles sent in as walking cases, these making nine casualties out of our regimental squad of 16 bearers for the day, two of which proved fatal. The glorious deeds of the Australians will be remembered because of this gallant stand.

The rain reduced the battleground to a perfect loblolly, but Anzac soldiers navigated the mud seas and the mud mountains like miracle men. I talked to Field-Marshal Haig yesterday. He was full of admiration for the men and the absence of whimpering under the worst possible conditions.

'They are not afraid of the worst punishment the Germans have yet offered,' he said, 'but the entire history of Flanders shows that mud is always the soldier's worst enemy.'

Notwithstanding the night's heavy rain the troops formed up for the morning attack and progressed along the entire front from the Ypres–Roulers railway to our junction with the French on the southern edge of Houthulst Forrest. Throughout this front we captured many defended localities, fortified farms, woods, and concreted strong points, taking a number of prisoners. The fighting was severe on the slope of the main ridge west of Passchendaele and the main ridge itself south of Passchendaele.

Heavy rain recommenced this morning and continued to increase in violence all day long, impeding our progress.

CHAPTER 15

THE ANZAC COVES

'Anderson and Brittlebank, the pianist and scenic artist we had with us for some time, were blown to pieces the other day in their dug-outs.'
Daily Telegraph reporter[85]

Besides Anzac Ridge and Steenwerck, another name that cropped up was Anzac Cove, synonymous with Gallipoli. However, one file referred to the 'Anzac Coves'. I discovered that they were a group of 'entertainers' commissioned by Sir Winston Churchill's brother, John, by order of General Birdwood, for a secret reason. He surmised that the soldiers needed some form of therapy for their post-traumatic stress disorder, long before the phrase was coined. Birdwood's aim was to provide soldiers with a fun show after each battle to calm their nerves and give them a break. However, this approach fell far short of the treatment needed for shell-shock or gassing.

This also proved dangerous for the performers, often working only metres from the frontline. During one show, several were blown to pieces. Muddy battlefields, pouring rain and freezing temperatures were challenging environments in which to produce live shows. Blackouts were also an important prerequisite in the trenches, to hide soldiers from overhead surveillance and bombing threats – but they were not conducive for the performers. Lack of materials for costumes was yet another challenge.

A valuable secret

Staff Sergeant Rannall Carlisle (1880–1927) was listed as a theatrical manager when he embarked for the war from Sydney on 22 December 1915.

For a while after Australian troops arrived in France, their entertainment had mostly been left to chance. But when Carlisle arrived, given his entertainment background, he recognised the wealth of theatrical talent among the Anzac units. He was appointed their supervising manager.

He soon established 'The First Anzac Concert Party'. All the members had been under fire, some having been wounded, and two had been in the original landing party at Gallipoli. Carlisle's efforts significantly boosted troop morale and provided much-needed relief and distraction from the harsh realities of war.

The Sun[86]

December 1917. Major John Churchill (Winston's brother) was Camp Commandant, 1st Anzac, and with the hearty approval of General Birdwood, formed a Corps Concert Party for entertaining the troops. The Comforts Fund Commissioner supplied the funds to purchase a piano, music, and stage properties of every description.

The pantomime troupe, humorously called *Anzac Coves*, are giving London a splendid tonic at the Court Theatre, in aid of the Australian Repatriation Fund. Their variety entertainment, which is both varied and entertaining, has more spirit than many a monster revue. The performers have the fresh, breezy style that seems natural to those who come 'direct from the firing line.'

Born comedians and sweet singers, they are not only masters of back-chat and rag-time but can sing a patriotic song or tell a tale of war with genuine feeling. Their melodrama is full of broad fun, with the result that they have to give two or three shows nightly. Even then, many lads are turned away each night. The number of the present cast is 13, and the work they perform is marvellous. The price of admission is one franc for officers, and half that for soldiers. Their records show that more than 150,000 Australian troops have heard them. Funds of over £900 raised in the first six weeks were used to buy coffee and such likes for the frontline soldiers.

The Register[87]

Often, after having given a show in their *theatre* they have hurried away in the darkness, with their piano and a few props in a motor lorry, to entertain troops coming out of the line. They completely uplift the spirits of war-worn infantrymen a few hours returned from some of the most violent hand-to-hand fighting of the present war.

The Coves put on shows in pouring rain and have carried on a programme with 15in. shells landing within 100 yards of their theatre. Sergeant Carlisle selected most of the cast members. 'As a party of entertainers we are the closest of all to the firing line,' he says, 'and have to put over our show under the most trying conditions. Shells and bombs play a big part. Sometimes these drown the performances, and the earth appears to shake. We all have to wear steel helmets and gas masks and have some very exciting times.'

Rannall Carlisle, *Darling Downs Gazette*[88]

When the Anzac Coves come over next Monday, London will be able to see entertainment exactly the same as that which men of Australian battalions in reserve, close behind the lines, nightly visit. Shows are performed free of charge for the wounded in hospital wards.

Not many weeks ago they were playing their great pantomime, Dick Whittington. The snow lay on the ground outside; but about 400 Australians, and perhaps another 200 British troops, had filed in a regular slow theatre queue past the box office in the big barn of a place which acted as a theatre, and sat inside the dark, freezing vault, their blue tobacco smoke curling into the shadows, greeting with gusts of laughter each favourite sally or buffoonery.

The performance had reached the scene with von Tirpitz, or it may have been the apache dance, when the petrol engine, which had been grunting in the snow in the yard showing signs of a most distressing cough, suddenly choked. All the lights went out. The actors flung a tag or two at the expense of the engineers in general, and of the poor beggars who were sweating outside over their enfeebled engine in particular.

The house roared with appreciation. By the time the laughter ended, the bad Old Lady and her reprobate husband were doing their dance upon the stage, with a guttering candle in one hand dimly lighting up their faces for the audience. An orderly, with his head bandaged from a recent gash, struck two dozen uneven candles where the footlights ought to have been, and the performance went gaily on to its end.

'We played at a command performance a few nights ago for H.R.H. the Prince of Wales, Generals Birdwood, Gough, Grimwade, and others. It is really a fine show. There are ten members in all – eight performers, one electrician, and myself as manager.'

A programme detailed the 22 numbers that were given at the command performance. The acts ranged from burlesque comedian's acts to chamber music.

Photographs show the troupe performing at Steenwerck in November 1917.

Leading lady Bobbie Roberts

'Leading lady' Bobbie Roberts was considered one of the finest female impersonators in the A.I.F. The following interview with Bobbie appeared in several Australian newspapers, giving an insight into the mindset of the 'leading lady'.

The Argus[89]

June 1918. The Anzac Coves name somehow conjures up a friendly atmosphere, and so it ought to. 'Cove means pal,' cast member Bobbie Roberts 'put me wise' during an interview.

'And is that why you called yourself like that?' I asked.

'Not entirely. On Gallipoli there is a famous Cove (with a grin), not a slang one this time, known as Anzac Cove. We are really named after that.'

'Do tell me about your performance at Buckingham Palace!' I said, for the Anzac Coves gave a show there before the King and Queen not long ago.

'Well, we went along early in the morning and rehearsed,' my Anzac explained patiently. 'A large stage had been erected for us in the Throne Room.

'We gave exactly the kind of show as those we give the boys in France. We had been told beforehand that we must not expect applause. But we had a lot of applause,' he informed me triumphantly. 'We were all very surprised and pleased. The King and Queen were both there. They came up and spoke to us afterwards.

'The Prince of Wales and Princess Mary were also present, and a good many members of the Royal Household besides. Altogether (my Anzac paused reflectively; evidently cherishing a liking for exactitude), altogether there must have been about one hundred and fifty people present. After we finished our performance, we had tea.

'You know it was not the first time we performed before the Prince of Wales,' he went on, leaning back in his armchair and exhaling smoke rings with a satisfied air. 'The first time was when we were giving a show near the firing line.'

'Oh yes, we have often given performances with shells whizzing around us as we played. We have also performed for two and a half hours in the pouring rain in an open stadium, with a piece of Macintosh laid down as a covering to prevent us from ignominiously slipping. Yes, I think we have performed under pretty well every possible condition.'

'Tell me about your costumes?' I cajole, seized with true feminine curiosity to know how the mere male managed.

'We make them ourselves. When we first started we had none at all, so we made up some black and white Pierrot costumes. Curtains come in very handy because, of course, when you are out at the front you have not much variety of material to choose from. It is a question of putting your wits together and making the best of what you can get.

'Once we contrived a suit of armour out of discarded biscuit tins.

'I was rather proud of my first dress. I remember I was masquerading as a woman, a heavy drama part. Burlesque, of course. Yes, I wanted to wear one of those clinging tragedy-queen-air gowns. You know the style! As I said, we had not much choice of material. I managed to procure red plush curtains. I stood while the boys pinned, draped, and then finally sewed this curtain on me.

'That's much the simplest way of making a dress, you know. Have it sewn together on you, then cut a hole to get in and out of it and there you are, finished and ready for action. Oh yes, women's dresses are quite easy to make.'

I shuddered at such simplicity, but he was so convinced that

I did not like to shake his faith. Instead I inquired humbly whether he had left his gown severely plain or employed a little trimming.

'Just a little. I cut out some flowers and sewed them on. Oh yes, my gown was quite a smart looking creation when it was finished, I can tell you. Perhaps the back view wasn't quite as perfect as the front, but the audience could not see that.'

I assumed he never turned around. A gallant Anzac does not show his back.

I asked about scenery.

'We had our own scenic artist. Oh yes, a professional. All the members of our concert party have been professionals before the war.'

How are they discovered when they are in the army?

'Quite easily. The Commanding Officer sends out a chit, for instance, asking for a professional scenic artist to be sent in. And when he comes along he is commissioned to join us. He has all kinds of *makeshift* canvases to paint on, though. We have often had to use the outer covering of the humble sandbag for a canvas.

'I have ten changes during every performance. It is some rush; I can tell you. I'd have to make up as a woman, re-make again as a man, back again to a woman, and so on! All in a few seconds. Oh yes, I know how a quick-change artist feels, all right.'

He told me of the tour in England, then broke off.

Gripping my hand firmly, (Australians know how to shake hands, no flabby clasp for them), he smiled genially at me and went – exited, I should say.

The Anzac Coves after the war

Between April and July 1920, the group toured the east coast of Australia, presenting the Anzac Coves variety show in Sydney, at the Parramatta Town Hall, in Manly and in country towns such as

Nowra and Wollongong, before appearing later in Adelaide, South Australia.

A 1920 *Illawarra Mercury*[90] article details the group's activities after the war:

> The Anzac Coves, who are to appear in the Wollongong Town Hall, is a concert party composed of artists who enlisted early in the war, and who got together over there and amused the Diggers during many wearisome moments, Bobby [sic] Roberts, female impersonator, who appeared at the command performance before H.M. the King at Buckingham Palace, is appearing with the above.

A *Daily Telegraph* article dated 19 May 1923 stated that Roberts produced a show titled *Bits and Bubbles* to raise funds for the babies at St Margaret's Hospital for Women in Darlinghurst.[91]

CHAPTER 16

STRONG LANGUAGE

'My soldier had brought the letter back with him ... It was a beautiful letter and the last words I shall always remember, "from thy brother who adores thee".'
M.G.S.[92]

So much drama has been written about the war by the soldiers and doctors, so I found it a refreshing change to read some lighter stories from the nursing staff.

This theatre sister's report about the use of – or lack of, in some instances – strong language within the wards, especially within her hearing, gave further insight into the respect that the nurses gained from their patients. She chose to use only initials, although this article was reprinted numerous times in newspapers.

M.G.S., nursing sister's report, *Cobram Courier*[93]

1917. France. 2nd A.C.C.S., Steenwerck. Strong language is often, in fact nearly always, a strong man's outlet in times of severe pain. Yet never have I heard an oath from a suffering soldier. Our orderlies may have heard something stronger, but when a sister is present, the soldiers behave accordingly. Within the last two years in my hospital work amongst these wounded and distressed soldiers, I have had endless opportunities of observing their chivalry in the wards. They never take our services for granted, and their gratitude is boundless.

I was theatre sister and had charge of a small surgical ward. Sitting one day beside a very stalwart gunner, who had just come out of chloroform, I found him greatly distressed. After some questioning, I finally discovered what ailed him. He wanted to know if, under the effect of chloroform, he had used bad language!

'It wouldn't matter for the blokes, the surgeons, you see, Sister. But it would be awful if I done it before you.' I hastily assured him that he'd slept like a lamb and never even bleated.

Once I entered one of the larger wards and found an impressive Court-martial scene proceeding. If there had been any officers about, they would have been much tickled.

The offender was charged with using profane language in the presence of a ward sister. The defence was that the sister was halfway out of the door and therefore, technically, not in the ward.

I suggested that the case be settled by asking the sister what the profane word had been and abiding by her judgment. A tactful sister had heard nothing, so the Court was dissolved, with a threat of *Confinement to Barracks* if the offence was repeated. These may seem small matters, but an army that respects womenfolk can be trusted all the world over.

Many things happened in Belgium in the early days of the war that our soldiers could not bring themselves to speak about. They spoke, however, of security for the fleeing refugees only to be found in and around our trenches.

One well-known Highland regiment was proud of the fact that a party of nuns, fleeing from the Huns with their schoolgirl charges, found sanctuary in a trench filled with fighting Highlanders, who next day formed their escort to the rear. These were stern days. Helpless women and girls were in deadly peril, but their appeals for help found an ever-ready response from every available soldier in our army. A soldier told me a story of this kind. When I then praised him for his share in it, he modestly said, 'Oh, any other bloke would have done as much for my missus and kids.'

That is the spirit in which our soldiers proved their chivalry. It ought to hold a foremost place in our memory, even in these days crowded with dreadful deeds.

'Taking-In-Night' – that is the name we gave to our nights for receiving the wounded; and they were often an education to we sisters in more ways than one. Worn and tired and muddied, the men arrived in blood-stained khaki, clinging to kit bags, heavy or light as the case might be, but all carrying "souvenirs" for loved ones. The first demand was always, 'Where are we? Can you give us a post-card to let our folks know we're all right?'

That *all right* was often pathetic from a surgical point of view but they, poor chaps, felt that to be back in "Blighty" anyhow was a bit of "all right" and would be good news for home.

In many cases the newly returned soldiers had sad duties to perform. Messages from comrades, now dead, were not always easy to remember or deliver. Yet they were the first thing to be seen to after arrival. In many cases, there was often no time for words, and a ring from a dead hand was often the only solace they could bring to an aching heart.

One of my patients had been easing the last moments of a Frenchman who seemed anxious about a letter in his breast-pocket. The only word he was able to say was 'Send' – before he died.

My soldier had brought the letter with him. We found it was for a sister anxious for news of him. It was a beautiful letter. The last words I shall always remember, 'from thy brother who adores thee.' We enclosed the letter to the address given and broke the news as gently as we could to the bereaved sister, telling her of her brother's painless end and his last thoughts for her. We hoped it would be some poor comfort to know how much her letters were cherished.

Our poor soldiers have many difficult tasks in the day's work, but I feel sure this breaking of bad news is, to their sympathetic natures, their biggest trial. Many a man ungrudgingly shortens his five day's sick leave to go and see a pal's widow, because he was the last person with his pal, as it may soothe her to hear all about it.

I am still going around the country as one of an operating team. It is interesting, but there is one drawback; one never gets any rest at all.

As soon as one finishes at one place, a push commences somewhere else in the line, and we are immediately sent on there. Usually, the visiting team is put on night duty and, when a push is on, the theatre people must do 16 hours' duty. I have been on a team now for eight weeks, while attached to our *abdominal* operating centre with a field ambulance. I had a good opportunity of seeing things that would have been quite impossible otherwise.

But in nursing these soldiers, I have finally come to this conclusion, that if soldiering makes patients of their stamp, the sooner humanity, "en bloc," become soldiers of some kind the better. Their rare courage and single-hearted devotion are beyond the range of ordinary comprehension. One can only reverently wonder at it and thank God!

CHAPTER 17

SMOKE AND DEBRIS

'Next second, there was a roaring, blinding crash almost on top of us.'
Jim Armitage[94]

A further chapter from Jim Armitage's diary, shortly after his arrival at the Western front, describes his move to a new subsection, and several close encounters with exploding shells. The use of poisonous gas within the trenches was another hazard Jim encountered. He soon realised the importance of keeping his gas mask handy, while learning the duties of an S.O.S. guard.

Jim Armitage's diary[95]

12 *May* 1918. On Sunday I was sent up to the guns to replace a casualty. I went up that evening on the ration cart and, to use the favourite expression, somewhat had the wind up. When we got quite close to the battery position, a German plane came right over us, flying low, spotting us and evidently the battery as well.

Our gun pits were just behind the village of Ribemont, and the Battalion Headquarters was in an old house inside the village. I reported to B.H.Q. and was told to wait outside for a minute. During this minute, which lengthened into ten, Fritz took it into his head to shell the village. I had never heard a shell coming before, as the sound usually arrived a second after the explosion, and it did not take me long to decide I did not like that sound. I later came to dislike it even more.

The shells were bursting about 70 to 100 yards away. At first, I could not understand the whistling noise which accompanied the explosion of the bursting shell. I would be eventually rescued and taken to the Operations Commander who had his headquarters in the basement. I was told to report to the sergeant in charge of 'D' subsection gun.

On emerging from the basement, I was just in time to see a cottage on the other side of the square go up in smoke and debris.

The 'D' sub fellows were all very nice to me, and welcomed me to their home, consisting of a hole in the ground about 8ft square by 5ft deep and roofed with iron and about 6 inches of earth. They told me I had come at a good time as the right half of the battery was doing all the shooting that night as well as the S.O.S. guard. We could therefore look forward to an undisturbed night. Accordingly, the five of us took off our boots and leggings, put our gas masks at the ready and slumbered peacefully.

Sometime after 5 am, I was awakened by a harsh voice shouting into the dug-out. A red-faced and dust-covered officer yelled, 'Get out. Make for the trenches to the left. It's getting too hot up here.'

This was all Double Dutch to me but, as the other chaps were scrambling into their boots, I followed their example. Not realising the extreme urgency of the situation, I was the last to leave.

As I got my head above the ground, I had a vision of the other men lying flat on their faces in all attitudes. Next second, there was a roaring, blinding crash almost on top of us. Bits of things fell all around me, and I was blown back into the dug-out. Someone shouted, 'Out of there, tout suite.' I picked myself up and rushed out again, nearly falling over a man lying near the entrance to the dug-out with half his head blown off. I saw where the others were heading and ran like a hare after them.

All that day and night we crouched in the old trenches about 150 yards to the flank of the battery while our guns were blasted.

The 108th Howitzer Battery had just vacated a position close to us. They left some of their own gas shells to collect later. German shelling exploded these, and the gas drifted down onto us, resulting in our wearing gas masks for many hours.

That day another man from our subsection was hit, a namesake of mine, Corporal Jedda Armytage, a Victorian. When they took him away – not badly wounded, I think – he left his tunic behind. It happened to be my size. As mine had already been damaged, I souvenired it and wore it until later, when it was blown off my back by a gun backfire.

It rained all day and most of the night; the trench got incredibly muddy, and half flooded. At midday, two men volunteered to go to the cook-house in the village for some food. The cook-house had been strafed too. They eventually ran and crawled back to us under heavy fire and gas. They made it alright, but we had a very gassy stew. That night we manned our guns, what was left of them. I took my turn at S.O.S. guard and was told that, when the lights shot into the air, one below the other and suspended by a parachute, it was to be recognised as a call for help in the way of a protective barrage from the infantry in our sector.

My job was to rush and wake everyone, rush back to the guns, which were already loaded and laid on fixed lines of sight, and fire them off one by one, and continue to fire until the gun crews arrived, (which was usually a matter of seconds). It was a wonderful sight to stand on high ground at night looking over the line, watching the way the gun flashes lit up the trees and the innumerable flares the Germans sent up. Occasionally, a great red flare came from an incendiary shell reflecting in the clouds, or a distant ammunition dump on fire added to the effect, which made the scene weird and beautiful.

We had another casualty that night, a signaller who had come up to the battery with me. He did not see much of the war. Gravely wounded, we heard afterwards he had been sent back to Australia eventually, as a cot case, with 20 pieces of shrapnel in his body.

We had four shoots that night and, as I had passed the gun layers test in England, I was put in the layers seat. We fired off our specified number of rounds at our specified target and got back to our trench before the counter-fire started.

14 *May.* We handed over our battered guns and position to the 11th Battery and made our weary way back to the waggon lines. I did not think there was anyone more relieved than I to get away from that place. It was my first experience of the line, and I was still a bit dazed and shocked by all of the gas and after-effects by being knocked head over heels back into the dug-out. The following morning the battery packed up and began its march to the back areas. I only had a few days of it, but the rest of the chaps had been in action for months and were desperately needing a spell.

The 3rd Division moved out of the line that morning, with the mounted Brigades, the Field Artillery, Divisional Ammunition column, and the Army Service Corps. The procession covered kilometres and made quite a sight on the road. Anyway, a couple of German planes thought so. They were most interested. We were glad to be moving out of, and not into, the line. As it was, they could not do much. We were too far back to have artillery directed at us and, as they seemed to be on a reconnaissance, they only had machine guns.

We went through Vauxin towards Abbeville. We had camped at Vauxin before, beside a large aerodrome on our way up. Our battery camped in some open fields the first night of our withdrawal, and at 4.00 am continued on our way. The weather was hot, the roads dusty, and the gunners had to tramp beside their guns. The gun limbers were loaded with all our gear and camouflage nets, and we had to half run to keep up with the horses.

We finally arrived at Epangs, our destination, about four miles from Abbeville and 30 miles from the line, averaging 15 miles a day on our march. At Epangs we were billeted in the beautiful grounds of an old chateau, where the officers were billeted. We camped under the trees, and bathed every afternoon in the Somme, which flowed at the foot of the grounds. There were battery manoeuvres with the rest of the brigade in the mornings. Our afternoons were free. The Germans flew over us every night to bomb Abbeville. They did a lot of damage and one night killed a number of W.A.C.S., who were attached to a military hospital.

CHAPTER 18

THE OLD INNS

'As long as this old inn stands, it will be haunted by gallant ghosts of men who fought in the great, bad war.'
Philip Gibbs[96]

The small eateries known as estaminets were often located in little towns or villages, although they could also be found within the front rooms of private homes.

The estaminets also served as lively gathering spots where soldiers could relax and chat away from the battles, meet locals and learn more of the language.

The Daily Standard[97]

November 1917. Our trouble this winter will be the same as on the Somme during last – a winter of evil memory. It will be the trouble of getting supplies to the lines and of getting shelter and any decent comfort for the men in the front and supports. They get their reward when their division is relieved and comes out of the line from that bad country beyond Ypres for a spell.

In the billets of small Flemish towns, the lucky ones make the best of a good time, cleansing themselves of the grey mud in which they have been living and sleeping and eating, and

THE OLD INNS

cleansing their minds of things they have seen in the fields of death. It is bright and warm in the estaminets.

It is good to play a game of dominoes in the Church Army hut, where there is always a cheery padre and sometimes a piano and a gramophone to take men's minds away from the war, with the comforts of an older kind of life... These are great places for men just down from the battlefields. The people who run them play the game well, keeping things merry and bright.

For officers, there are new clubhouses in the towns behind the lines, not far behind either, still well within shell or bomb range. Here officers, covered with wet mud can get a wash, and sit down to a good meal and look at the latest illustrated papers, before tramping off again, to the hellfire corners of the front, or going further back.

Best of all these officers of the fighting class like to get into the old inns on the roads of war where they sit with a few pals round a small table, eat long and leisurely and take their time over a bottle of red wine, with coffee to follow and a good cigar. There are little lamps on the tables, white tablecloths, and the glasses are all sparkling. It is like a dream of an extremely nice and friendly heaven to soldiers who have been fighting in the mud.

There is one old inn I know like that, up north where what's left of the road goes to Ypres. For three years officers on their way to the salient have come here for their last dinner out of the line; sometimes for their last dinner.

Thousands of them have dined and gone on. If they come back, they dine here again and say how good it is, how "topping."

It is an old inn, built before the French revolution sent some of its customers to the guillotine. It has a cobbled courtyard with old pumps and horse-troughs. As one goes in, one looks into a vaulted kitchen where the buxom cook is busy with the *soupe a l'oignon* and the *ragout du boulettes*, so that savoury smells are wafted to the nostrils of hungry young officers before ever they got to the big *salle-a-manger*, where little tables are spread, and lamps are lighted.

In daylight, one looks through the windows across the fields of Flanders. At night, the sky is all lurid with flushes of shell-fire, while searchlights grope across it, seeking the night raiders who are bombing the villages round about. But the blinds are drawn tight, for Madame keeps to the letter of the law. The room is good enough for officers who have been living in the mudholes.

Some come in with the mud upon them still, up to the tops of their marching boots and up to the collars of their waterproof coats. They peel off the coats, look down at their muddy boots, and smile at Mlle. Suzanne as though to say, 'Pardon, Mademoiselle.'

Mlle. Suzanne sits behind the desk touching her curls with her fingers, smiling at the looking glass on the opposite wall.

Friendly young men shift their chairs to catch a glimpse of her, because it is good to see a pretty girl after so much ugliness. Mlle. Suzanne acknowledges these glad eyes with just the right touch of recognition, neither too little nor too much of welcome, for she has had those glances from half the officers of the British Army, and the Overseas Forces. She is clever as well as kind.

In the next room is a piano. It is played by young officers. Ragtime tunes, and old songs are sung by some of their comrades and hummed by all of them. Sometimes a man comes in and smiles when he sees the piano. He says, 'Good Lord, it seems a thousand years since I touched a note!'

He sits down and plays something with the touch of a master's hand, so that men at the little tables, who have been talking of the last show and their rotten time in places such as Polygon Wood and Passchendaele, are suddenly quiet and listen with a far-off look in their eyes. At the end of the piece they say, 'Jolly good! Now play something else.'

A young Canadian officer came in one night with a strange box under his arm. 'Is there anyone here who plays the piano?' he asked. Presently, Madame, who keeps the inn, was ready to play, so out of the box the soldier took an old violin. He had the face of a pugilist, roughly hewn, but he played with a fine, strong touch, and with a sob in the heart of his instrument. His unit was for Passchendaele. I don't know whether he came back again.

In the old courtyard of the inn there is a clatter of hoofs over the cobbles, with that click-clack which one hears on the stage in costume dramas, when The Three Musketeers or some other romantic fellows come upon the scene. A gust of wind blows through the door and into the room troops another group of muddy officers, a brigadier and his staff of cavalry officers.

Into the old hostelry on the Ypres road comes every type of an army which has a thousand types of soldiers. They stay an hour or two and then go after a good dinner, a bottle of wine, and a smile from Suzanne. Something of their spirit remains behind, so that as long as this old inn stands, it will be haunted by gallant ghosts of men who fought in the great, bad war.

There are other places like that in towns behind the lines. For men out of the line they are little sanctuaries where, for a spell, the doors are shut against the enemy and all his evil deeds.

CHAPTER 19

MADEMOISELLE FROM ARMENTIERES

'A ribald song no longer.'
Bartlett Adamson[98]

The soldiers' song 'Mademoiselle from Armentières' was popular during World War I. The lyrics raised the sensitive issue of sex on the battlefield, a topic that could only be elucidated by someone there at the time. Over 130 verses of the song have been identified.

The following article, written after the war, discussed the secret meaning of the song.

Bartlett Adamson, *Smith's Weekly*[99]
Stigmatised, out of the past she came, to cheer the Diggers as they drank forgetfulness in the estaminets in France and Flanders during the war years. Into the past she goes, no longer stigmatised and, going, she turns and smiles and, smiling through the mist of time, reveals herself in an unexpected light.

Seen so, the Diggers realise that she, who had come to them in ribald song, was in fact a healing presence in brave disguise. Where the nurses, living actualities, had so often saved them from physical death, this mythical girl from Armentieres had even more often saved them from mental death. No wonder that

Diggers have tended more and more to idealise her as the years have passed until today she, who was the subject of every ungallant jest, has now become 'a symbol of every romantic memory', to awaken tears in the eyes of men who, in those dim days, thrilled the world by their fierce courage.

The response given today to 'Mademoiselle from Armentieres' might seem sentimental. It is so, and that is no dis-compliment. As a people we too greatly fear the emotional frankness known as sentiment.

During the war years Diggers were game for anything, except sentiment. That was one region in which they dared not intrude, in which they could not trust themselves. War is no place for human emotions. But today even the Diggers are game to be sentimental if worthy occasion calls for it. Yet something more than mere sentiment plays a part in the response to Mademoiselle from Armentieres.

There is subconscious recognition of gratitude due to the mythical Mademoiselle who helped the Diggers to escape from thought when it was dangerous to think. In those days they would march casually into the black clouds of death. They were unfaltering against a human adversary, but they had to retreat from thoughts. To escape, they made jokes, sang ribald songs, twisted sentiment to obscenity, emotion to casualness.

In that mood, in that need, out of the past came Mademoiselle from Armentieres. She, more effectively than any other visitant, soothed war-tense nerves with an opiate of song.

Yet, was there more even than this? Mademoiselle was an escape, not only from war's horror, but from the sex starvation which the war imposed. Most of the Diggers were young, vigorous, at the age for affection, fond of this or that girl, or even these or those girls, whom they had left behind. In their need for feminine companionship they leapt, protectively, to the other extreme. Jocularly they sought to deride such femininity. Defiant ribaldry was the simplest way to stifle their sentimental hunger. Here the mythical Mademoiselle was at most an anodyne, as in the other sense she was an opiate.

No other song could so effectively satisfy. Mademoiselle was easy to sing, and infinitely responsive. There were innumerable variants of her lines, and she could be dressed up in new stanzas at will. There was no monotony with Mademoiselle. Most important of all, she was a personality, and in prime need for such a song, a female personality.

There were still other considerations. Mademoiselle, a girl in a drinking song, gradually became something of a symbol of life away from the trenches, of companionship freed from filth, menace, death, and mutilation; companionship enjoyed, for however brief a while, in some degree of rudimentary comfort.

Mademoiselle thus became associated with thoughts of happier interludes, even though those interludes were marred by knowledge of this or that mate who would no longer join in the ribald chorus.

Finally, there were other incidents, more intimate, more tender; when this or that village girl, or even this or that vivandiere, seen for a moment, known for a day or a week, an hour, or a night, gave contentment, ecstasy, romance. Occurring in such circumstances, those brief encounters must remain as memories, growing more vivid with the years, tending more and more to become moments of high adventure or tender recollection, awakening to life most vividly when again the air vibrates in deep-voiced chorus to Mademoiselle from Armentieres.

The years have woven together all those memories of estaminets and drinking songs, of sudden release from horror, of comrades seen no more, of pleasant companionship, of girls whose presence flashed across the path of life, until all have become symbolised in the little Mademoiselle from Armentieres.

Mademoiselle is the one song which all Diggers sang at some time or another, which many of them sang most of the time during estaminet interludes, the one song which they remember as having been sung by comrades now dead, the one song most potent to revive the memory of those incidents most worthy to be remembered. So, with the years Mademoiselle has changed.

The genesis of that change was the return of the Diggers to their homes.

The song was too popular to be discarded, too ribald to be freely sung. Words, phrases, and incidents were varied to suit new circumstances.

As years passed, Diggers found that variations more suited the moods which the song now awakened. It was varied yet more, not at dictates of politeness, but of inclination.

Diggers were beginning to be game to face the emotions which that song symbolised, game even to be sentimental. With these changes, Mademoiselle more definitely than ever revivified the past, especially the romantic past when this or that village girl, when this or that vivandiere, brought solace to men hungry for companionship which only a woman can give.

Mademoiselle has thus become an actuality, no longer ribald, but romantic – dark eyes flash under distant stars, and strange words spoken thrillingly low, when …

>They laughed and loved in the old French town, Parley-voo!
>And her heart spoke out of her eyes of brown, Parley-voo!
>But the time fled by and there came a day
>When he and his cobbers marched away. Inky-pinky,
>   parley-voo!
>Quiet the old estaminet, Parley-voo!
>No more the Diggers will come that way, Parley-voo!

May your heart grow light with the passing years,
Oh, Mademoiselle from Armentieres. Inky-pinky,
parley voo!

Thus has come about the strange metamorphosis of a song.

It inverts the normal rule. Usually a sentimental ballad deteriorates into a ribald parody. Mademoiselle, beginning as a ribald drinking song, has become sublimated into a sentimental ballad of genuine artistic merit and sincere human appeal ...

Mademoiselle belongs to the Diggers. As they and their deeds fade into the past, so into the past Mademoiselle goes with a reluctant step. But as she goes, she reveals herself as a gracious creature who dared to masquerade in ribald disguise to save the sanity of men, as a benevolent and beautiful memory, worthy of the tears which she can at times awaken in the eyes of Diggers.

A mathematical constant
Listening Post[100]

Mademoiselle is what the mathematicians would call a constant. Some time ago, it was reported that the real Mademoiselle had died but, as a Dickens character would have said, 'there weren't no such person.' Like Bairnsfather's Old Bill, she was a type and not really an individual ...

It was the Great War that introduced the town and the lady to the men of the new armies, but the song into which they were thrust is as old, almost, as the army itself – and just as wicked. The ballad was evidently picked up from Prussian soldiers by Wellington's men during, or just after, the Waterloo campaign. Its sentimentality was a fair target for the British soldier's unholy skill in the black art of parody. Even in those days, the origin of the music was lost in the mists of time. This was the song we all stopped singing when padres or nurses approached or reproached.

Snowy and the nurses
Bartlett Adamson, *Western Mail*[101]

We have heard what hard-doers some of the lads were in the way they put the roughies across, but some of our nursing sisters could put it across too, in a more classical style.

For instance, I had to undergo an operation at the Base Hospital about the end of 1919. While chatting with some of the lads in the same ward, they kindly informed me that while a man is under the dope he gives away all his secrets. The day before the operation, two of the Sisters came to me. 'Cheer up, Snowy,' one said cheekily, 'we are going to get all your war history tomorrow, all about your Mademoiselle from Armentieres and that English girl.'

What with the tale of the lads, and then these two Sisters, I didn't know what to buy for it. To crown it, in the evening the Matron came along with two Sisters. She cheered me up by saying, 'Well, Snowy, all fit? You have to be good now because we are going to hear all your lovely history tomorrow. Good night!'

As I came to (after the operation the next day) I saw Matron and the same two Sisters in attendance. Later on the trio came to my bed, all business of course. One pulled out a book which, to my horror of horrors, was a Pitman's shorthand notebook. The Matron then said, 'Do you understand shorthand, Snowy?'

'No, Matron. I do not,' I replied.

Turning over six double pages of that confounded notebook she went on, 'Well, my lad, here is the history of your last few years. What shall we tell your wife?'

I could see a mischievous look in their eyes, but I could not see through the joke. It was only when reading 'The Diary of a Doctor' in *The Western Mail* of December last (12 years after) that I discovered that speech under anaesthetic is impossible.

To think that my Cobbers were in on the act!

CHAPTER 20

COBBERS

'There are fair-weather friends; there is no such thing as a fair-weather cobber.'
Staff-Sergeant Frank Mattocks[102]

The secret society of cobbers

Frank Mattocks was an Australian journalist who enlisted in September 1914. Assigned to the Australian Army Service Corps, he wrote a number of articles during the war. The following is about the mateship of cobbers on 'the barren strip of Gallipoli, how the old khaki-coloured life, with its teeming incidents and crowded memories was swiftly fading'.[103] As he states below, soldiers had few secrets from each other in war.

Maitland Weekly Mercury[104]

Cobbers! Of all that is worthwhile in this new life of ours there is nothing finer than the contemplations of one's cobbers. To those who have ever been denied the privilege of being in the field with the Australian army, it would be difficult to form and estimate of the value of a cobber. When you hear returned soldiers talking of 'me and me cobbers,' I am sure you must fail to realise the value of the expression.

In civil life staunch friends are a splendid asset. You require them only on rare occasions. With cobbers it is different. You always need them, and what is so grand about them is that they never disappoint you.

The secret of having a friend is being a friend; the secret of having a cobber is being a cobber. You simply cannot help having cobbers in the army. In this huge concern, and in the ranks especially, you perceive the nearest approach to Socialism we shall ever have. There is so much inter-dependence one upon the other. This is so glaringly self-evident; there is such a complete breaking down of stupid conventions and ridiculous barriers of the old routine of things; there is such a close community of interest that one cannot fail to remark upon this extraordinary relationship between soldiers.

Soldiers are notoriously Bohemian. They spend lavishly; they share everything; their money, their pleasures, their troubles, their ideas, their clothes, toilet gear, their spare time, their experiences, past and present, their hopes for the future and, lest we forget, their love stories.

If, after nightfall, you chance to be chatting with a cobber or perhaps two, and you happen to drop only an eyelash by way of encouragement, your cobber will produce his pocket-book and extract a photo of the girl (or girls; soldiers are a lot like sailors) and give you details of a charming little romance, and in all probability conclude with a panegyric on Australian types of beauty, and their easy ascendancy over girls of other nations.

Maybe your cobber is a married man. He shows you photos of the wife and several little Australians. As he passes them over to you one by one, you're favoured with a running commentary on the virtues of each, and many remarkable incidents connected with their small histories. I venture to say I have seen more photos of pretty girls, and more photos of Australian babies during the past couple of years than I have ever seen in the thousands of glances I used to have in Ernie Cameron's window.*

I have listened to more love stories with settings in all parts of Australia than I have read in popular magazines. I have acquired some knowledge about Australia, in conversation with soldiers from all parts, which has caused me to admit shame-facedly that what I knew about Australia, before quitting it, was infinitesimal.

Soldiers have few secrets, but after all 'where's the harm in cobbers?'

It's remarkable how many cobbers a fellow has. They come from all parts of Australia. There are the cobbers you knew while you were in camp in Australia; on the journey across; in Egypt; on the Peninsula; and so forth. You are continually running across old cobbers, fellows you have not seen for, say, three, six, nine, twelve, eighteen months, sometimes two years. You meet them in the most curious places and at the most unexpected times. Chaps who have been home to Australia; others who have been convalescent in England for months. Here they are back in the line again. Though their greetings take different forms, they are all hearty.

I have a dozen nicknames; 'Maitland' is one of them. 'Hullo, Maitland, how in _____'s _____ are you?' Shake.

He may be one of those big, hefty fellows you last saw in Gallipoli – back-woodsmen, Australian giants. Shake.

He knows how to shake. I have a fair-sized mitt myself, and reckon I know how to shake, but it often happens this way. Your hand disappears completely in his. He applies pressure, and if you're unprepared, you will find yourself smiling back through set teeth. They are great, these cobbers.

In the army, as I have pointed out, you are so dependent upon one another that you are always requiring favours and small services. You're no sooner out of some difficulty and trouble than you're up

---

*   Ernie Cameron, photographic business in Maitland.

against another obstacle. But never worry, your cobbers always see you through. I have been in scores of difficulties myself, yet not once have I been left in the lurch. Wonderful fellows these cobbers.

I often wonder how a fellow is going to square up the credit and debit sides of the ledger. Opportunity to repay a good turn does not always occur. As Emerson observes, 'We cannot render benefits to those from whom we receive them, or only seldom.' But the benefit that we receive must be rendered again, line for line, to somebody. So there it is. You can only pass on these moving acts of kindness.

I have a very tender and sincere regard for the word *cobber*. I was sitting one afternoon in Shrapnel Gully, just below Steele's Point, feeling tired and drowsy. Days and nights without sleep are not conducive to wakefulness. I couldn't lie down because there are always urgent calls for water and ammunition for the line, and sometimes a helping hand in the line itself.

Presently a boy put his hand on my shoulder and said, 'Come on, cobber.' He was sniped in the breast and was bleeding profusely. I gathered him up and took him around a corner to an English Captain, a doctor of whom I had made a cobber only a couple of days previously. He was a fine fellow, a Scotchman, who had served through both the Balkan campaigns. He took care of my Australian cobber for me. Ever since then, if a stranger calls me 'cobber' and asks for something or for some small service, I have to do it even if, as sometimes happens, the request is a bit over the fence.

The Grand Order of Cobbers is the greatest fraternity I know. Its numbers are legion. There are no paltry distinctions of class or religion in its constitution. All its members are men of blood and iron. Its purposes and ideals are beautiful, so simple, and the only password is *cobber*, the open sesame to all that one soldier can do for another.

'Comrades in arms' is a phrase that has a heroic swing about it, but I shall always prefer to think of my comrades as cobbers.

CHAPTER 21

FINDING BILLETS

'Never mind the four unfortunates. We'll leave them by the fire till we get something definite.'
A.H.B.[105]

Away from the battlefields, soldiers needed a place to rest – somewhere they could obtain food, wash themselves, clean their mud-coated belongings and enjoy a roof overhead. These places were referred to as billets. The logistics of finding any suitable, but safe, accommodation, over a vast area to house up to hundreds of men at a time, proved to be a headache for assigned officers. Battalions were constantly on the move, so finding billets for the night often became a logistical nightmare.

The following diary entry from soldier A.H.B. recounts life in the billets. Place names were redacted, as was required at the time so that the enemy would not know where to bomb sleeping soldiers. Real place names included Bapaume, close to Steenwerck, and Péronne and Cambrai, further along the road.

Daily News[106]

December 1917.
'One officer and four orderlies will report to Area Commandant at C_____, by 2 pm. Monday, 6th inst, arrange forward billets, A.A.A.' Thus read the Brigade order.

Sunday, 5th inst. One officer accordingly, to wit your humble servant, with four faithful orderlies in attendance, arrives at C_____ at 2 pm, in a smother of mud and rain, and duly reports to Area Commandant. 'Who are you?' asks that worthy individual.

You tell him briefly name, number, rank, unit, and a few other of the numerous Army requirements, including present mission. 'Well, I don't know where to put you,' says the A.C.

Not knowing either, you receive the intelligence with a stony silence that spurs him to a further effort. 'Better try B_____ I think. Yes! B_____ will be the place. See the Mayor and arrange everything with him! Yes, yes, quite certain! Good day!'

B_____ is five miles back along the road you've just come. Never mind! Off we go. The Mayor will arrange everything, good old Mayor. In due course, we run the Mayor to earth in the awful parlour of a small grocer's dwelling. He is very old, and very suspicious of Colonials. It seems that once upon a time an Australian battalion was quartered upon the Commune, and the inhabitants still consider that those ancient peoples who complained of the plagues of flies and locusts did not know when they were well off. You explain who you are, and that the war is still going along somewhere. So, in due course, you receive your billets.

A hasty tour shows them to be fairly good. After solemnly warning the owners to hold out against all comers till you arrive next day, you return to the four cold and weary men waiting in a corner of the marketplace. And there you meet your old and trusty friend, the Staff Captain, obviously bursting with information.

'Ah! Here you are,' he begins with a remarkable show of jovial animation, quite sufficient in itself to raise a cold wave of suspicion in your sophisticated breast. 'I've just arranged for you to billet in P_____.'

'In P_____? But, dash it, I'm fixed up here. The Area Commandant…'

'Never mind the Area Commandant. You'll be in P_____.'

Gone the joy and animation. Stern officialdom rides supreme. With a weary sigh, and four wet soldiers, you depart for P_____, another two miles onwards.

Arriving in the square, you deposit the retinue in an estaminet in open defiance of all rules and regulations and once more seek their Mayor. He is a genial, open-hearted countryman, and shows you two farms, adjacent and suitable, in about two seconds. Off you go again.

Farm No. 1 is a poor and dirty place, estimated to accommodate about 150 men, and with reasonable space for half that number. Madame is apathetic – if the soldiers are coming, well so be it. Something desperate is always happening – two nights ago an aerial torpedo fell in the field. *C'est la guerre!*

Farm No. 2 is different altogether. The yard is clean and well-kept. The inevitable hideous cesspool in the centre is comfortably filled with clean straw onto which a tall red rooster and numerous scraggy chickens are disporting themselves gaily. On one side the open stalls show housed cattle; from the other comes the pleasant hum of a threshing machine standing in a covered way between two huge barns stacked high with fresh sheaves. Madame is doubtful.

Round the machine are clustered the attendant satellites, three of them old men well over sixty, and the fourth a youth with a wooden leg and minus one arm.

A curious glance reveals an old horse walking on an endless treadmill as the moving power of the concern, a typical peasant idea.

Madame is within, it seems. You advance to the attack in open order and recite carefully to Madame that the Mayor has sent you, that you have 80 men to place, with certain officers; that you would like a mess room; and that of all the soldiers of the Allied armies yours are the most childlike and bland, *'Bons garcons, toujours convenables.'*

Madame's cold gaze does not waver, nor does the stern old mouth relax. She has just got rid of 50 soldiers that morning. Everything has just been cleaned up. They stole her wood and robbed the hens' nests; and the time before that they left without paying for their straw.

Furthermore the barns are full of the newly gathered crops, and soldiers smoke in bed.

Truly a bad outlook. The enemy preserves an unbroken front, but the old eyes are kind, and the creases in the weather-beaten face were not put there by ill-humour.

'If Madame will believe it, one is much annoyed to be forced to intrude on a lady's household and can only plead in extenuation that one must do one's duty, fully realising the sacrifices made by the long-suffering civilians, and not a little surprised at their unfailing kindness to the strangers within their gates. Monsieur le Maire has said that Madame's is the best.'

'Eh bien, Monsieur! Now if there were no crops, perhaps one might …

'But suppose one promised personally that there should be no smoking. And many of the soldiers would gladly do a day in the fields, to relieve the pressure. They are good lads, and so tired. All this weather in the trenches and the mud. Has Madame any sons at the war?'

'Ah! Monsieur! J'en ti cinq. Mais entrez, Monsieur, entrez! Two went away the first week. They lie at Verdun.' The stern old mouth twitches. 'My third boy, Henri, he won the Croix de Guerre on the Somme – her eyes glisten proudly – but he also will come no more. Pierre is without, you have seen him. *Ah! Mon Dieu! Mon*

Dieu! Quelle vache de guerre! My last boy, Jean, my baby, he is but a month gone to join the Chasseurs.' Gently rocking to and fro the old dame weeps silently, but not for long. 'You will stay here for tonight, Monsieur. Tomorrow we shall see! Perchance the further barn.'

About 8pm I was about to turn in to a fresh, clean bed, having seen the four orderlies safely filled with eggs and coffee and well settled, when a rap was heard on the door.

'*Voulez-vous du lait, Monsieur?*'

Just before we swung out of the yard a week later, en route for Messines and glory – some of them got it too, poor lads, I wrung the hard old hand with great respect and all the goodwill in the world, which I feel sure was reciprocated. Waving her arm towards the forming ranks the old dame smiled.

'Just like my Jean,' said she. '*Bons garçons, toujours convenables.*'

Imbibing Australian
Weekly Judge[107]

We were billeted in a big barn at Steenwerck and had just finished tea. Twilight was deepening. Here and there the gloom of the interior was specked by the glimmer of a candle. Outside, greedy hogs were foraging amongst the wealth of the farmer's backyard, grunting contentedly as they un-mucked an empty beef tin.

The Diggers for once were in a musing mood; their brief rest was to end next day. What conversation there was rose and fell in drowsy modulations, then died away. We all listened.

At the rear of the barn the farmer's daughter began to milk their cow. We heard the milk spurting into the pail. Softly she began to sing as the family milk-source was encouraged to accelerate her flow by the words, 'Over the top, with the best of luck,' repeated again and again to a little haunting air of her own. We had become quite abstracted under the spell of her gentle voice when, suddenly, with the surprise effect of an unlooked-for shell, there was an explosion. 'Put your foot back, you #^&%,' she rasped.

The spell was gone. When we had recovered from our astonishment, someone drawled, 'Who's been teaching her English?'

'I don't know about English,' sadly replied the religious member of our platoon. 'I think it's Australian she's been learning.'

No mail for you!

During the war, the most disappointing thing that a chap could hear was the phrase, 'No mail for you.' Sergeant-Major Alan Shilling described what it was like in a letter he wrote home, which was later published.

South Western Times[108]

If you only knew the pleasure it gives us out here to hear from our old friends in Australia, you would feel amply compensated for the time spent in writing. Up to yesterday I had received no mail from Australia for just on three months.

Yesterday I got nineteen letters all in a bunch so that was not too bad, was it? By Jove, though, the weeks and weeks of waiting with no letters are up to mud, so to speak. The letters must have been delayed somewhere. I hope you get my letters. All the boys are complaining about not receiving any word from their homes. I think I know the reason why.

S.S. *Mongolia* has been sunk with a fortnight's mail aboard from Australia. This is very bad news for us, as the mail days are looked forward to with much interest, more than anything else. We would sooner miss pay day than lose our mail.

'No letter for me again! All right; two can play at that game.' That is the kind of thing one hears nowadays when mail is distributed. The disappointed soldier turns away grousing, to wait another twenty-four hours in the hope of receiving a precious envelope, bearing the stamp of Australia.

Don't let this sort of thing happen! Do not let the boys out here get into their heads that, because the war goes on and on, you are forgetting them. There is enough to grouse about, heaven knows. And the longer the war continues the more necessary your letters become if the 'blues' are to be routed.

Parcels are scarcer; but we can understand that. Letters do not cost any more than they did in 1914; and they are much more valuable to us than ever they were. So write often and write at length. It is easy to say in an occasional letter, 'We are always thinking of you,' but this is hard to believe unless we receive the evidence of frequent letters.

CHAPTER 22

BACK FOR A REST

'To illustrate Flanders, let me give you a bunch of random memories from my near past.'
Augustus Muir[109]

Life in the trenches is difficult to imagine for anyone who has not participated in war. The constant tension, the knowledge that one could be blown apart at any moment, left nerves frayed and minds on the verge of melancholy or madness. One thing that kept these soldiers alive was counting the days until they were relieved from the trenches and sent back behind the lines for respite.

I stumbled upon this lively article from the Scottish journalist Charles Augustus Muir (1892–1969), printed in 1916, contrasting the differences that a rest made, depending on where one was located within the arena of warfare. From the horrors of Gallipoli to the relative calm of a small Flemish village, his fertile imagination ran wild. As he offers us 'a bunch of random memories',[110] we glimpse the detailed days and nights that constituted 'back for a rest'.[111]

Augustus Muir, *The Evening Star*[112]

February 1916. 'Two more days in the trenches, boys, then we go back for a rest!' For fighting men going back is indescribably sweet. During the long, weary hours of watching in the trenches the thought of it is a joy, that sweet, quiet time.

It means sleep – hours of it! It means food – heaps of it! Food washed down by a dozen delectable drinks. It means leisure. That shattering strain of trench life is removed. It means doing what one jolly well chooses.

But the fighting man in Gallipoli has different views. His memories of being behind the firing line are not enticing. His imagination has nothing to cling to, nothing pleasant, nothing soothing or redolent of home. Unless the battalion is moved altogether from the peninsula, he has less to look forward to than before going into the trenches, for the best spot in Gallipoli is the firing line. Here are fewer fatigues, less uncooked food, and less chance of being ordered at quick notice to pack your traps and trek. At Gallipoli, the news that they are going back for a few days of rest is not received with joy.

To illustrate Flanders, let me give you a bunch of random memories from my near past. A dark night, cloudy and damp; the crisp rattle of rifle fire down the line; a row of dark figures waiting in the inky dimness of the trench. Every man is standing to, equipment on, his rubber sheets rolled up, not an article of value but what is stowed away in capacious knapsacks and bulky pockets.

The company is waiting to move. It is a thrilling time, that hour of listening; not for the Boches, but for feet in the communication trench, the steady tramp of the relieving company who are coming to take over. Thud-thud-splosh-squelch. At last come the footsteps of the new platoon filing in. The officers converse. Points of importance out in front are explained. The best dug-out is indicated; ammunition, bombs, and 'what not' are handed over and signed for. 'Follow on, Fifteen platoon!' and the subaltern plunges into the muddy ooze of the communication trench.

Our rest has begun. Midnight. A village. A shivering officer steps out of the darkness. He is the billeting officer. 'These are your billets. Take them, good night.'

The Quartermaster-Sergeant gets busy. Our section files in through a doorway. Someone lights a storm lantern. It is a cosy little barn with a hay loft. The place is about breast high in delicious, fragrant straw.

We ascend the rickety ladder as shadows flicker around the roof. Equipment is dropped, rifles are stacked, blankets unfurled. The softest of soft beds are cunningly scooped. It is good to be here. Felicity. Peace. The guns are far away.

You awake at dawn with a chilling surge of fear, lest you have been asleep at your post. It is habit reasserting itself, but the scented hay and the mingling snores set doubts at rest and lull you back to slumber. There is no hurry to rise yet.

Parade? It is a pleasure to be on parade again. Platoon Commanders examine rifles, chins, and feet, then you are free till evening. Free, that is, to conduct an organised raid on every emporium in the district and taste the beer of every estaminet within range.

Gallipoli. In a thin drizzle of night rain, we left the firing line at Gallipoli and went back to rest after thirty days in the trenches. Rest was necessary, as these had been days of strain, with little sleep at night. Food became sickening in its sameness; life was not worth living.

It was in a gloomy frame of mind – and with a shaken state of nerves – that we went back behind the firing line to renew our strength. The rest camp was on the beach, just shallow holes in the earth and rock. In the darkness, we stowed ourselves away as best we could. Rain was falling seriously. The ground was thirsty after long months of dazzling sunshine, else we should have been wholly washed out. A strange, sickly-sweet odour wafted from the wetted scrub.

Two hospital ships in the bay could be recognised by their brilliant lights. All else was in darkness.

Morning. Tea, biscuits, salt bacon, the same old grub, the same old round, but with this difference. At the rest camp, you are shelled daily, while in the firing line you are generally free from these malign and snarling visitants of the air. No man is advised to venture from his gully in the ground, for at any moment the shelling might start.

My imagination played me the worst tricks. I recalled Flemish villages, the small cafés, the clean cook shops. On that barren, pallid peninsula, little coloured pictures emerged from the storehouse of my memory; letters from pals, firelit pictures of warm interiors, the homely faces of the peasantry.

Ricketts and I were in the desert in '15 when a letter from an Australian girl blew into his hand. Together we read it. In a moment of idleness I wrote her, signing Ricketts' name. Some months passed and a reply came to Ricketts.

Unknown to him I replied in a romantic way. Again a reply came. Ricketts, feeling the joke was on him, wrote to her in a grief-stricken manner, informing her that 'Mr. Ricketts had been blown up with his gun,' and signed my name to it.

In due course I received a letter from Miss commiserating with me on the loss of my friend. Naturally, I replied that I, meaning Ricketts, was still alive and 'Apparently some spiteful person was trying to come between us.'

We came to France shortly after and Ricketts received a photo of a beautiful Australian girl. 'She'll do me,' he said. 'I'm going on with her.'

Back he went to his battery. After he left I recounted his *romance* to another friend. I had just reached the point of telling where he wrote to her of his death when the field telephone rang.

'Is that you, Gus? Joe here. A shell just landed on Ricketts' No. 1 gun and killed him.'

CHAPTER 23

CHRISTMAS AT STEENWERCK

'Let nothing you dismay.'
Philip Gibbs[113]

With the war lasting for years, events such as Christmas came and went. Stories about a ceasefire on that day had various themes – one of a fleeting hour of camaraderie, others of treachery, tragedy and death.

The following stories cover Christmas in different years, each with distinct outcomes.

Christmas of 1915
Philip Gibbs, *The Advertiser*[114]

December 1915. Christmas and Cannons. I heard no carols in the trenches on Christmas Eve, but afterwards, I sat in the elegant drawing-room of a French chateau, among a company of men who were wet to the knees and slathered with mud. There was a pint of water in each of my boot tops. A friend of mine raised his hand and said, 'Listen', smiling as he spoke.

Through the open door came the music of a mouth-organ. Someone was playing an old, old tune to which he knew the words:

'God rest ye merry gentlemen, let nothing you dismay.
Remember Christ our Saviour was born on Christmas Day,
to save us all from Satan's power, when we have gone astray …'

Outside the wind was blowing across Flanders with a doleful whine that now and then leapt into a savage violence that rattled the windowpanes. Beyond the booming of its lower notes was the faint, dull rumble of distant guns. 'Christmas Eve!' said one officer. 'Nineteen hundred and fifteen years ago, and now – this!'

He sighed heavily, but a few moments later told a funny story, which was followed by loud laughter.

So it was, I think, in every billet in Flanders and in every dugout this Christmas Eve, where men thought of the meaning of the day with its message of peace and goodwill, and contrasted it with the great, grim horror of the war, speaking a few words of perplexity. After a quick sigh (how many comrades have gone since last Christmas Day?) he had the courage of laughter. For while there is life, there is laughter. 'Let nothing you dismay.'

The words came into my head on this Christmas Eve, as I saw the undaunted courage of humanity which not even Satan's power can kill. The Divine Sentiment in the human heart could not be destroyed, even by war's foulest brutalities.

How strange to find the spirit of Christmas, the little tenderness of the old traditions, the toys and trinkets of its feast day, in places where death has been busy, only yesterday, and where the spirit of evil lies in ambush.

'All quiet?' I asked a man who sat with his back to the parapet, staring into a broken piece of mirror fastened to a stick, which gave a safe view of the enemy's trenches.

'Nothing doing,' said the man. 'The Germans want a quiet Christmas. I don't blame 'em. They could have a noisy one for the asking.'

I went back out of the trenches and into the shelled town, where I heard a slow tramp of feet. Presently through the slashing rain came a draped coffin on a gun-carriage, and soldiers marching slowly with reversed arms.

A gallant colonel, who fell to a sniper's shot, was going to spend his last Christmas in the dug-out to which all men go before the great stand-to. Young officers who walked behind his coffin had their heads bent to the drift of the rain. It was not a glad picture on Christmas Eve.

Throughout the night our men in the trenches stood in their waders.

The dawn of this Christmas Day was greeted, not by angelic songs, but by the splutter of rifle bullets all along the line. A sad business! Yet in the heart of it is gladness, a wistfulness which belongs to youth, whatever its perils may be, or its discomforts of life.

Christmas of 1916

Lance-Corporal William Bodger, who trained at the Warrnambool Camp, recalled events about the Christmas of 1916. He mentioned having a brother killed at Gallipoli.

Warrnambool Standard[115]

On the night that we received our gifts, we were sitting around a smoky fire inside our little hut. It did one good to see how our platoon of young warriors sprang up and crowded round the platoon sergeant as he came in the door, labouring under the weight of some 30 Xmas gifts from Australia. At that time the parcels were doubly welcome, as we had only just come back from the trenches, and smokes were becoming scarce.

After the excitement had subsided, we sat round the fire and smoked good old Australian cigarettes and tobacco. We naturally talked of home until well after midnight, when we turned in and sucked Australian lollies until sleep closed our eyes.

Christmas of 1917

John St Clair wrote about an unusual Christmas. Among the many secret impossibilities accomplished in this war, one Australian battalion successfully transplanted Christmas 1917 from its immovable date on 25 December to 16 February 1918.

Engaged on the Messines front in December 1917, this regiment was coming out of the line during the early hours of Christmas Day.

After spending several days at Wulverghem, a little to the rear, the battalion went back to the line on the night of 1 January, with no time for festivities. Their commanding officer, unfettered by tradition or red tape, decided to put off celebrating Christmas Day to a more convenient time.

The opportunity came six weeks later when the regiment was at rest in Aldershot camp, situated off the road leading from Steenwerck to Neuve Eglise, almost within sight of that famous town of Armentières.

The Register[116]

16 February 1918. The deferred festivities took place on the appointed Christmas Day. The Britisher celebrates largely through the media of food and drink, so all canteens in the vicinity were visited with the object of augmenting regular rations and other supplies. A vastly creditable array of foodstuffs gladdened the troops.

It was whispered that several empty bottles, which might have contained beer at one time, were found in and about the camp the next day.

As high judicial sanction exists about not drawing conclusions from circumstantial evidence, it might be inferred that the search for evidence of alcoholic beverages was not attended with success.

The Australian Comforts Fund authorities, with usual lavish generosity, made possible by the unremitting thought of those at home, provided Christmas presents of tobacco, cigarettes, pipes, matches, chocolates, sweets, and other desirables dear to the soldiers' hearts.

The kindly curtain which veils the future from the present was drawn taut that day in the Officers' Mess where, under the sway of Christmas Spirit, good cheer and revelry prevailed.

No shadow fell across that gathering of the tragedy awaiting the battalion upon its next occupancy of the line.

On the night of 1st/2nd March the front line was taken over at Hollebeke. Evidently the enemy had secured information, or successfully made deductions, for they organised a raid on the battalion sector that night – an ideal time for a raid owing to slender knowledge of the ground by the regiment going into the line and the confusion which necessarily prevails during the period of 'walk-in, walk-out'.

Well primed beforehand, the Germans made a dash for the company's headquarters, and succeeded in capturing the C.O. The bullet received while the Major was being escorted back towards the enemy's trenches proved fatal. He was spared the indignities and inconveniences incidental to life in a prison compound.

CHAPTER 24

THE AUSTRALIAN CORPS

'My own command at that junction still comprised the
3rd Australian Division, which I had organized and trained
in England, 18 months before.'
Sir John Monash[117]

General Sir John Monash was especially proud of his 3rd Division troops, who he previously said were living up to his expectations. In this stirring chapter from Sir John's diary, he recounts farewelling the mud of Flanders.

Third division moving out
Monash diaries and letters, published in the *Daily Telegraph*[118]

The early days of the year 1918. My own command at that juncture still comprised the 3rd Australian Division, which I had organised and trained in England 18 months before. It was on March 8 that the 3rd Division bade a last, but by no means, regretful farewell to the mud of Flanders and Belgium, regions which it had inhabited for the preceding 16 months.

The division moved back for a well-earned rest, to a pleasant countryside at Nielles-les-Blequin, not far from Boulogne. It was laying there, enjoying the first signs of dawning spring, when the curtain was rung up for a great drama in which Australian troops were destined to play no subordinate part.

The Germans attacked the front of the 5th British Army on March 21.*

Divisions, situated as we were in reserve, and, for the time being, entirely out of the picture, had to depend for our news partly upon rumour, which was always unreliable, and partly upon severely censored communiques; framed as to allay public anxiety.

Nothing definite emerged from such sources, except that things were going ill, and that fighting was taking place on ground far behind what had been our front line near St. Quentin. This hint was enough to justify the expectation that my division would not be left for long unemployed.

On the same day, March 21, instructions were issued for all units to prepare for a move, to dump all unessential baggage, to fill up all mobile supplies, and to stand by in readiness to march at a few hours' notice.

Later came detailed instructions that the division was transferred from the Australian Corps to 10th Corps, which later was to be G.H.Q. Reserve, and that the whole division moved the next night to the Doullens area, the demounted troops by rail, and the artillery and other mounted units by route march. Entrainments commenced at midnight on 25th and continued all night. At daybreak on March 26th, after assuring myself that everyone was correctly on the move, I proceeded south by motor car, endeavouring to find 10th Corps headquarters and to report to them for orders.

My fruitless search on that forenoon revealed to me the first glimpse of the true reason for the far-reaching disorganisation and confusion which confronted me during the next 24 hours.

---

*   Second Battle of the Somme.

Over three years of trench warfare has accustomed the whole army to fixed locations for all headquarters, and to settled routes and lines of inter-communication. The powerful German onslaught, and the recall of a broad section of our fighting front, had suddenly disturbed the whole of this complex organisation. The headquarters of brigades, divisions, and even corps, ceased to have fixed locations where they could be found, or assured lines of telegraph or telephone communications by which they could be reached. Everything was in a state of flux, and the process of getting into personal contact with each other suddenly took a responsible leader hours, where it had previously taken minutes.

I sought the Tenth Corps at Hauteloque [sic], where they were supposed to be. They were not there. I proceeded to Frevent, where they were said to have been the night before. They had already left. In despair, I proceeded to Doullens, resolved at least to ensure the orderly detrainment of my division and their quartering for the following night, and stay there to await further orders.

A despatch rider was sent off to G.H.Q. to report my whereabouts and the fact that I was without orders.

Arriving at Doullens, I tumbled into a scene of indescribable confusion. The population were preparing to evacuate the town en masse, and an exhausted and hungry soldiery were pouring into town from the east and south-east, with excited tales that the German cavalry was hot on their heels.

Influenced by the persistency of these reports, I determined to make immediately dispositions to cover the detrainment of my troops, so that some show of resistance could be seen.

Soon after my arrival, I learned of the presence of Major-General MacLagan. This news, implying as it did the presence also of some at least of the Fourth Australian Division, was a gleam of sunshine in an otherwise gloomy prospect. I found MacLagan near Basseux at about 4 o'clock. His division had already been on the move, by 'bus and route march, for three days without rest.

The position to the east and south-east of him was obscure, and he also had posted a line of outposts in the supposed direction of the enemy and was arranging to dispatch his 4th Brigade to Hebuterne (which the enemy was reported to have entered), with orders to recapture that town.

That the enemy was not far away became evident from the fact that the hut in which we were conferring presently came under desultory long-range shell fire. There was nothing to be done except to arrange jointly to keep up an effective and as far as possible, continuous line of outposts towards the south-east, and to await developments.

Having made these arrangements, I returned along the same crowded road which was now also being leisurely shelled by the enemy, to my headquarters at Couturelle.

On the Ancre
Monash diaries and letters, published in the *Daily Telegraph*[119]

That night, after many conflicting instructions, I was ordered to report personally, without delay, to General Congreve, commanding the 7th Corps, at Montigny. In black darkness, on unfamiliar roads congested with refugee traffic, I did not reach Montigny until after midnight.

General Congreve was brief and to the point. He said, 'At 4 o'clock today my Corps was holding a line from Albert to Bray, where the line gave way. The enemy is now pushing westwards, and if not stopped tomorrow, will certainly secure all the heights overlooking Amiens. What you must try to do is get your division deployed across his path.

'The valleys of the Ancre and the Somme offer good points for your flanks to rest upon. You must, of course, get as far east as you can, but I know of a good line of old trenches, which I believe are still in good condition, running from Mericourt-l'Abbe towards Sailley-le-Sec. Occupy them if you can't get further east.'

At that juncture, General MacLagan arrived and received similar crisp orders to bring his division into a position of support on the high land in the bend of the Ancre, west of Albert.

CHAPTER 25

A DEFINITE CRISIS

'When Haig left, we all felt confident not only of our own success, but that there was a brain at the head of the army capable of handling any offensive with conspicuous ability.'
Alexander Jobson[120]

Before the bombing

Many earlier sources had commented on the *charmed life* around Steenwerck, but the relative calm of the little town would be shattered when a shell suddenly exploded in the main street in March 1918. It was a portent of dangers to come within the month.

Brigadier-General Alex Jobson was the Acting Commander of 3rd Division in General Sir John Monash's absence at Steenwerck. He wrote about British Commander-in-Chief General Haig's visit to Steenwerck, which instilled an air of confidence in the soldiers. However, they were still living in the midst of a war zone, and the explosion in the main street of Steenwerck would soon bring the conflict closer.

Brigadier-General Alex Jobson, published in *The Sun*[121]

Early in the year 1918. General Haig first came to Steenwerck to inspect the 3rd Division A.I.F. on a raw, cold morning when the land was covered with mist. Detachments of various units of the division assembled in a small field in review order. Not review order as far as the glory of dress was concerned, but in order of assembly.

It was a muddy field. Cold, damp air made everyone cheerless, and the mounted horses were fretful. The Commander-in-Chief did not keep us waiting long, for presently he and his staff appeared on the road. His staff was confined to a few officers. It was not difficult to pick him out. There was no mistaking the clean-cut face and determined expression. As he rode down the lines, he spoke in his usual courteous way to each officer as he was introduced, and later expressed himself in moderate terms as pleased with the look of the men.

This part of the inspection completed, the C-in-C took up his position near the gate, where each unit marched by him in fours. Their marching and general physique had impressed him considerably, for he said several times to General Monash, 'You've got some fine men here.' The men marched well. When it was over, the General rode away with his staff, heading down the road to the next division, leaving behind a general feeling of satisfaction.

I next saw General Haig at Steenwerck, just over a year ago, when he came to discuss with the Divisional Generals his plans of the Messines offensive, then about to take place. Brigadiers were ordered to be present and were questioned as to their preparations.

General Haig on this occasion was attended only by one officer, a heavy artillery Corps Major-General. What struck me more than anything when he came into the room was his firm, healthy appearance and his keen, but sympathetic, eyes. His skin was clear, and he looked what he was, a clean-living man of action.

There was no loss of time, for he promptly got to business. Various operational maps were displayed on the walls. He asked

General Monash to state his plan for the offensive. This the General did in his usual thorough manner. The general plan of action was given, then followed by actions to be taken by the individual brigades.

From time to time the Chief put cogent questions to our generals, proceeding when he was satisfied with their answers. The need for this was on the whole rare, for the Chief was thoroughly conversant with proposed plans, while our General's own story of the projected offensive was as full as it could be. After hearing General Monash fully, the Chief asked each Brigadier in turn to relate what task had been allotted to his brigade, and what preparations he had made to ensure success.

Monash listened keenly, but patiently, for the most part deferring his searching questions until each one had finished. It was not, perhaps, as severe an ordeal as we had expected. All throughout, the Chief addressed us in a kindly manner and put his questions in such a way as to put us at our ease, and to get the best out of us.

When we had ended, he expressed himself satisfied that preparations were thorough, and that it only remained to carry them through effectively. He advised us to see that our men were fit and well. Moreover, he was particularly insistent that every possible thought should be given to considering the problem of dealing with enemy machine-guns. His attitude was distinctly optimistic, and full of determination.

When he left, we all felt confident not only of our own success, but that there was a brain at the head of the army capable of handling any offensive with conspicuous ability.

The fateful explosion

The following entry describes the fateful explosion of a shell in the street of Steenwerck, which preceded a later German attack.

The Sydney Morning Herald[122]

8 March 1918. Sergeant T. Walters, formerly Health Inspector at Mosman, who returned yesterday, sustained injuries from a shell that exploded six miles behind the firing line, whilst he was working at Steenwerck. The Germans were making desperate efforts to bring down an Allied observation balloon near Lille, and in order to baffle those attempts, the balloon was shifted about. The Germans used a shell with a particularly soft nose, designed to explode on the slightest concussion. One of those shells was fired at the balloon. It exploded in the centre of the Steenwerck roadway, seriously injuring Sergeant Walters' legs.

Telegram communications after the bombing

The following telegrams reveal the dangerous situation in Steenwerck in the weeks after the initial bombing. The Germans advanced in the region and clashed with Allied forces. They captured several nearby towns and would launch a military offensive on Steenwerck in mid April.

United Press Correspondent, published in *Brisbane Courier*[123]

30 March 1918. Long-range guns bombarded Bethune, Estaires, Laventie and practically all the villages and towns in the back areas of Arras. The Germans used several of their fresh divisions, Marshal von Hindenburg perhaps hoping to break through the flank position from the north, though his exact intentions remain to be seen.

Reuter's telegram, published in *The Sun*[124]

10 April 1918. Fighting on a front of 30 miles, the Germans have advanced their centre seven miles from the original starting point, Estaires and Steenwerck being now in their hands. The loss of Merville, on the Lys river, has again created a definite crisis. It is reported that the Kaiser's troops have at last secured Messines which, combined with the Passchendaele Ridge, is a key point of the battle.

A refugee fleeing Steenwerck

The following unsigned letter from another refugee recounts their family's experience fleeing from Steenwerck's destruction on that fateful day in April. The letter was posted from France to a friend living in South Australia. Unlike Jeanne Plouvier's experience of escaping alone, this family had each other and relatives to turn to in Nantes, a town situated over 580 kilometres from Steenwerck. The writer gives a brief dramatic account of their plight.

West Coast Recorder[125]

Nantes. 10 April 1918. We had to leave Steenwerck, as the Germans were near Steenwerck, and everything was on fire. We had to run away from the guns and bullets, and it was terrible to see civilians and soldiers get killed that day. I shall never forget it. We had to leave everything, as we could take nothing with us. The Germans are in Steenwerck now and are near Hazebrouck. You know all those places. Mother, father, and I had to walk for two days, then we took the train. We stopped in the train for two days with nothing to eat; 6,000 civilians were in the same train. We stopped one day where the soldiers were billeted before the war, and next morning we had to move from there, and they sent us to a village just the same as prisoners. We stopped there for two weeks, then we asked the officer to let us come to Nantes. Father has a sister here, and the officer gave us a pass.

A definite crisis reached

On 13 April 1918, the front page of *The Sun* (Sydney) newspaper printed the banner headline, 'DEFINITE CRISIS REACHED'.[126]

Underneath the banner it issued a compilation of news from Reuter's telegrams, London correspondents' reports, and articles printed in *The Times*.

One report informed the nation that Messines – defended so valiantly by Australian troops – had been captured by the German army and then stated *'the ground in front of our lines is strewn with corpses.'*[127]

The report stated, *'the nation is watching with anxiety, unprecedented since the beginning of the war, the progress of the critical battle in northern France.'*[128]

Field-Marshall Sir Douglas Haig's telegrams were also printed in the edition, stating 'severe and continuous fighting occurred last night',[129] and reported on prolonged fighting and counter-attacks.

One telegram by Percival Phillips read:

> 11 April, 1918. Troops and guns crossed at a number of points to support attacks in the Steenwerck region, while divisions around Estaires endeavoured to advance along the river in the direction of Merville.[130]

The day that Steenwerck burned

The fateful day described in Jeanne Plouvier's letter to Doctor Davenport arrived on 10 April 1918. Official war office announcements and other reports from newspapers of the day told of fierce fighting in Steenwerck against the advancing German troops. Of great priority was the evacuation of wounded soldiers and nursing personnel from the 2nd Australian Casualty Clearing Station, many expressing terror at the thought of being left behind and the fate that would await them at the hands of the enemy.

Out of necessity, and with great difficulty, the clearing stations became mobile. The German army was now in possession of Steenwerck, and given the significant military resources left behind in the rushed evacuation, Monash had to make a decision. There was no other choice than to bomb Steenwerck themselves – to destroy the township that had played such an important role as their secret headquarters' location.

Extracts follow describing these crucial moments, including General Monash's comments of the loss of key personnel. Later entries by Monash on 20 and 21 April describe the bombings.

Monash diaries, as published in *The Daily News*[131]

12 April 1918. There was fierce fighting at the village of Steenwerck, and fighting is now proceeding at Nieppe and Steenwerck, two miles north-west and three miles west of Armentieres, respectively. This would show that, in his first rush, enemy troops made considerable advance as the village mentioned is fully seven miles west of the position held by the British, but the counter-attacks made by our troops evidently decreased this gain.

War Office Announcement, published in *The Sydney Morning Herald*[132]

12 April 1918. The War Office announces that during the recent retirement some casualty clearing stations fell into the enemy's hands. All the doctors, nurses, and patients were safely removed, and deficiencies had since been made good. The Australian and Canadian medical authorities generously helped, lending doctors and nurses. During the evacuation, which was carried out under heavy fire, a number of casualties occurred among the medical and nursing personnel.

Monash diaries, as published in *The Daily News*[133]

12 April 1918. Up to the present my casualties have been very small, with the exception of the loss of Lieut.-Colonel

Churchus, who, with his adjutant and intelligence officer, was killed by one chance shell which entered the hut where they had their headquarters on a hill. My aide-de-camp and I arrived at the spot ten minutes afterwards, but the shelling had then stopped.

This has been my most serious loss up to now, although three battalion commanders have been wounded ... The Boche has walked into Armentieres, Ploegsteert Wood and Messines. Steenwerck is burning, and Bailleul is threatened. It is a deplorable business. If we only had 20 more divisions like the 5 Australian, 4 Canadian and 1 New Zealand, there would have been a different tale to tell.

General Haig, as published in *The Sun*[134]
13 April 1918. Further retreat. We counter-attacked south eastward from the direction of Bailleul and from the north towards Steenwerck, but we did not succeed in pushing back the enemy, although we punished him heavily.

Brigadier-General Jobson, as published in *West Echo*[135]
20 April 1918. There were determined hand-to-hand encounters at Messines and Wytschaete, which were taken and re-taken several times, the Germans being eventually driven out. Similar scenes took place at Steenwerck. We heavily bombed the Merville, Estaires and Steenwerck railway junctions.

General Haig, as published in *The Scone Advocate*[136]
21 April 1918. Despite the weather four and a half tons of bombs were dropped on the railway station, an ammunition dump, and other targets. Our night flyers were most active, dropping 16 tons of bombs on Armentieres, Warneton, Estaires, Bapaume, and the railway junction at Chaulnes, and directly hitting four trains, one

of which, judging by the explosion, was full of ammunition. All our machines returned.

The moving war front

With the significant sites of Armentières, Bapaume and Steenwerck now in ruins, the war frontline moved to new battlegrounds in the Somme region. Meanwhile, General Monash was absent, involved in the Battle of Hamel, over 50 miles away to the east of Amiens. As the 3rd Division's acting commander, Brigadier-General Jobson remained in charge of this region. He kept in close contact with Field-Marshall Haig, chief commander of the British Expeditionary Force. Jobson resumes his story below.

Brigadier-General Jobson, as published in *The Inverell Times*[137]

June 1918. I did not see him [Haig] again, but through the battle we still felt that his interest in us was a deep, personal one. A few hours before the actual offensive, as I sat in the brigade battle dug-out making final arrangements, I received a personal letter from Major-General Harrington, General Plumer's chief of staff. In it he expressed the wishes of his Generals and of himself for our success. They had every confidence in our ability to carry out the task successfully.

This personal touch gave us confidence, for we felt we were still in the minds of those up above. In the Second Army, and I understand too with the Chief, the value of personal touch is never forgotten. We next heard of the Chief's interest in our portion of the offensive when news came through that, on the second morning of the attack, he had motored down to Bailleul to see General Godley at Corps Headquarters.

A heavy enemy shell fell in the street close to his car. Fortunately, although the staff car sustained damage, the

Commander-in-Chief was unhurt. When a new car was obtained, he proceeded on his way as if nothing had happened.

It is sad reading for many Anzacs to learn of the devastation of Armentieres, Bailleul, Steenwerck and intervening villages. In this district every Australian division has, at one time or another, spent a well-earned rest. Estaires, a pretty little township, hardly touched after two years of war, was well-known to the Fifth Division; while Bailleul, Armentieres, Nieppe and Steenwerck were as well-known to the Third Division as are their own home cities.

Fourth Battle of Ypres, Battle of the Lys: 7–29 April 1918

It was during the Fourth Battle of Ypres that Steenwerck and the surrounding areas were overtaken by the Germans in their Spring Offensive. The once peaceful town was now burning as the residents fled for their lives.

On 8 April, the Australians of the 1st Division moved south to support the Somme offensive but soon became engaged in heavy fighting near Merris and Meteren due to the Battle of the Lys.

The town of Hazebrouck was crucial for supplies, and its loss would disrupt British communications in the area. Commander-in-Chief of the British Army, Sir Douglas Haig, made requests to French General Ferdinand Foch for extensive aid. These requests were largely ignored as Foch focused on conserving reserves for future attacks. However, Foch did send two divisions to General Plumer's 2nd Army and positioned General Maistre's Army in the Authie Valley as a precaution. As the situation worsened, Haig issued his Order of the Day to the British Army on 11 April.

'There is no other course open to us but to fight it out! Every position must be held to the last man: there must be no retirement. With our backs to the wall and believing in the justice of our cause, each one of us must fight on to the end.'[138]

The 1st Australian Division reached Hazebrouck on 12 April after General Haig ordered them to cover the railhead there as a matter of urgency. The town's railway delivered half of the Allies' daily food and munitions supplies. Had Hazebrouck fallen into German hands, the consequences would have been catastrophic.

Haig directed all Commonwealth forces to hold their ground against the advancing German divisions, who were desperate to achieve victory before American troops were expected to arrive in large numbers. Despite overwhelming odds, Allied efforts bought time for the Australians to take up the fight and close the breach in the British line.

Their advance temporarily halted, the German divisions regrouped and attempted to advance up the valley between Meteren and Merris, but were met with a hail of fire from two Australian battalions. Meanwhile Haig searched for more mounted regiments to bolster the weary Allied fighters who were at the end of their reserves.

On 14 April 1918, the Germans attacked the nearby Mont de Merris, which was defended by Lieutenant Christopher Champion of the 3rd Battalion of the A.I.F. The Germans captured Gutzer Farm in front of the Australians, enabling them to flank Champion's forces. Throughout the afternoon, Lieutenant Champion and his men repelled multiple German attacks and stopped a final assault at 7 pm.

Unfortunately, Lieutenant Champion was killed by a bullet to the head. He was not found until a farmer discovered the remains of four Australian soldiers in 2003, 85 years later.

The decisive but largely forgotten battle at Mont de Merris prevented the Germans from breaking through the British defences and gaining access to the coast. In his despatches, Haig praised the valour and sheer determination of the Allies' armies against the 'titanic onslaught'[139] of the German forces. He stated that 'no more brilliant exploit took place during the whole offensive'.[140]

CHAPTER 26

A CONSTANT STREAM OF BULLETS

'There was suddenly a terrible rushing, wobbling scream overhead. A huge driving band of metal, apparently from one of our own big 12-inch guns in the rear near Glisy, dug itself into the ground … It could have just about cut a horse, or a man, in half.'
Jim Armitage[141]

Jim Armitage recollects his brigade on the move through various war zones including Villers-Bretonneux, and the experiences in sharing the trenches with his best friend, John Roxburgh.

Jim Armitage's diary[142]

June 1918. *Epangs Chateau.* We enjoyed the freedom of swimming in the Somme, of practising our battery manoeuvres in the mornings and watching enemy planes fly over each night on their way to bomb Abbeville, but our rest further back came to an abrupt end.

After packing our kit and managing the horses, we tramped out of that quiet chateau to take our place in the line. The first day's march took us through Liercourt to Hangest. The Huns tried to drop bombs on us during the second day, but they were attacked by British planes. One British and one German fighter crashed nearby.

We passed through Amiens and Camon, both towns being knocked about considerably. Amiens received an 8" shell as we left, just to remind us, I suppose, that there was a war on!

In an orchard, under a railway bank behind Glisy, we established our waggon lines. We were not favourably impressed with the position at first, as this line was the main line from Amiens to St. Quentin and La Fère. It was joined about 500 yards away by the main Albert-Amiens line. These facts alone should be sufficient to condemn such a place as a long-range artillery target. To add to this, there was an English 12" railway mounted gun hidden on one line, and a 13" French gun on the other. We expected a lively time from enemy fire drawn by those two guns. We were quite mistaken. The waggon lines turned out to be ideal. We are only losing a lot of men through sickness, two from Trench Fever. Another was run over by a limber, crushing his leg.

4 June. We took over from the 4th Division behind Villers-Bretonneux and straight in front of Amiens. The badly shelled gun pits took a lot of cleaning. Their 'D' sub pit had been blown sky high, gun and all but, after a great deal of work, we cleaned up the place after a fashion.

The Huns were shelling about 100 yards to the right of the road as we brought our guns up. Roxburgh and I shared a 4'6" by 6' trench which we made our home. The weather was hot and fortunately very dry. We sometimes got a bit of gas, and, because of the lowness of the ground, it hung about for hours.

One peaceful evening John Roxburgh and I were sunning ourselves in shorts just outside the battery headquarters dug-out. Suddenly the screech of a heavyweight long-range shell caused John to dive headlong into the dug-out. He ripped a foot-long gash in his thigh. My reactions being slower, I fell flat. The shell burst harmlessly in a shell hole 100 yards away. I took great glee in pouring black, strong iodine all over his wound. John's comments were impressive.

One night during a routine shoot, an S.O.S. signal went up in our front sector. We quickly changed to our barrage range and, after 15 minutes of strafing the Hun, the raid petered out.

On our right was a French battery. Their guns were beautiful pieces with a split trail, which fired a shell about 5 inches in diameter. They had long-range guns and did all their shooting at night. They used a charge which seemed to make less noise than our 18 pounders and had less flash.

Their gunners lived in great dug-outs 40 foot below ground, where they also built a small mess room. Their dug-outs had gasproof curtains at the entrances. We lived in holes 4′6″ by 6′ by 8′ with galvanised iron and 10 inches of earth over us. We were friendly with the French gunners (who always had wine). They said, when we asked them why they troubled to build such elaborate dug-outs, 'Why Monsieur? No dug-out, no *après la guerre*.'

Behind us was a battery of British military aircraft guns receiving considerable attention from German 4.2-inch *whiz bang* high velocity shells. These things travel so fast that the scream of their approach comes after they explode.

Major Walker won everyone's admiration by his coolness and manner of taking all the difficulties in his stride. One day, Colonel MacArthur King came to escort a tribe of bigwigs and brass hats from divisional headquarters to inspect the brigade. When they arrived at our battery and saw the shattered state of everything, and the multitude of fresh shell holes around us, the bigwigs decided it was not a healthy place to spend the holiday, and suddenly remembered that they had left their smelling salts back at H.Q.

They hurried off in that direction, just as a 5.9″ *woolly bear* burst right over us. This did nothing to postpone their departure.

A woolly bear is the name given to German high explosive shells fitted with time fuses or delayed action fuses, exploding into a mass of brown and white smoke. They are used for ranging as observers can see where they explode. One can expect a strafing to follow.

9 *June*. We went forward to dig pits for the centre section gun, which would occupy a ridge some 3,000 yards in front of the main batteries. It would serve as an anti-tank section, only going into action in the event of a tank attack. This ridge was under open observation from the German lines. As we started work, we were spotted by the Huns and came under machine gun and whiz bang fire. One man, in his haste to fling himself onto mother earth, flung himself onto me, accidentally stopping a piece of shell splinter with his shoulder and saving me a nasty crack.

We learned a valuable lesson. Henceforth, we worked only at night. As we crawled away from the site, Fritz made it uncomfortable for us all the way back to the battery. This was to be accomplished by a series of short wild runs, always terminating in the bottom of some old shell hole, before crawling through a wet and very damaged wheat field.

That evening we went into Villers-Bretonneux to search houses for flour to help our gas-damaged food supply. A constant stream of machine bullets passed overhead. I picked up a return ticket to Amiens on the platform of the wrecked railway station, as a souvenir.

11 *June*. We were relieved by another detachment of gunners and then went back to the waggon lines for ten days' *rest*, which usually consisted of Reveille at 6am, watering and grooming horses and feeding them; breakfast, the identical breakfast that men have eaten since the war began, being a dessertspoon full of pork and bean stew or else a piece of boiled bacon, 3 inches by 2 inches, and sometimes a piece of bread.

After breakfast, we turned the horses out to graze on the flats and worked on building earthwork revetting, cleaning up the horse lines till 11.30, when we mustered the horses and groomed for an hour. Lunch always consisted of a spoonful of deplorably watery stew and an army biscuit which was quite inedible, unless soaked in tea, known as an *Anzac wafer*.

In the afternoon we worked on the revetting, to protect the horses from shell splinters. We made them from big cut tufts of rooty grass from the flats of the Somme. These walls were about 2 foot thick at the base and 1 foot thick at the top, a bit higher than a horse's back. The walls ran both front and behind the horse lines, with subdivisions between.

At 5 pm our tea consisted of one thick slice of bread and one large spoonful of jam, or margarine, or cheese. Not all three.

Every second night we were up all night, carting ammunition to the battery or doing horse line picket duty. On one occasion, I'd been up with a full load of ammunition as an attack was expected. In a pitch-black night we lost the track several times. On our second trip up from the ammunition dump, we ran into gas and were shelled while unloading at the guns …

The Germans had a huge gun of 12-inch calibre away back, whose sole task appeared to be to shell Amiens at dusk. We would hear this distant boom when things were quiet. About 30 seconds later, we would hear the great shell whining high overhead. Another 30 seconds afterwards came the crash of its explosion in the town. Later in the evening, a big railway gun would go off with a blinding flash and an earth-shattering crash. We would hear the great shell shrieking through space, probably searching for that spiteful gunner of Amiens.

Gunners in the waggon lines relieved those at the guns, the centre section having moved their guns up into the new anti-tank positions, so that is where we went. We unloaded our waggon in a sunken road about 150 yards behind the guns. While helping to unload, I met Bob Shute who had been relieved. He did not say much, but what he did say was right to the point. 'Don't waste too much time getting across that open stretch of ground between here and the guns. When you get there, keep your bloody head down. Bye!'

I did not wait to ask questions as most of the fellows were on their way. I picked up my kit and went for my life.

At the new position, we dropped our kits and started to take stock. Everything was calm and peaceful and the view from the ridge was beautiful. I think, for the moment, we forgot there was a war on. I certainly forgot Bob's warning. We were rudely brought back to earth, diving into the miserable holes the former occupants happily called dug-outs.

The place I found myself in with two other fellows, John Roxburgh and Arthur Ranken, was dug into the chalk bank. It had 4 inches of soil and shock over it, together with sandbags full of stones and several logs thrown on top with bits of iron to act as *bursters*. The dug-out was 4 foot wide, narrowing to 3 foot at the base, the entrance 2.5 foot by 6.5 foot long. The floors and walls were crumbling clay which fell in handfuls if touched. We gained entrance to this burrow by crawling down three chalk steps headfirst, a bit like crawling down a ladder headfirst.

There was nothing to do all day but play cards and sleep. We kept one man on watch day and night with just his head sticking out, listening for an S.O.S. or gas attack. In the event of such an attack, our orders were to keep going for as long as possible and, if necessary, to blow the guns up in case of capture. There was no chance of getting them out.

Secret enemy tunnels

The opportunity to explore enemy trenches or dugouts was fraught with danger, as some were mined or otherwise booby-trapped by departing troops, provided they were not leaving hastily due to the enemy's arrival. Below, another soldier recounts his experience of exploring such a passageway of tunnels.

North-Eastern Advertiser[143]

Sausage Valley was a few miles from town where the road winds around till it gets up into a saucer-shaped gully, about two miles wide, and the same length. Before the offensive move started in July, it was one of the very strongest points in the German line, full of deep well-built dug-outs. In one place, showing around the slopes on the rim, the many entrances to underground passages were hewn out of solid chalk, and well-timbered too.

It is not a fragrant place by any means, but we went down a flight of steps about 60 feet into a large passage running right around that particular mound, and saw rooms of all sizes, with stoves and light fittings in every direction. They had interconnected tunnels so that, in case one exit got blown in, they had other means of escape. These dug-outs were built of steel rails and heavy timbers with beds let into the walls ship fashion and triplex glass gas curtains.

Fitted up like a house underground, the walls were pine-lined or papered, with cupboards; linoleums or carpets on the floors, and in some rooms they had bedsteads with mattresses, chairs and tables; in fact, everything one could think about. It was a great piece of work and must have taken them months to fix up. One could barely believe it without seeing it.

Evidently they thought they were there for keeps when they settled down in that spot.

In the valley itself, along the road were our camps, kitchen cookers and stores, ambulance waggons and other gear, with different battalions utilising the old trenches as best they could till the time came to do their turn at various points along the line.

Guns were there in hundreds, of all sorts and sizes, and occasionally they would all get going, and then it was some row alright. Shells from Fritz's guns were always dropping in here and causing more damage. As it was one of his own former spots, he had the range and direction to a nicety, and had a fancy to pelt the road every evening from about the middle of the afternoon when he thought our ammunition limbers and stores would be coming up.

It used to be an anxious time for the drivers till they got their loads off and were away. Then the teams and limbers used to clear out at a gallop. I have often seen Vern Hand go down with his limber in a cloud of dust and wondered if they would get clear. Amongst the teams in the clearing, I could hear him roaring at the horses to get a move on. Our line was in front of Pozieres, where the Germans held the next ridge.

CHAPTER 27

DESPERATE TIMES

'It is a horrible thing to record, but when the girls went to remove the amputated limbs, the bundle was too heavy for them to lift.'
Sister Millicent Armstrong[144]

While the soldiers fought on the battlefields, the nurses fought behind the scenes to sustain life for the wounded and to ease the pain of the dying. The graphic descriptions in this chapter deal with the unpleasant topic of the amputation of limbs. This procedure was often necessary to save a life.

Many of the nursing staff went above and beyond what was required of them, often paying from their own pockets for additional help at critical times. Describing the constant pressure of 14-hour working days, they also greatly appreciated having a rest, although I recall one nurse writing that, after a break, she 'was very glad to get back amongst the soldiers again'.[145]

Sister Perry Handley
Northern Star[146]

June 1918. We have had a desperate time the last two weeks. I thought after four years in the war zone in France I had some idea of the horror of it all, but we have yet to learn a great many things. Encourage as much as you can the Red Cross workers for, without their help and support, we and many others would have gone under.

As you perhaps have seen by the papers, the fighting near us has been one fierce struggle… Don't worry for our safety, for we shall be sent back if they advance, but I have spent almost every penny I possessed, both that sent over by you and my own money, to help the struggle. There has been one steady stream of people day and night passing through from the invaded areas; penniless, homeless, and foodless.

It is well that those who live in luxury cannot see the misery of it all, or rather it is a terrible pity.

Now that our own position is so insecure I think it wiser to cable than wait two months for a reply to letters, for if the Germans get nearer to Paris there may be trouble getting money from the banks. We are not alarmed, but we are told to prepare and have our handbags packed ready to leave at a moment's notice.

Should the news be bad, we shall be *Somewhere* in the south of France. You will know before this reaches you how things are.

The work came with a terrific crash. We expected something to happen, but no one had any idea it would come with such force in our sector. Without any warning, and without any equipment or facilities, we were swamped with thousands of wounded.

You know our bed capacity is only 250, so stretchers were left everywhere; in the corridors, the halls, the college boys' dormitories, the courtyards, and the parks; anything and anywhere were employed to get them from the battlefield.

Am enclosing a diagram from today's paper showing our position (can't mention places). We have French, American, and German wounded, all brought in together – such terrible wounds. Operations (for haemorrhage, gas, gangrene, amputations, etc.,) were so urgent that, within 24 hours, I was called upon to equip ten operating tables and get them into action.

We have been working day and night for two solid weeks without stopping, except for one hour. I implored them to call a halt to get rid of the debris.

For three days and nights our small staff of ten nurses had to cope with it all and for two days and nights, without stopping, Miss Palmer and I had to 'hold down' the operating rooms, with the help of three French maids whom I pressed into service and some refugees, whom I paid out of money you sent over. We were all hard pressed. I employed and paid people, wherever I could, to facilitate work. After three days the American Red Cross came to our help, sending thirty nurses, doctors, and necessary supplies.

We are all now working at a solid, steady pressure of 14 hours, but we are getting rest and good food.

This village has certainly lived through tragedies, but it is a satisfaction to feel we were here, otherwise there would have been nothing for the men. Our being on the spot saved many lives.

Units are being quickly established in front of us. As soon as they are ready, we will be relieved of this pressure. Every day new tents are springing up in the park and extra help pouring in. During our tremendous work in the operating room, I was called upon to provide surgical supplies for 26,000 men who had arrived at the next village, after four days and nights march, footsore and without any equipment.

They had lost everything and were just done. All I could give them were a few old field dressings and some torn rags. An onlooker might think it bad management that things like these could happen, but everything changes so quickly, one hasn't a chance to act.

I'm sitting up in bed writing, nearly asleep. Have had two hours' rest. I must get up, and once more go into the endless machine of the operating room, where everything is orderly and systematic, but being done with speed, for many are lined up in corridors, awaiting their turn.

Yesterday there were over 100 patients ahead of us. Today we caught up to 60. If there is not another rush in the night, we hope to get ahead of the work.

I have estimated 600 operations in one week ...

•

The graphic stories from the nurses and soldiers indicate what life was like on the battlefields and how they coped with horrific injuries in the aftermath. It is sometimes hard to fathom that these were mainly young people in the prime of their lives, struggling to make sense of an unimaginable situation out of their control.

In particular, I need to constantly remind myself that Jim, despite the maturity of his writing, was just an eighteen-year-old teenager when he and his classmates enlisted.

They had to grow up very quickly.

CHAPTER 28

CORBIE ON THE SOMME

'The earth shook. The mind boggled at the concussion.'
Jim Armitage[147]

Friendly fire

Mustard gas was one of the horrors of war devised by the Germans in their use of chemical warfare. But another horror was that of friendly fire when our soldiers were slaughtered by our own weapons. In the heat of battle, miscalculations occurred, as Jim Armitage describes below.

Jim Armitage's diary[148]

July 1918. Our orders had been to keep going as long as possible, or else destroy the guns if in danger of being over-run, but thankfully, there was no need to blow them up. From our ridge we had a splendid view of Corbie, Windy Flat and Corps Corner and the shelling those places received, Corbie in particular.

All the enemy's shells passed over our heads as they were behind us. We were between them and the German guns. One could never be sure when one of the shells would drop on us. It was an unwritten law that no more than one man should leave the dug-out at a time, in case one had to beat a hasty retreat into the clumsy entrance, so we lived like rabbits coming up for our food, which was often cold tack, and going down again to eat it.

There was a cleverly camouflaged battery of 18 pounders behind us on Windy Flat. Later I learned that this battery was the 49th, which included John Brunton[*] and Rob Wilkinson.[†] John looked a bit of a wreck the last time that I saw him. He was a big man and had lost so much weight.

We acquired a great respect for German artillery. At dusk, when our observation balloons were hauled down, they started shelling along our ridge and continued at half-hour intervals all night. It was always an anxious time for S.O.S. guards, identifying numerous lights going up in the front line, ducking for cover from shells, and sniffing for gas. The Germans pumped a lot of gas into the low ground around Corbie.

Our carefully used cook-house, a hole 5 foot by 4 foot and 4 foot deep, got a direct hit with a German 5.9" mustard gas shell. All our food was ruined. We had no food or water till the evening of the following day. We all got a bit of mustard gas but miraculously lost only two men. It took all night, working in those cumbersome gas masks, to beat and burn the gas out of our dug-outs. One dug-out had to be abandoned.

One night a Hun plane dropped a bomb on the trail of 'C' sub gun, blowing it to bits, and setting the camouflage alight, which exploded some of our ammunition. At the same time, it cut a swathe through the protective wheat crop for a radius of around 5 yards.

During this affair, Sergeant Hans Marker of 'D' subsection was awarded the Military Medal for preventing the destruction of our ammunition supply.

---

[*] John Moffitt Brunton, Jim's school friend. Sydney Grammar WWI Honour Roll.
[†] Robert 'Rob' Wilkinson, another classmate from Sydney Grammar School.

Portrait of General Sir John Monash, one of Australia's most distinguished soldiers during World War I. In France, from 1916 to 1918, he was Commander of the 3rd Division, Australian Imperial Force (A.I.F.). In May 1918, he took command of the Australian Corps.
AWM A01241

Australian soldiers play the popular game of 'two up' near the ruins of Ypres. October 1917.
AWM E01199

Soldiers haul guns by hand along Anzac Ridge in the Ypres sector. Boggy ground would have rendered it impossible to use horses. 26 October 1917. AWM E01055

The Anzac Coves performing. Standing on the left is female impersonator and 'leading lady' Bobbie Roberts. The former pianist and former props designer were killed in a bombing during a performance. 23 November 1917. AWM E01307

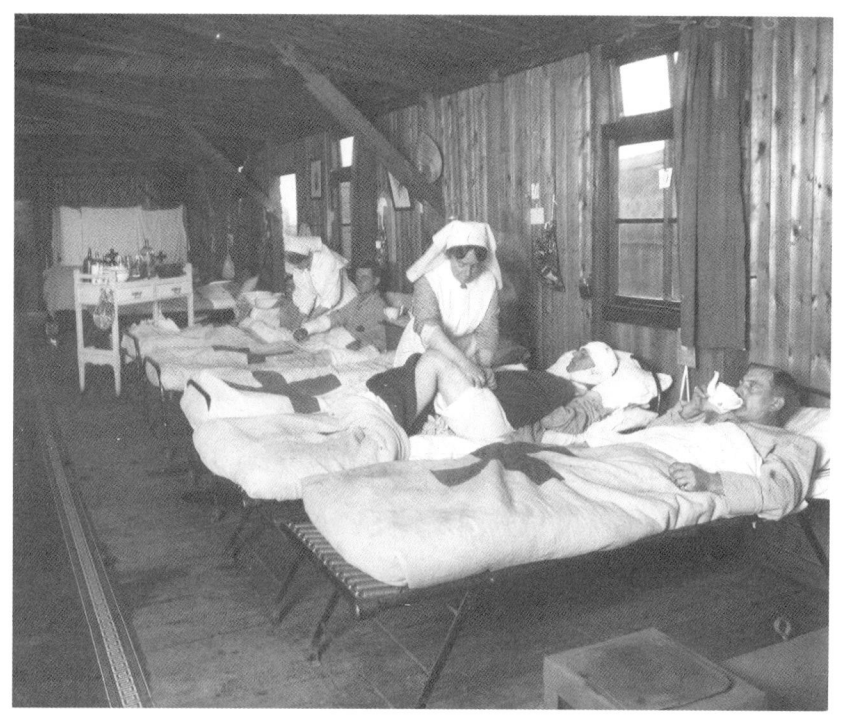

A ward of the 2nd Australian Casualty Clearing Station, based in the town of Steenwerck. Most of these patients were wounded fighting in the Third Battle of Ypres. November 1917. AWM E04623

The ruins of Steenwerck after the bombing on 10 April 1918, which forced Jeanne Plouvier to flee the burning town. AWM E02150

The Australian War Correspondents' Headquarters in France. Men cool their horses in the river. 17 May 1918. AWM E04884

The site codenamed 'Circular Quay' by the Somme River. Pontoons were hidden in the interior of the building by day and assembled by night to create a bridge. May 1918. AWM E04795

Men of the 3rd Division of the A.I.F. near Bray-sur-Somme in the wake of the Australian advance at Amiens, beginning the Hundred Days Offensive. The Emblem of the 3rd Division can be seen on the vehicle. 28 August 1918.
AWM E03070

Australian soldiers receive mail, one of the highlights of their days. During the war, many ships carrying mail were torpedoed. 13 October 1918. AWM E03560

Members of an Australian Field Artillery unit cook lunch, using a kerosene tin. 14 October 1918. AWM E03550

A meal break for the soldiers of the 7th and 8th Brigades of the Australian Field Artillery. The men were travelling along a road near Brancourt to participate in the advance battle at St. Quentin Canal, the first full breach of the Hindenburg Line. Jim Armitage belonged to the 8th Brigade. 18 October 1918.
AWM E03562

Jim Armitage, fourth in line. John Roxburgh, centre. November 1917.
Printed with permission from Jim's relatives, the Suranyi family.

Jim Armitage many years after the war, with his wife Lurline Armitage. They are riding horses at Killarney Station in Narrabri, NSW. Circa 1930.
Printed with permission from Jim's relatives, the Suranyi family.

After the mustard gas shelling, two men took it in turns to go down to the main battery every night for rations. This meant a two-mile walk, run, and crawl each way across open country under surveillance from German observation balloons. The countryside was raked by shell-fire at odd times all night, to try catching transports moving about.

Infantry coming and going out of the line used this place too, and so we had some rough moments. A Salvation Army chap had occupied an old dug-out in the middle of the Corps Corner, where he used to hand out cups of coffee to us harassed blokes. This magnificent bloke was always there with his quiet smile and his coffee urn. On arriving there one night, we found his dug-out blasted. There was no trace of the man or his coffee urn.

3 *July*. Started making preparations for a stunt. A brigade of 4th Division started digging gun pits on our left but were spotted and given a lively time. The battery of English Royal Horse Artillery, which pulled into action behind our ridge twice a week for 30 rounds rapid gunfire, finally desisted. We were exceedingly glad. They stayed about half an hour, then limbered up and galloped off. Their speed and precision were very impressive. They always managed to finish their shoot and get away before returning fire started.

We got the backlash intended for them.

After pulling out from our region towards the end of the month, we started carting and hiding vast quantities of ammunition across the Somme, into an open area. We had to cross the pontoon bridge* in total darkness and the traffic jam was terrible.

Australian engineers erected this bridge every night after dark, dismantling and hiding the pontoons every morning before

---

*   At Circular Quay crossing.

daylight. Well, one night we were hopelessly blocked by an English unit's waggon which had a wheel over one edge of the narrow bridge. After a while we could stand it no longer, so we unhitched the horses and tipped the waggon and contents into the river. The Tommies took a poor view of all this, but everyone else was pleased.

Battle of Hamel: 4 July 1918

The Battle of Hamel in World War I was the first operation planned by Lieutenant-General John Monash since taking command of the Australian Corps. A short but decisive and bloody engagement, it was the first time Australian and American infantry, tanks, artillery and air support fought together on the same battlefield. Utilising Monash's strategies, within ninety-three minutes, Allied forces captured 1600 enemy soldiers. Approximately 1380 Australian and US personnel were either killed or wounded in the battle.

The Allies aimed to take the high ground east of the village of Le Hamel, south of the River Somme. The Germans needed to occupy the ridge at Le Hamel if they planned to capture Amiens, about 20 kilometres west.

The Australian Imperial Force (A.I.F.) provided the Allied officers and soldiers with extensive training, including rehearsal exercises on a replica of the battlefield. The use of such innovative tactics, which were repeated on larger-scale advances, helped to end the war in November 1918.

Jim Armitage recounts the Battle of Hamel and its aftermath below.

Jim Armitage's diary[149]

4 July 1918. Got to our new positions and started setting progressive fuses at about 2 am and on the tick of 4 am every gun on this mile long, and God knows how deep the wheel-to-wheel guns were, fired simultaneously. The earth shook. The mind boggled at the concussion.

After a while, thick smoke settled into a fog, and we had difficulty seeing our aiming lights. This was the beginning of the assault on Hamel. We were drawn up between the towns of Villers-Bretonneux and Sailly-le-Sec.

The 3rd and 4th Australian Divisions went over the top, gaining their objective, a ridge beyond Hamel. We didn't have a single German shell near us, but the 4th Division Brigade suffered severely.

They had eight killed and some wounded in one battery alone. Another battery behind us also had casualties. This battery caused considerable trouble with premature burst, due to poorly made American ammunition. Since they were right behind us and shooting over us, we had one or two narrow escapes from flying shell splinters. One piece of red-hot steel, about 2 inches long, whizzed past my head and buried itself in the ground at my feet.

The attack was a complete success. The Australians took over 200 prisoners and over 90 machine guns. Those Germans who came back past us seemed weedy, noticeably young, and utterly shattered by the savagery of our barrage.

English tanks were in the assault and suffered badly. Planes dropped more ammunition and messages. The Germans counter-attacked about an hour later but, after we put up another short withering barrage, our infantry quickly drove them back.

9 July. Strictly speaking, no civilians were allowed within 12 miles of the front. Despite this, one old peasant and his middle-aged daughter continued to live and work their fields near our waggon lines.

One evening, I went that way and was talking to our brigade interpreter, a Frenchman, as we passed their field. We stopped then and started yarning and questioning the old man about being allowed to stay so close to the line. Was he not afraid of being overrun by Germans? He replied that everybody knew he was a loyal, honest Frenchman. There was no need to worry about the Germans getting through with Australian infantry in front of him. As far as an odd shell coming over, well, he was an old man, he could not be worried about that!

He said, 'I know in my heart they will never cross this ground again. I know, because the German Uhlan Officer who billeted himself and his men on us told me, laughingly, that two battalions of Australian infantry were marching through Amiens, to drive back the whole of the German Imperial army. We buried him that afternoon with several of his men while the Germans were being driven back through Villers-Bretonneux.'

CHAPTER 29

ENDLESS TROUBLE

> 'We eventually got it out from under the collapsed roof, turned our team around, attached the cart to the back of the waggon, then lost no time in getting out.'
> Jim Armitage[150]

Major Dallas Bradlaugh Walker, who was in command of Jim Armitage's battery, often sent the boys on escapades that had little to do with the war, sometimes getting them into more strife than they could handle. In the following diary entry, Jim recounts an eventful journey transporting ammunition.

Jim Armitage's diary[151]

July 1918. *Vauxin.* I was brakeman on a waggon carrying ammunition to the battery. The road through Lahausay and Bonneauville was badly knocked about. Our 5th Division was caught there one night rather badly. The road resumed through what was left of Corbie and continued down a long steep hill and along the left bank of a large, marshy lagoon.

After loading ammunition, Major Walker told us to go into Vauxin and collect a load of scrap timber from the shattered village, then take it up to a proposed new gun site about 1,000 yards in front of the battery's present position.

After we had done this, he told us to go into Sailley-le-Sec and salvage a gig he had seen there, which he thought he could use.

We started off. It was a bright, moonlit night and absolutely still in the gully's roadside depression. We went on and on, and thought we were never coming to the place. We quite expected a German to pop up from the roadside or find ourselves in No-Man's land, as the sound of machine guns was getting closer.

At last, we pulled up into the village under cover of a pile of rubble, which represented the village church. In the still night, we heard bullets chipping bits off the shattered buildings above our heads. Putting the lead driver in charge of the horses, we searched, crawling into every battered farmyard and stable yard looking for that gig.

There were numerous wrecked farm carts but finally we found one in fair repair, though badly chipped by shell splinters, a light spring gig. We eventually got it out from under the collapsed roof, turned our team around, attached the cart to the back of the waggon, then lost no time in getting out.

We were blocked just outside the village by an infantry transport column, which had been caught by shell-fire whilst we were in Sailley-le-Sec and had suffered heavy casualties.

We finally got past those people and into the gully below the big hill, when we struck gas, and decided to make a dash for it. In the middle of this dash the gig, to our dismay, started to work loose. I had to climb over the back of the waggon and grab the shaft, while the whole crazy outfit careered madly along the shell-pitted road. What an absorbing sight we must have presented in the early hours of a moonlit morning.

Our next, and almost last, trouble was encountered on the road where a bottleneck was jammed thickly with guns, men, horses, and waggons going to and from the line.

We were nearly in the centre of the village when the shelling started. Now the recognised procedure here is for pedestrians to get off the road the best way that they can, going through houses, ditches, alleyways; anywhere to give the teams a chance to get clear. We were going well when our leading horses went down in a shell hole.

The two wheelers bore down on top of them while the crazy gig swung out into the road and jammed a gun team dashing in the opposite direction. In a moment, the whole road was a tumbling mess of men and horseflesh. Miraculously, injuries to man and horse were minor, and everyone was on their way in a very short time. It's remarkable how men can work under fire, but the already somewhat dented gig was in no way improved by the time we got it back onto the road. The Major's ears must have been burning.

When we were nearly home, a German plane flew over, very low. It was daylight now but overcast. Our battery opened up at a low angle overhead, a few yards away. The blast almost blew us off the face of the earth. The poor horses, already badly shaken, nearly collapsed on the spot and broke the pole for the second time.

However, our work was not yet done. Before leaving our lines the previous evening we had been told on our return, to pick up a load of hay in a nearby field. We plodded wearily on in pouring rain, picked up the wet hay, returning just in time for the 6 am day's work.

Later that night, I was up at the guns. A German plane dropped an aerial torpedo right on our horse lines, scoring a direct hit between the tall bank and the revetting.

Sixty-three horses were killed or had to be destroyed. That ghastly sight affected me greatly. Luckily, only two men were hit. The replacement horses, an untrained lot, gave us endless trouble.

A lucky escape

Due to a malfunction of his artillery gun, Jim received a nasty jolt from the backfire. A portion of the explosive charge escaped through the gun's breach mechanism, which set his uniform on fire. The leather money-belt around Jim's waist took most of the brunt, badly charring his two-up winnings from the week before. A reporter would later joke that Jim playing two-up 'saved his life'.[152]

Jim Armitage's diary[153]

26 July 1918. After many horses were killed by an aerial torpedo which was dropped on our revetting, the new replacement horses give us a lot of trouble. I went up to the guns with the relief but, as D subdivision had received reinforcements, I was transferred back to my C subdivision. The battery was in an ideal situation 200 yards in front of Vauxin on a level stretch of ground between a little hill and a tree-lined road.

At our usual 20 yards interval the guns just fitted in, our pits being dug into the edge of a ripening wheat field. We changed our camouflage as the colours of the wheat changed.

Dug-outs were dug into the side of a hill under some scattered trees. An Officers' Mess and S.O.S. post was dug higher up under another fringe of trees. Having to cross that open enemy-observed ground to get there, we excavated a communication trench from the battery over to the Officers' Mess.

There were two worn footpaths 30 yards behind our guns; one made by infantry passing at night from the road to old support trenches on the top of the hill, the other path being worn by us. This latter path led from the trees past our pits, stopping suddenly 20 yards from the road. An aerial photograph showed this suspicious-looking path stopping just short of the road, so we promptly trampled an extension past our location. Both paths then looked like innocent tracks over the hill, except for a few brass shell cases not under camouflage, shining in the sun. This was soon remedied, and we only had one casualty in this position.

One night, during a late shoot, we had a backfire on our gun caused by a shell-case flaw. Small ports in the gun's breach mechanism provided for such an emergency, as a portion of the explosive charge escaped through them.

Unfortunately, I received most of this by-pass explosive charge, right in my middle. It blew half of the right side of my tunic and breaches away, badly charring my leather money belt, and most of my two-up winnings from the week before.

We were engulfed in thick, sulphurous smoke. When it had cleared sufficiently, I found myself sitting on the floor of the pit trying to put out my smouldering clothes. I was almost totally deaf for about 10 days. This was known as 'Gun Deafness'. I got no sympathy.

About this time, stories were coming in of German dawn patrols going out to relieve their night outposts but finding them deserted. There seems to have been quite a bit of this most mysterious and demoralising thing happening. I spotted dark shadows passing by one night.

It appeared that blackened Australian infantry parties would sneak out, surprise those outposts and, at the point of cold steel, bring them back without firing a shot. Pitch black nights and the noise of gunfire, used to advantage, covered any sound they made.

One day we received orders from headquarters to build a 'real' dug-out, for some future advance, into the hillside of our good position. A sapper was sent here to direct operations.

We started to drive two tunnels into the hillside, each about 6 feet high and a yard wide and both were heavily timbered. We took it in turns to work, two men at a time, for 1.5-hour shifts.

Personally, I thought that dug-outs did more harm than good because frequently we didn't have enough camouflage to adequately cover the freshly dug earth. Sometimes engineers would bring up timber which we were too busy to cover, and such fresh sawn timber might lie exposed for a couple of hours. Enemy pilots had very sharp eyes, and low-flying airmen didn't miss much. I'm positive that exposed timber was responsible for a bad strafing we got one night at the end of July.

S.O.S. duty was most unpleasant, owing to its exposed position in full view of enemy lines, but excellent from our point of view to spot enemy gun flashes at night and to pinpoint a German battery. Sometimes, during a German strafe, the unfortunate guard would spend his time dashing for cover in the nearby slit trench then rushing back to his S.O.S. board, to try to measure the angle to give him the position of enemy gun flashes. At the same time, he had to keep his head clear enough to recognise his own area S.O.S. flare signals against all of the coloured flashes the Jerries were sending up.

During this time, he was also expected to report the positions of enemy guns, calibre of shells fired, the kinds of shells and the rate of fire, amongst other things. Sometimes the poor fellow was too busy to run and wake his relief.

31 *July*. Three more of our balloons were brought down just behind us. That night Jerry opened up with a battery of 4.2s firing shrapnel. He was only raking the two innocent-looking paths on the chance of getting some infantry, but as one innocent-looking path went right past our camouflaged guns, we got the benefit of it. Only one man was hit, and he got a Blighty. One shell blew the side out of our gun pit, covering me with dirt. Shrapnel rattled against the gun shield and punctured some of our live shells without exploding anything.

Another shell exploded behind our guns where our sub-commander had been standing. I remember looking around to see where his remains had been blown to but saw him crawling, unconcernedly, out of a nearby shell hole, calmly brushing dirt from his tunic.

3 *August.* We manhandled ammunition up from the road all afternoon and right through the night, only breaking off at frequent intervals to give the Huns 60 rounds at gunfire rate on various parts of his support lines. Heavy batteries away behind us roared incessantly, while pumping gas and high explosives into the enemy positions.

At this stage one realised just how much of our artillery bombardments had been steadily increasing over the past two to three weeks. One can imagine how many new batteries must have been brought into action. We also noticed the Hun artillery didn't seem to be quite so keen to start an artillery duel, as his daylight work dropped considerably.

From dark to daylight, roads were becoming increasingly jammed with lorries carrying small and large ammunition, engineer's supplies, and every imaginable kind of equipment. The noise of the engines increased with the density of traffic, the shouting of drivers, and the curses of men. The heavy rumble of solid-tyred lorries added to the confusion, until we thought the noise would reach the German lines.

One night a Hun plane dropped a parachute flare right above the roadway. I expected to see wild confusion, but nothing stirred. There might not have been a living thing for miles. In the lightless yard the lorries stood motionless, their dusty tops matching exactly the colour of the road.

That night, the Germans heavily bombarded the valley area with gas, shrapnel, and high explosives. We thought the show must have been given away, but he evidently didn't guess what was going on and the strafe was just routine. Obviously, something big was about to happen and we were getting rather strung up, lest the Germans get suspicious and then have time to reinforce the area.

6 August. Moving forward in front of Vauxin, 'A' sub guns got into position beside our right section, which already had its guns there. For the past three nights our waggon lines have been carting ammunition to this new position. Now they started carting all of our spare ammunition from my gun pits. Bob Shute happened to be brakeman on one waggon. On his second load around midnight, I asked him what sort of a place we were going to. He vividly described it as an open field, bang under the noses of the Huns, with not enough cover to hide a cat. To get there one had to cross that constantly shelled pontoon bridge, get along a road through a swamp and, 'If you get off the road, you've had it!'

I said goodnight to Shute. I was crawling into my blankets when I was told I must go up to the waggons in the new position and learn as much as I could in the dark about the area so that I could act as a guide for the guns. By this time our waggons had gone, so cursing at the top of my voice, I ran after them and scrambled over the back of the first waggon I came to, only to find that it was from another battery. I rode with it until we came to the bottleneck on the pontoon bridge.

When I crossed that shaking, overladen bridge on foot, shells started falling in the village ahead and one could hear teams breaking into a gallop.

I jumped onto another team as it started its wild careering. The wrong waggon again. It belonged to the 29th Battery but near enough as I knew that, wherever we went, my battery would be right beside it. Such a wonderful, still night with hardly even a distant shot until those shells started falling in the village. The noise of many hundreds of horse teams and their clattering guns and waggons was enough to wake the dead. The infantry, walking along the roadside going up the line, cursed us, yelling at us to slow down and to make less noise, but once this sort of momentum started, it was hard to stop. Why the Huns weren't alerted I shall never know ...

I knew we were close to the frontline. The German Verey lights were so bright they looked close enough to fall on us. There were large piles of ammunition everywhere, covered by long, dry grass. The night seemed utterly pitch black until a flare went up and in the light I could see horses, harnesses, waggons, and tin hats, all shining dangerously bright.

The first man I ran into was Frank Cody, our C section sub-sergeant. He asked what the hell I was doing there. When I told him, he let off steam, telling me that John Roxburgh had already been sent up as a guide for the guns. After exchanging mutual opinions on the ruling powers, I made for the road, jumped onto a passing limber, and headed home.

CHAPTER 30

THE SECRET OF CIRCULAR QUAY

'The value of stealth, audacity, and imagination are written along the south bank of the Somme. Not that frontal attack can be avoided yet or its price foregone.'
A. S. Wallace[154]

Codenamed 'Circular Quay'

As the Germans regularly bombed strategic bridges and crossings, a secret pontoon bridge was devised at a location codenamed 'Circular Quay'. Constructed after dark and dismantled before dawn, access to the bridge was very congested overnight. The pontoon pieces that formed the bridge were stored beside the Somme River in an old building with *Circular Quay* painted on the side. Jim Armitage explains that the soldiers knew what this location was. If the enemy or spies overheard the reference, they would hopefully assume that it related to Circular Quay in Sydney, Australia, not to the secret night crossing on the Somme River.

Jim Armitage's diary[155]

Another roadblock at Circular Quay pontoon bridge. This time another Tommy waggon was half over the side. They sent a man back to report for orders to their Commander miles away. To Tommies' horror, this was also quickly tossed over the side.

I wondered how many waggons and limbers had already gone over. When heavy shelling started again, even the Tommies stopped protesting.

7 August 1918. We knew we were close to the *big thing*.[*] At midnight we gave the Hun sixty rounds of gunfire with the last of our ammunition, by firing shrapnel as percussion to try and deceive him. The horse teams waited behind us to limber up immediately after our last shot was fired. We took our guns across Circular Quay, queuing up with hundreds of other vehicles quietly enough, with only an occasional shell dropping down in the background.

We got onto flat marshy country where our guns were to be sighted. It was utterly still. Vehicles made no sound on the marshy ground. There was no talking, only occasional random bursts of German machine-gun fire and an odd gun going off in the distance. The constant display of enemy Verey lights going up from their trenches worried us.

The silence played on our nerves a bit. As we got our guns into position, you could hear drivers whispering to horses and men muttering curses under their breath. Still the silence persisted, broken only by the whine of a stray rifle bullet or a long-range shell passing high overhead.

We started putting out our lines of fire, calculating our charging fuse settings, so that our shells would keep bursting ahead of our advancing infantry. Some clown along the line had trouble with his fuse board and lit a match. When he pulled himself out from under the mass of men on top of him, he was covered in marsh mud and straw.

---

[*] The coming Battle of Amiens.

Each crew's world centred around their gun. We could feel that hundreds of groups of men were doing the same, preparing for the heaviest barrage ever launched.*

At 4.29 am, silence reigned. Jerry appeared to be sleeping peacefully, unaware that hundreds of men had their fingers on hundreds of triggers. Away to our right, we heard the stutter of some battery whose watch was a few seconds fast. All hell broke loose, and we heard nothing more. The world was enveloped in sound and flame, and our ears just couldn't cope. The ground shook and our little sphere simply heaved.

I was the gun layer. Eventually I looked down and realised I'd been mechanically sighting and firing for 10 minutes. The gun was lurching so badly that the bubble on my chronometer jumped wildly. The only way I could sight it was to catch the bubble as it became more or less level, pull the trigger, and hope for the best. I was relieved after half an hour, which was about as much as any gun layer can stand at that pace. Sound waves beat against my head, and I looked around to find us half-buried in shell cases.

There was no wind. Lots of men were made violently ill by the discharge of cordite fumes. Smoke hid our aiming posts to add to our difficulties, but we were not fired on once.

As the sun rose, the smoke lifted a bit, and we could see what was going on. In front of us was the village of Hamel. Our barrage had lifted well beyond it and our tanks and infantry were passing through. On either side of us, as far as we could see, was a great wall of field guns, which the newspapers were to describe later as 'a wall of guns, wheel to wheel, along the entire front.' Actually, the guns were at 20-yard intervals, but that was close enough.

All guns were still in position. The sight of all this massed artillery, right out in the open without a spot of cover, was a sight

---

*   Zero Hour.

to see. From that day forward, we forgot about sandbag shelters and gun pits and fought out in the open.

A long way behind us the heavies were still pounding away, the 60 pounders were about 1,000 yards beyond that. We fired continually until 8.30 am, lifting our barrage every 15 minutes. The operation was an outstanding success. Our infantry advanced 9,000 yards.

The Germans, shattered and stupefied by the suddenness and force of the attack, offered little resistance. A good many of them thanked the thick pall of smoke for their escape.

The advance was made in three stages. First, the frontal attack with very heavy barrage; second an open warfare attack with creeping barrage and third; explosions and digging in. Exploration parties had a great time digging detached parties of Huns out of hiding. At 9 am, we limbered up our guns and started our advance into captured territory. What was left of the roads after our shelling was blocked with traffic. Until now, we hardly had a shell returned to us. However, we now learned that all had not gone so well to our left. English troops had been held up and ran into big trouble on some bad ground and had been unable to silence the enemy guns in their sector. In consequence of this, when we did make our advance, we were under flank fire from enemy guns.

Things were uncomfortable until we entered a bit of sunken road, where we were given 10 minutes of hell. A German battery of 5.9" guns was dug in to our right and had an open site target on all of us. In a few minutes of unmolested shooting, the Huns had our column a mass of blown-up tanks, guns, waggons, men, and horses.

The mess was indescribable. Horses went down with their drivers and gun wheels were badly shattered. We decided to get out of there. It was amazing how our drivers stayed with their horses and tried to get them free. A gun team from some other battery, trying to gallop away across the top of the bank, was literally blown on top of us, horses, guns and all.

Snowy Hamilton, a mate of mine, and I nearly got our heads kicked off by wounded horses. When we got clear I clambered over the back of some waggon that was galloping away. Sadly, a 4th Division battery, ordered into action against this German battery, was blown off the face of the earth before it got its guns unhitched. They had 80% casualties.

When the English troops had been reinforced after taking their objectives, we returned to try and salvage our damaged gun. The sight was beyond description. The debris consisted of vehicles, men, horses, and shattered guns. Our kits, tied to the waggons, were scattered in rags everywhere. My gun was hardly worth salvaging but, with help from Ordinance, we got replacement parts, eventually getting it back into service.

My gun team survived this horrible business with extraordinary luck. Only one of four of us was killed and two were wounded but our horses didn't fare so well. We had a few bad minutes, the worst I have had. It was a horrifying business, struggling there and looking down the barrels of a battery of 5.9" guns firing point blank at us!

Battle of Amiens: 8–11 August 1918

Jim's diary entry for late in the night on 7 August noted that they knew they were 'close to *the big thing*'. The Battle of Amiens marked the beginning of the Hundred Days Offensive, dating from 8 August to 11 November, a string of Western Front offensives that successfully led to the collapse of the German army, thus helping to end the war.

In late July 1918, troops from the United States had arrived to reinforce the war effort, while our Allied Forces held the superior position as the stalled Marne offensive exhausted the German soldiers.

French General Ferdinand Foch devised an attack in the Amiens region of northern France with the aim of protecting the vital Paris–Amiens railway, and securing several strategic transport hubs. The Allied forces began the attack on 8 August.

Jim's entries recount his experience in the Battle of Amiens.

Jim Armitage's diary[156]

9 *August* 1918. The battery pulled into action on the crest of a ridge just to the left of what had once been a thick wood. The rubble of Cerisy-Gailly was somewhere to our right, our waggon lines just behind. We had received orders to engage in open action any target that presented itself. We did not have much shooting to do that night as the Hun did not feel like presenting himself and, without a gun, our section had no action. Some batteries were less fortunate. One made their waggon lines in an old German dressing station. The Hun got right onto them and next morning their lines were a shamble of horses, waggons, harness, and gear.

That evening an English heavy battery, way to the rear, started dropping huge shells in Cerisy Wood, around which our brigade was situated. We could not stop them. It was some time before they discovered their mistake. Someone had given the wrong map reference.

S.O.S. guard duty was nervy work that night as no one was quite certain where the Huns were, or if they would make an expected counter-attack. Furthermore, we were on some newly captured territory which could have been mined, in which the Hun certainly had every important point accurately pinpointed for artillery fire.

During my watch in the still, creepy hours, I did see something moving. My first thought was 'Oh God, we've been surrounded.' I nearly panicked and started an alarm!

It was a man. In the bright moonlight, I could see his face. I nearly shot him but, as he seemed to be making very painful progress and was staring at me as he crawled towards me, I finally went towards him.

He let out a croak and said, 'Not shoot, not kill me.' When I ventured closer, I found a badly wounded German. He had a leg blown almost off and a bad wound in his side. I got help and we dressed his side. We could do nothing about the leg.

At first, he was certain he was going to be shot, but we managed to reassure him and, while keeping a sharp eye out for any tricks, persuaded him to tell us, in very poor English, that he had been wounded in our advance. He had laid in a thicket all night, afraid to come out until the pain forced him to.

The dope we gave him eased his pain a bit. Amongst other things, he gratefully forced on me a second-class order of the Iron Cross. When he was carried to the dressing station, he was again sure he would be killed. He might have been right. A couple of hours later another German shell landed right on the dressing station and blew it to hell.

The next day a spotter plane, looking for artillery targets, was brought down close to us. We rushed over and hacked off souvenirs from the remains. Things were strangely quiet. The Germans had been shattered by the ferocity of the assault. They had lost thousands of men as prisoners. They were not in a position to make an effective counter-attack, and their troops were not in any condition to stand more action for a while.

In this position, our waggon lines were short of water and the horses, two at a time, had to be taken a considerable distance to drink.

In the afternoon, we pulled out of the line and camped for the night at Windy Flat, near Corbie, well out of range of enemy fire. The next day we moved into the line again to take up new positions.

I should mention meeting the Gurkhas – small, nuggety, smiling men, totally ruthless. They are very proud of their felt hats, like the Australians wear, as other Indian Regiments wear turbans. They advanced through our lines at dusk with horrible looking long blades strapped to their backs. They wear the *kukri*, a large knife, a curved affair about 18 inches long and 3 inches wide and they believe in drawing blood every time they use it. They even offered to bring us back some German heads as souvenirs. It would be a brave man who would stand up to these fellas in the dark.

12 *August*. We moved southwards towards Pozieres, where we finally encountered the Canadians. They told us that the storming troops of the whole offensive consisted mainly of colonials. There were 82,000 Canadians, 80,000 Australians, 35,000 English, as well as New Zealanders and African troops. At this point, we were a good distance inside captured enemy territory. Enemy dumps, guns of all calibre, every kind of equipment littered the roadside.

We, like almost every other battery, now sported a German service waggon to carry our surplus gear. Horses caught roaming around had probably never been harnessed into a heavy limber waggon before and caused some problems.

Near Pozieres, we made our waggon lines in a valley which had formerly been a large German ammunition dump. A light railway ran through it, now run by the Canadians. Hundreds of thousands of shells were arranged in neat piles around the valley. There was every kind and every calibre from high explosives to gas; not an ideal place for waggon lines especially as Hun bombers came over at night. However, we were not molested while we stayed in reserve waiting for orders.

Horse watering facilities were bad, but the only ones for miles around. Consequently, a continuous queue of at least 1,000 horses waited to drink.

The Germans knew this and had it ranged accurately, but for some reason, only fired a shell once or twice a day. One can imagine the scatter when the shell did come over, and the subsequent rush to beat other fellows back to that trough when shelling stopped.

There was a hitch somewhere in the arrangements. Our infantry took longer to fight through to the new objective and met with stiffer opposition. While advancing quietly along a road, we were shelled rather erratically. The forward columns broke into a canter. Heading for some woods on our left, we crossed a lot of open ground and found ourselves looking straight at the guns of a battery of German 5.9"s, only a short distance in front of us. They must have seen us out in the open like sitting ducks but continued their ineffective shelling of the sunken road we had just left. They missed an extraordinary opportunity to blaze into us with open sights at point blank range.

We got our guns into action in the wood, our horse lines made against a steep bank facing the enemy, in front of the guns. It was the only possible place, the only protection we had from open observation by the Huns.

After we got there, a battery of Royal Horse Artillery galloped up with their little 12-pound guns and went into action. Bang on top of our bank they opened up on the German battery. Of course, they drew fire. When things got too hot, they cleared out leaving us to whatever the Hun chose to throw at us, which was a lot. We interested him quite a bit.

I got a big shell splinter through my tin hat. Fortunately, it was not on my head at the time. I was so annoyed but my mate, Snowy, could not see what I was upset about. He said that my hat had never contained anything of any value!

In this position behind the bank, we were shelled all night with high velocity 5.9" shells. This bank saved us because high velocity shells had a low trajectory and, to clear the bank, the shells had to burst some distance behind where we were crouched. He chased us up and down the gully all night.

Here I lost the only stripe I ever had. I was limber gunner in charge of the gun's efficiency and cleanliness. While I had the breech mechanism in parts, I thought Jerry was going to sweep to the left with his shelling, but he started sweeping to the right, the way I had moved. A shell burst on top of the bank above and covered me and everything else with barrowloads of dirt. My superior showed little sympathy over my loss of one or two breech block parts.

German planes had already bombed us three times that night. On the fourth attempt, they dropped a flare. Fortunately for us, the pilot's attention was caught by a column of infantry passing nearby who showed up in the glare of the powerful flare. Those poor, wretched men were practically wiped out. This must have satisfied the pilots because, although they knew we were there, we were left alone after that.

We christened this place 'Eight Inch Gully' because of three huge 8" German guns in it, captured by the 45th Battalion. Further around was a captured battery of 5.9" guns and also a battery of whizzbangs. The Diggers got these batteries into action against their previous owners.

There was a great quantity of gas shells scattered around those guns, and everyone who passed by picked up a couple and fired them off at extreme range. Where they went no one knew, but a couple of thousand gas shells fired into enemy territory must at least have given some people headaches!

It was decided to try to fire the 8" guns, but a careful examination showed that, of these apparently intact guns, two had been booby-trapped. About 50 men manhandled the remaining gun and, using our instruments, we trained it on a large German marshalling centre. The shelling must have been unexpected, because our own heavies had not yet had time to move forward. In fact, the speed of our advance made the cumbersome, heavy artillery useless.

We tried another German heavy gun but took no risks. We tied one end of a long piece of telephone wire to the trigger and took the other end into an old German dug-out about 100 yards away. We pulled. There was a shattering crash. We crawled out to find the gun carriage standing partly where we had left it. The whole piece, the barrel, and the breech mechanism was buried in the ground behind. Heaven only knows where that shell went. We hoped it got as far as the enemy lines. The cunning Hun had taken off the recoil buffer, removed the springs, then carefully replaced everything.

Early next morning Jerry opened up on us with Howitzers. This meant it would drop shells right over the bank onto us, so we had to evacuate. A few casualties occurred before we could get the horses out. I dashed down into the gully as anxious to get out as anyone, grabbed the first pair of horses I came to, jumped on bareback and without bridles galloped along the gully with the rest.

Our search for water for the horses brought us to a small village where German cavalry had been in action against Australian infantry. The street was full of dead Uhlans and their heavy type horses, but there were comparatively few Australians dead. The fighting had been hand-to-hand and grim.

That day I lost my gas mask. I have never been windier or more nervous about it. One feels helpless against gas without one's gas mask, as there is always a chance of running into gas. That night we were ordered to move our waggon lines back; a thing we were only too happy to do as they were still in front of our guns. We moved to a position near Cerisy. Here, to my great relief, my gas mask was miraculously returned. One of the fellows in the battery saw it hanging on a tree, picked up by some passer-by. My name was scrawled all over it. I had dropped it while watering the horses.

•

Jim's mention of commandos and Gurkhas passing in the dead of night intrigued me. I spent hundreds of hours trying to find the identity of the main commando. Without a name, army archives were useless, and most of that information was on a need-to-know basis only. As at other times in my research, I stumbled upon my find out of pure luck, or perhaps a nudge from beyond the grave.

While entering the keyword 'ghost' about a different matter entirely, a reference came up for 'Ghosts of Western Snows'. As I read the article, I had chills. Here was the commando himself: Lieutenant Dalton Neville, telling his story in his own words, but printed decades after the war. Now that I knew his name, and who he was, I had to find out where he was buried.

CHAPTER 31

GHOSTS OF WESTERN SNOWS

'He was a huge, powerful man. It was impossible to get close with him, so although I didn't want to fire, I had to shoot.'
Lieutenant Dalton Neville[157]

In the Sydney publication *The Sun*, I finally found the story that I had long searched for. It was under the heading 'World's Super-Raider'. I would never have thought of searching under that keyword, but the other reference was 'Ghosts of Western Snows', 'ghost' being a keyword that I used on a different project. At last I had discovered the identity of the secret commando Jim Armitage mentioned in his diary as passing him one dark night.

The Snow Ghost finally revealed
The Sun[158]

1918. France. Lieutenant Dalton Neville, M.C., D.C.M., Croix-de-Guerre, is the kind of man whom people turn to look at twice. A glimpse of his profile stirs the mind sharply and leaves the impression that a familiar face has passed, but one which the memory cannot label. As people half turn for the second glance they murmur: 'I know that chap. I've seen his face somewhere before,' and puzzle in vain to recall him …

There is no grimness, but a striking suggestion of casualness and enduring humour. In vague and weirdly distorted shapes this cameo of Lieutenant Neville has impressed itself on a million minds.

Strange stories passed from the front lines of the Australian army right back to the base; tales of a mystic shadow which swept down onto lonely outposts at night and left dead men, or a more terrifying nothingness, behind.

The legend said that sometimes it was a white ghost gliding noiselessly across the snow; others that it was a vague, black shadow which rose out of the mud beside men in the trenches and struck them down. So realistic were the visions inspired by these tales that there are men in Germany who repeat in nightmares the hours of nervous tension spent in dark and isolated listening posts.

These tales have a more crystallised form in the records of the A.I.F. They arise from the fact that for three years Lieutenant Neville played at Red Indians in real earnest on the battlefields of France, gliding silently among belts of barbed wire, and down the sides of shell craters as his war ancestors had moved noiselessly through leafy forests or down the slopes of canyons.

He became known as the super-raider of the A.I.F., the super-raider of the war, for the men he trained and led across the darkness of No-Man's land at night had no equal in the art of silent warfare. Their comings and goings were visitations from the unknown which struck terror into the hearts of the soldiers who were pushed forward into the lonely outposts of the German trenches.

'These Australians are terrible, inhuman,' wrote a German non-com to his friend in southern Germany. 'We go to our outposts afraid even to whisper because we never know when they will creep up unheard and rush upon us, leaving us no chance to escape. Sometimes when we go forward to relieve our comrades, we can find nothing of them – not even the trace of a scuffle.'

This letter, with the corporal himself, arrived back in the Australian lines under the escort of Neville's silent fighters. There was nothing left behind to show how, or where, the corporal had gone.

The effect of these raids on the enemy's morale was so disastrous that the Germans placed a price of 10,000 marks on Lieutenant Neville's head.

Though the group's primary object was to capture, killing was inevitable – desperate hand-to-hand fighting with the raiders struggling to strangle the cries of their victims, feeling for their bodies in the dark with their knives, trying not to use their rifles lest the noise reach the main trenches and the air be filled with Verey lights and every inch of No-Man's land swept with machine-gun bullets.

The ideal raiding party consisted of twelve men under the leadership of Neville. They were armed with rifles, bombs, revolvers, and knives. A system of signals was arranged so that no noise was made. The men would advance for sixty yards, sink slowly down onto their knees to get a better vision of the skyline, turn in an arranged direction, and watch for any movement. If there was none, the leader would wave his hand, the men would rise to their feet, move forward again, repeating the process until they were within one hundred yards or so of the outpost they were attacking. Then they would drop down on their stomachs and crawl slowly forward.

When within twenty yards, the leader would decide whether to risk discovery by crawling further forward, or to rush the post from that distance. Then came the final push, the frantic effort to kill or capture without noise. Each man was taught the German for 'Put your hands up quickly!' He would whisper this into the ear of the terrified enemy whom he had taken by surprise, over whom he stood with a raised knife.

Once in the outpost there was nothing nice about the work. Each raider picked his man and gave him a fraction of a second to decide – surrender silently or be killed.

'On one occasion,' said Lieut. Neville, recounting some of his experiences, 'we raided an outpost at Villers-Bretonneux, early in the advance in 1918. Three of them made no resistance, but the fourth, a corporal, defended himself with the butt of a heavy revolver. He was a huge, powerful man. It was impossible to get close with him, so although I didn't want to fire, I had to shoot. The outpost was about thirty-five yards from the main German trenches, and the man made a rush to get back to his own lines. I shot him again, but he dropped on his hands and knees and started crawling forward. I had to shoot him twice again before he stopped. I told my men to get back and crawled over to search him for information. One of my men came to help me and we were ripping off his shoulder straps when we heard a noise.

'We looked up to see a German officer and a private within five yards of us. They saw us at the same instant, but we had our revolvers up quicker, and each taking his man shot them both dead. Before we could get away the effect of the shooting had its result. We were surrounded and had to fight our way back to the patrol waiting for us in No-Man's land. There we settled into a real battle, but all managed to get away without a scratch.

'Sometimes there were wide belts of barbed wire to cut through. Absolute silence was necessary, for the slightest sound might cause the Germans to flood No-Man's land with their machine-gun fire and catch us in the wire. We experienced of this on the Butte de Warlencourt in March 1917. No-Man's land at the place of that patrol raid was 1,800 yards wide. After going about four hundred yards we came to a wide belt of barbed wire. We cut a laneway and followed through in single file. A hundred yards further on we were held up by more wire, more than 15ft thick. Well within fifty yards of the German forward trenches, we came to another belt. While we were working our way through this, one of the parties clanked his rifle against the wire. Immediately three white Verey lights went up from the German trenches.

'Every man stood dead still. It was impossible to drop to the ground because the men were still in the wire and any movement would have been seen instantly.

'There was an interval of a few minutes before more lights went up, but no one moved, knowing that the absence of the black blurs, which the Germans must have seen by the first lights, would strengthen their suspicions. Then, directly the second batch of lights had died down, we rushed the trenches. There were seventeen of us in the party, but we tackled a front of one hundred yards, killing every one of the forty men who occupied it.

'The alarm had been raised. To get back we would have had to pass through a laneway of machine guns which were directed onto the wire. The only thing to do was to stop with Fritz. We did this, diving for the nearest shell holes in which we were up to our waists in water. We stayed there until the firing died down, the Germans believing that we must have all been caught. Creeping forward, we crawled through the wire. About four hundred yards from the trenches, I called the men together and we walked back, not one man being hurt.'

This is the extraordinary record claimed by Neville that, although his only work on the line for three years was to lead raiding parties into No-Man's land, not one casualty was suffered by his men during the whole time. He bears an ugly scar on the back of his head, but this is not counted as a casualty, because it did not take him out of the line. How he received it is a story typical of the desperate character of the silent fighter's work.

When on a raid Lieutenant Neville always carried a revolver in each hand and made it a habit to fire both when shooting at a man. On one occasion his party met a counter patrol in No-Man's land. During the firing he emptied both revolvers without realising it. A little later he came face to face with a German. He pulled both triggers, but there was no shot. Realising what had happened, he dropped his revolvers, sprang at the man, and attacked him with his knife. It was a double-bladed knife with a knuckle-duster handle, but the blade struck a breastplate which the German was wearing and snapped off.

The German seized him by the head and pressed his thumbs into Lieutenant Neville's eyes, while the Australian gripped him by the throat with one hand and with the other pounded his face with the handle of his broken knife. During the struggle, the German rolled over on the ground, managing to pick up the broken knife blade with which he slashed the Lieutenant behind the ear. This appalling struggle between man and man ended only when Neville choked the German to death!

One of Lieutenant Neville's schemes was responsible for the stories believed by the Germans in the early days of the Diggers in France, that many Australians were black troops. In their raids, he and his parties blackened their faces and hands, having discovered that, on dark nights, it was possible to see the uncovered faces of the men at a short distance.

To complete their safeguards, they rusted any gleam off their rifles and varnished their tin hats with mud. On the Somme, during the nights when snow was on the ground, they wore white overalls, which hid their dark equipment, and made them absolutely undistinguishable.

His armament, he says, is two big revolvers, a double-edged knife, and a big, loaded club studded with nails, which he found in a German trench. He naively described himself as a walking tank.

Those two revolvers will not go into the proverbial melting pot. On the butt of one are eight little nicks, and on the butt of the other, fourteen. Each records the death of a German caused when Lieutenant Neville played a deadly game of Red Indians in France.

He has one other relic. It is a black, charred pipe with a cover over the bowl.

'I smoked it every time I went on a raid,' he said. 'But it was not for bravado. Once we got down to our work, I was never worried, but at the start I was always in a deadly funk. It was so real that I couldn't keep my teeth from chattering. I used to grip this pipe between them for the first half-hour so that nobody should know.

'I'm in the centre of the world's greatest battle, and by a miracle am still alive and well. It is intensely cold, always drizzling, and our crowd is in a great shell hole full of mud. Our condition is bad enough, but Fritz must be in a terrible state. The Australians have made a great name; other troops greet us with joy. I have been fighting for the last five months, and only had slight wounds.'

In August Lieutenant Neville was badly smashed, but his cheerfulness and constitution pulled him through: 'We were out on No-Man's land when it happened. I was in charge of a patrol, and we met an enemy party. A fight started. I shot one Fritz; and another shot me. I shot him through the chest. It was a heavy fight; a lot were killed and wounded. Another chap and I dragged each other back to our own trenches inch by inch. He was shot in the head. My leg was broken and twisted. It was agonising to crawl, but I was determined not to fall into German hands.'

Headquarters, Australian Imperial Force, British Expeditionary Force
June 6, 1918.
Dear Neville,
I write to convey to you my heartiest congratulations on the Military Cross, which has been awarded to you for your conspicuous gallantry and devotion to duty, when in charge of a patrol near Villers-Bretonneux on May 17. Knowing that identifications were urgently needed, and having located two enemy posts, you decided to attack them.

You led your men with such dash and skill that the enemy were caught unprepared, and you succeeded in taking three prisoners and in inflicting casualties on the garrison.

You displayed excellent leadership in withdrawing your patrol to our lines under heavy enemy machine-gun fire and in face of a counter-attack. It reflects the greatest credit on you that this action was carried out without a casualty, and I thank you so much for your good work. With all good wishes,
Yours sincerely,
W. Birdwood.

•

Dear Lieutenant Neville,
My search for you and your fascinating story had led me on a merry chase for years, but I think that you already knew that.

As a researcher, I hate loose ends, so when the Australian War Memorial website stated that you are buried at Wamberal cemetery on the Central Coast, I appreciated the irony, having searched for you half a world away in Flanders.

I taught, part-time, at Wamberal Primary School for years, and was driving past your grave every week, as the cemetery is close to the school.

I remember the day that I sat beside your grave and asked you to let me know more of your story. You obliged in a remarkable way, for I found a reference that afternoon to your young engineer, the one who had the vermeil medal, along with a quirky, cryptic clue about keeping one's keywords secret. How was I to find out more, if I didn't know the right keywords? But the right keyword was already in front of me, for in searching for the meaning of the 'vermeil' medal, the other frustrating and major loose end of one part of this saga was revealed in a remarkable little story, printed in a newspaper in Brisbane, Queensland, many years after the war ended. Thank you so much.

Gratefully,
Patricia Skehan

CHAPTER 32

ZERO HOUR

'This fog is a God-send. Fritz seems to be a bit uneasy by the way he is throwing those 5.9"s at us; but I don't think he knows we are here. Three hours more to Zero. Ugh, it's cold!'
Captain-Chaplain Herbert Green[159]

A masterpiece of shrewd deception

The Monash diaries were critical to understanding the context of warfare under General Monash's command of the Australian forces. He went to great lengths to keep his plans secret until the last minute, to achieve the element of surprise.

Newspapers in every Australian state published extracts from the diaries. For example, the *Sydney Mail* published a lengthy article spread across four pages, titled 'Australian Victories in France' in 1920.[160] Extracts from Monash's own memories show his master plan and operational orders for smashing the Hindenburg Line, from this article republished in numerous newspapers.

Daily Mercury[161]

7 August 1918. 7 pm. The share of the A.I.F. including many MacKay men, in the launching of the offensive along the Somme played an important part in the staggering blows delivered against the enemy on that occasion. The plan of a quick thrust under unorthodox conditions was designed by General Monash.

His broad plan was a masterpiece of shrewd deception, and his operational orders were classic of defined duties. To conceal the steady arrival of such large reinforcements, he sent advance parties of Canadians and other Australian divisions on distant missions. For instance, Canadian field hospitals and staff units turned up in northern France, whilst Canadian combat troops were frequently dressed in Australian uniforms. The Air Force kept check of all troop movement which was to be only by night. Any daytime activity that could be distinguished by enemy reconnaissance planes was guarded against.

The famous order issued by Monash read: *Zero Hour will be 4.20 am, August 8, 1918. Watches will be synchronised 8 pm tonight, 7th Inst, at the quarry. Orderly officers of all the brigades will attend.*

At 4.20 on the morning of August 8, 1918, whilst the fog blanketed a dreary night, the concentrated fury of the Australian artillery that had been moved into the open fronting the enemy lines broke out. Australian and Canadian divisions began to cut their way through the Hindenburg Line.

Extracts from General Sir John Monash's book, published in various newspapers[162]

The idea is being circulated that the Canadian Corps is being brought to the south to take over the role of Reserve Corps at the junction of the British and French armies in replacement of the 22nd Corps, which occupied that role until it was ordered to the Champagne front.

In order that the enemy may be deceived as to the destination of the Canadian Corps, in the event of his discovering that it has been withdrawn from the Arras front, some Canadian wireless personnel have been sent to the Second Army area (in Belgium), where they have taken over certain wireless zones.

In order to deceive our troops as to the cause of the coming down here of the Canadians, rumours are going abroad that the Canadian Corps is being brought down with the object of relieving the Australian Corps in the line.

To most Australian Corps this would appear to be an obvious reason for their coming, as the idea has been mooted on former occasions.

The secret was indeed well kept, and the *camouflage* stories circulating proved to be so effective that the King of the Belgians forwarded a strong protest to Marshal Foch because the Canadians were about to deliver an attack in his country without his having even been consulted or made aware of the plans.

The Canadian headquarters in London complained to the War Office that Canadian forces were divided and were being sent by detachments to different parts of the front instead of being always kept together, as the Canadian Government desired.

It is said that even Mr Lloyd George knew nothing of the intention to attack until late on the day before the battle.

To preclude the possibility of detection by enemy aircraft, I issued orders that all movements of troops and transport of all descriptions should take place only during the hours of darkness, whether in the forward or in the near areas. In order to keep an effective control over the faithful execution of these difficult orders, I had arranged for relays of *police* aeroplanes, furnished by our No. 3 Squadron, to fly continuously by day over the whole of the corps area, in order to detect and report any observed unusual movement.

Surprise has been from time immemorial one of the most potent weapons in the armoury of the tactician. It can be achieved not merely by doing that which the enemy least anticipates, but also by acting at a time when he least expects any action. It was a weapon which had been employed only rarely in the previous greater battles of this war.

The offensive before Cambrai, planned by General Sir Julian Byng, and then the battle of Hamel were rare exceptions to general procedures of heralding the approach of an offensive by feverish and obvious activity on our part, and by a long-sustained preliminary bombardment of the enemy's defences, designed to destroy his works and impair his morale.

CHAPTER 33

THE DARKEST DAY

'… The black day of the German Army in the history of the war.
This was the worst experience I had to go through.'
General Erich Ludendorff[163]

The great onslaught

The Allied forces' surprise attack on German troops at the Battle of Amiens marked a significant turning point in the war. In the following article, a soldier recalls the events of those decisive days.

Reverend Thomas Joseph O'Donnell, as published in
***The Advocate*[164]**

August 1918. Lihons. In March, the great onslaught by the German forces which had ended so disastrously for the Allies, and nearly ended the war in favour of the enemy, had staggered the world. How near we were then to defeat has not yet been told. The enemy drove the Fifth army before them like clouds before a storm, and after a few days there were all the elements of a complete disaster.

For thirteen miles before Amiens, the key position, there was not a man. The way was opened to the enemy to take the city and so rush to the Coast and separate the British forces from the French. We know how the Australians were rushed in on that occasion and, before Amiens, stopped the rush and saved the situation. Then he made another attempt before Hazebrouck, and once again the Australians saved the situation. Later he pushed on further East and was repulsed near the Marne. His big attempts in open warfare had failed. But he was satisfied to be allowed to sit down for the winter and recoup his forces and gather fresh strength which he was sure could be used in the spring to open at last the gates to victory, and to world domination.

General Monash conceived a plan of frustrating his designs, and when these plans were elaborated, they were accepted by the British authorities. General Foch[*] himself marvelled at the daring of the Australian general and his forces.

Monash worked out his plan and was given practically a free hand. For the first time in the war five Australian divisions were to fight together. That in itself was a remarkable fact. With them he wished the four Canadian Divisions to be associated, and besides there was one English Division. Monash worked out a plan of attack on a wide front which he estimated would stagger the enemy and set him on the run.

The first essential for this grand attempt was secrecy. To his credit, in spite of enormous difficulties, that secrecy was maintained until the morning of August 8, when the attack was launched.

For such an attack it was, of course, necessary to gather on the allotted front enormous supplies of war equipment, ammunition, guns and stores. How to bring the men and supplies into such a limited area without the knowledge of the enemy was the puzzle. But it would need to be accomplished.

It was necessary to have many tanks on the front line for this attack. How to get such noisy engines of war into position without

---

*   Ferdinand Foch (1851-1929) French General, Supreme Allied Commander WWI.

the knowledge of the enemy, who was observing from aeroplanes and war balloons, was a mystery. But it was done, nevertheless. The tanks were brought up by night while hosts of aeroplanes flew over the enemy lines, not so much to do damage by bombing as to hide the noise of the moving tanks by their own noise. The ruse was a success. Hundreds of tanks were brought up and hidden in the woods by Hamel and Villers-Bretonneux.

So, too, the guns were brought and placed in position: great howitzers, sixty pounders and others. They were there in thousands, all ready for the grand attack now definitely fixed for August 8.

The Australian divisions took their places. The first Division was hurried there by train and motor coach from the North to a position close behind the main line of attack. The men were then let into the secret of the great offensive. An army order was read to all the troops telling them of the great attack that was to be launched and calling on them to give of their best. Every man of the Australian Army and the Canadian Army was keyed up to the highest pitch. At last, it was announced that Zero hour, the hour of attack, was 3 am* on the 8th.

The 7th passed quietly. It was evident that the enemy had not the slightest idea of what was awaiting them within a few hours. Feint attacks were made at other points along the line, but from captured documents it was quite certain that the enemy had no notion of the great attack that was awaiting them in the Hamel to Villers-Bretonneux section. The hours passed slowly. Midnight came and everything was tranquil.

In the Australian and Canadian lines men were working with great earnestness. Gunners were at the guns. The tanks were manned by their heroic crews, the planes were tuned up, the

---

* Time stated by Rev. O'Donnell four years later in *Burnie Advocate*, a Tasmanian newspaper.

signal corps had their instruments perfect, the infantry stood ready with rifle, bayonet and bombs for the onward rush; the army medical corps stretcher-bearers were all ready. At 2 am word was sent along to warn all of the approaching hour.

From the enemy lines there came not one sign of anxiety. Half past two and the tension grew greater. The minutes passed slowly. At ten to three every man was straining as it were like a racer to be let past the barrier. Then a few moments of highest tension, and out from the silence came the loud booming of two thousand cannons. Zero hour had arrived.

The Australian and Canadian troops were making a grand united thrust at the heart of the enemy. The old tanks came wandering out of their hiding places, over roads and trenches, on through barbed wire entanglements right into the enemy lines. The sky was immediately lit with enemy flares and lights so well known to every Digger. Tanks passed over the ground and immediately the Australian and Canadian soldiers followed them.

The suddenness and strength of the attack completely staggered the enemy. They did not resist. They fled in horror or surrendered with their hands up and their faces pale as death.

Right along the line success was achieved. Out in front of Villers-Bretonneux, where the enemy was in strong force, there was a little resistance, but nothing could stop the onward rush of the Diggers. War sites such as Frevent, La Motte, Bonneauville, Harbonnieres and Cerisy-Gailly were soon in the possession of the A.I.F. By mid-day, an immense area of country was taken. Prisoners began to pour back until over ten thousand were in the hands of the Australians alone.

Reports came in which showed that the attack had been completely successful. Advanced guards went as far as Vauvillers and Reincourt. At one place a train full of Germans was taken. A hospital with several German nurses was captured, and from other sectors there was evidence of the hurried flight of the enemy, now stricken with terror.

The Canadian advance was just as successful. They also reported great advances, plus the capture of many prisoners and war material.

The English Division was held up at Chippily Ridge. This took a little from the general success unfortunately, adding greatly to the Australian casualties, as they were enfiladed from the flank as well as from the front.

The enemy went so fast that it was hard to locate him. At the close of the day the position was uncertain. But one of the most wonderful feats of the war had been accomplished. The enemy lines had been pierced for a distance of ten miles, and he had been driven in disorder and panic before the advancing overseas troops.

The 9th was used as a day of consolidation; guns were brought forward, and our supplies renewed. Passing over the ground captured on the 8th, on all sides were evidence of the great fight of the day before. The enemy dead were everywhere. Many of our brave boys were seen lying where they had successfully fought a machine-gun post or a nest of snipers. Around Harbonnieres were now vast numbers of troops. The enemy aeroplanes were active and succeeded in doing much damage with bombs. There we witnessed many thrilling fights in the air between our planes and those of the enemy. Every now and again a plane was seen to burst into flames and crash to the earth.

Under the existing conditions, it was not possible to have everything to perfection, and our men had to go on short rations, but they never complained. Orders were given for a new attack on the 10th at different portions of the line. We were ordered to move into a position beyond Harbonnieres and reached our location at midnight.

This was one of the elaborate winter quarters the Germans were getting ready. It consisted of immense underground houses with beds, electric lighting, and all kinds of conveniences. The tired men threw themselves down to rest; but at 4 am came the order to rise and get ready to go forward. A hurried meal was served, then the brave Digger bands got into line, and we set out towards Lihons Hill.

It was surprising to see what blunders could be made in war. We were now making one; under orders, of course, but one that was to cost us much. The position of the enemy was not known; yet we were ordered to advance against Lihons Hill in broad daylight, instead of making an attack in the dark, following a heavy bombardment of what seemed a most likely position for the enemy. As we moved across the plain that lay in front of that hill, one would not think there had ever been a war in the world. It was a beautiful morning, and there was a silence like that of the grave. The only evidence of any upheaval on the days preceding was here and there a broken tank or a dead German.

Zero hour for the attack on Lihons was fixed at 8 am. We walked to the foot of the hill and reached it at 7.30. When we were about to ascend it there came a fusillade from the old trenches at the top. From front and flank the enemy was attacking us with machine guns. Men took shelter where they could in old trenches or shell holes. Then was added a new terror.

Enemy planes came over and swept us with machine-gun fire. Lying in a shell hole with bullets bristling all round I waited. At 8 am the guns boomed forth, but the barrage was placed 800 yards too far forward.

Then I witnessed a sight that never can be forgotten. Those men rose up from the places of shelter and went up that hill through a hailstorm of bullets and bursting shells. Not one hesitated. Everywhere one could see men fall, but the others went on until they reached the top, and there battled with the enemy in the trench. The Hun fled before them. They pursued him and gained complete possession of the hill and nearby Creepy Wood, where a desperate fight ensued. It was a wonderful performance.

The 11th Battalion had been one of the first to land at Gallipoli, but they admitted that in this new encounter they lost far more men than they did on Anzac Day. Of 30 officers we lost 17 either killed or wounded, and of less than 500 men, 75 were killed and over 200 wounded within an hour. Aid posts were set up in old trenches, and soon the wounded came through in hundreds. The other battalions were engaged in the same fight at different portions of the line, and the wounded were numerous.

The principal dressing station was established in an old hospital. During the day hundreds of men, some of them frightfully wounded, were carried in. The ambulance arrangements were not good, and these men had to be carried back a distance of two miles or more. The day was a scorcher, the heat being terrible.

On the hill the battle continued. It was not possible to go out to get the dead. Many more died in the dressing station.

There were no men to act as gravediggers. Even the batmen and battalion staffs, such as cooks, were gathered up and sent out to help at critical positions. There were 24 men awaiting burial, so I asked the colonel of a medical corps to give me some of his men to bury them. They were not good diggers. As we were at work the enemy, watching from a balloon, saw us and probably concluded we were digging a gun pit and sent a great shell within a few yards. The men disappeared. After some time, I was able to get them again and there we laid to rest captain, lieutenant, sergeant and private – Anglican, Methodist, Presbyterian and Catholic, all laid to rest side by side on the honoured field where they fell. In another grave 50 men of the 5th Battalion were buried together.

The authorities had fixed a certain line as our final objective and it was arranged that when that was reached, we were to dig in and remain there for the winter. But so great was the success, so complete the defeat of the enemy, that General Foch urged that the attack be continued.

No one expected the war to end for at least 12 months; but this attack was so successful that it continued, and the war was to end less than three months later. The enemy had been broken. The great blow of his final defeat was inflicted by Australians and Canadians and being continued, ended in his utter overthrow. General Erich Ludendorff, the German military strategist, said that August 8 was the darkest day in the war for Germany.

Later on, the attack was continued with equal success, the storming of Mont St. Quentin by the Diggers constituting one of the most splendid feats of the last war. The enemy was completely routed and, disorganised and being broken in his strongest position by overseas troops, our attacks at other places were easily brought off. The Hun was sent streaming back to the Fatherland – degraded, defeated, and disgraced.

Whatever is celebrated on any other day of the year, there can be no doubt that the deed of August 8 was the most wonderful, thrilling, and successful feat accomplished by the Diggers. Australia should always remember that day, which was indeed the darkest day for Germany and the grandest for Australia. It terminated the war 12 months before anyone thought it was possible. It ended in the rout and overthrow of the German army and destroyed forever the menace of German domination.

No one would be so foolish as to say that the Diggers won the war; but no one can justly say that without their wonderful feats in March and on August 8 and following days, it would have ended with such a great triumph for the Allied forces. Had the war been lost, Australia today would be a German colony. The proud Hun would be marching through our streets, and we would be but serfs under his haughty sway.

Whatever sacrifice we made in men and money, whatever the toll we paid, was it not worth it to keep Australia free? Australia was the greatest prize in the world, and there was none that the Germans desired to possess more.

No one wishes to glorify war. War is hell and is hateful and abominable, but we would have been a recreant race if we failed to do our part to save our country in the hour of danger.

The Diggers did it, and the whole world resounded with the splendour of their deeds.

Future generations will appraise at its true value the sacrifices made and all the wonders accomplished.

The bravest men that God ever made sleep out there on the hills of Gallipoli, at Lihons, at Amiens or under other Flanders fields. It may be truly said that their names live forever.

The timing of Zero Hour

Interestingly, discrepancies in the exact timing of Zero Hour vary between letters, reports and locations.

Reverend O'Donnell wrote that the time was 3 am, but most memoirs state 4.20 am on 8 August, the time confirmed in the Monash memoirs. Jim Armitage mentions the silence at 4.29 am in his diary, 'before hundreds of men had hundreds of fingers on hundreds of triggers'.

One soldier, Lieutenant McConnel,[165] remembered being on the Hamel Road, a mile or so behind the line, at Zero Hour, hauling heavy guns toward the frontline. He recalled the planes buzzing overhead to drown out the sound of the horses and limbers – a ploy devised by Monash, as such sounds travel more at night.

CHAPTER 34

A MILITARY SOLOMON

'One could not help wondering what sort of shambles it would turn into if Fritz only knew.'
Lieutenant McConnel[166]

Lieutenant K.H. McConnel

Lieutenant Kenneth Hamlyn McConnel, from 1st Australian Infantry Battalion, embarked for the war on 10 December 1914, returning to Australian in May 1919. His insights into the daily life of the average soldier under his command proved to be enlightening. The lieutenant related his memory of their battalion's location at Zero Hour. He also recalled an amusing incident that warranted this chapter's title.

Glen Innes Examiner[167]

It is truly said that 'an army marches on its stomach.' Some small meed* of honour is therefore surely due to the men and animals who fill that stomach.

After seeing life as a trooper in the Light Horse, and a platoon and company commander in the Infantry, it fell to my lot in 1918 to skipper the 1st Battalion's transport section. Never before

---
*   Earned reward.

had I commanded – nor could I hope to command – a finer body of men.

Casualties in transport sections were light as compared with those in the fighting companies. One result of this was that the section was full of *old originals*, many who had seen service with the rest on Gallipoli. And although the casualties were light, it need not be supposed that the transport was a home for those afflicted with *cold feet*. Nobody who has not travelled up to the line astride half a team with a full limber behind can properly appreciate the amount of nerve required for the job. Too often, when 'all was quiet on the Western Front,' the roads would be receiving the special attention of Jerry's batteries.

A pedestrian on a road, hearing a shell coming, dives into the nearest ditch. Not so the driver, he has to sit in his saddle and take whatever comes to him. The horses knew when one was coming their way. Some of those, who had previously been wounded or had a teammate killed alongside them, were regular shell-shock cases, and would tremble and rear, till it took a good man with nerves of steel to keep them in hand. May I say that it was a strictly enforced rule that no driver might gallop his team without express orders from his officer.

Night after night these chaps went up, delivered their loads, waited around at company or battalion headquarters to collect any gear that had to be taken down, and then padded back the same way. Nerves were on edge from start to finish, but none of them would admit it for a moment.

On August 8, 1918, although the 1st Brigade was only a supporting brigade, our transport section was on the Hamel Road, a mile or so behind the line at Zero hour. That road was packed four deep with infantry and artillery transport stretching back for miles. One could not help wondering what sort of shambles it would be turned into if Fritz only knew. But Monash's low-flying aeroplanes drowned the noise of the wheels, and never a shell came near us; Glory be.

Within an hour of 'zero' our last limber was over the old German front line and then began one of the hardest fortnight's work I have ever known. In that fortnight, to the best of my memory, our transport lines were never in the same spot for more than two consecutive nights; and every night before any man turned in for a wink of sleep, every horse was dug in shoulder high.

On the third day of the attack when the 1st Division moved up through Harbonnieres, I remember we had the cookers up with the battalion. All of a sudden, a machine-gun and a couple of whizz-bangs opened up. The cooker teams quietly trotted up, as if on parade, hitched up, and walked back with the cookers. None of them was hit, and the dinner went on cooking.

In the trenches in Flanders

I was intrigued by the mention of the travelling kitchens, so researched the following articles.

Private J. Whitcombe, *Ultima and Chillingollah Star*[168]

The field kitchens cook as they travel along, and as soon as we halt for meals there is a hot dinner ready. We have two kitchens for about 700 men.

As soon as one meal is served up there is another to be prepared. There is no rest when the battalion is in billets either, only rather more work than at other times. Many a man, stumbling out of his barn in the early morning to swill himself at the pumps, finds us cooks already dressed and at work.

The Telegraph[169]

Last night we heard heavy footsteps, an odd noise … I peered into the darkness and within a few feet of my head was a fat pig.

He was more frightened than I and decamped. We followed and in five minutes, Mr Cochin [sic] was tied to the wheel of an ammunition cart. He grunted all night long. Next morning, men from the neighbouring battery heard of our interesting capture and claimed it as theirs. What cheek! We squabbled… Suddenly shrapnel began falling in the midst of this debate. Did Prussian shells stop the row over that pig? No, sir! For ten more minutes the bullets flew; the pig squealed; the squabble continued… Then along comes the captain. "In the name of heaven," he exclaimed, "get back to your 75s. Cut the pig in two." A military Solomon has solved the difficulty, and both battalions had pork for supper that night.

Lieutenant K.H. McConnel, *Glen Innes Examiner*[170]

We then had the whole transport section in some old German gun-pits in an orchard, about half a mile behind the line. It was nice and handy and we could get hot meals up to the boys. Then someone on the staff got wise to us and said it wasn't safe, so we were sent back to the plain behind Harbonnieres. Poor little Bunty, beloved little pack mare, got it in the neck as we pulled out, and her leader nearly cried, but we managed to get her patched up at the field veterinary section, and she came back with us.

That plain, as everyone knows, had hell bombed out of it every night, and it was fairly strewn with dead horses. That some of ours were not among them was due partly to luck, but more especially to the fact that every horse was dug in. We had three bombs right in our lines late one night without losing a hoof.

There were two trips to the line to be done each day. The rest of the time was spent in scouring the country for petrol tins in which to send up the water, and then in boiling them out. We used to reckon that the boys in the line ate petrol tins; we never seemed to get any back.

About this time — what with greasy heels and one thing and another — we were a bit short of horses and, as the artillery and the Tommies had the first pick of all remounts, the transport sections were supposed to put up with any old thing that came along. One horse we got was actually blind! This was a bit too thick, so we reckoned we had better exchange him for a nag from a neighbouring Tommy battery, which we knew could always get a decent one from the remounts. But this battery had met the Aussies before and so had a couple of sentries on duty with loaded rifles and fixed bayonets. However, Corporal Wigley and I rode up to their lines this night, one of us on the blind nag, and said we were looking for a horse that had strayed. We were sure it was on their line.

'Nay, chum. Hain't no horse o' yourn here,' said the sentry.

'Well,' I replied, 'how many horses have you got on your line? Let's count them.'

Dismounting, I walked up the line and back with the sentry and found them all correct. We rode away well satisfied. Yes, very satisfied, for was I not astride a perfectly good black gelding with four good legs and two good eyes. Wigley had worked the changeover while the sentry and I were counting. We cut his fetlocks and hogged his mane, and next morning rode him through the British battery to see if they would recognise him, but it was all too much to expect. I'll bet they did not keep a brand register.

CHAPTER 35

THE MAJOR'S PET CHARGER

'This business of almost walking into enemy territory was occurring far too often.'
Jim Armitage[171]

Once again, Major Dallas Bradlaugh Walker would land Jim Armitage in trouble. Given Jim's farm-raised background and his familiarity with horses, he was tasked with looking after the major's prized charger, his own fiery chestnut steed and the horses of his limber team. Quite an equestrian workload!

Jim Armitage's diary[172]

16 *August* 1918. We came back through Villers-Bretonneux to Corbie, without going into action after all on the Pozieres section. We passed through just after the village had been shelled by long range guns and a lot of artillery reinforcements had been caught in the fire. There were some casualties and for most of the men it was their first battle experience. The soldiers were sitting about in holes and gutters smoking, calm but with that stolid, vacant sort of expression one sees on men who have just come through this sort of thing.

20 *August*. We moved up to Cerisy and made our waggon lines behind the same bank that had sheltered us before, and the next day

our guns went into action on a new line. We then established our gun limber lines handy to the bank of the Somme canal, 500 yards behind the guns, in case we had to get them out in a hurry.

I was given the Major's pet charger to look after. He had two horses and expected me to be a sort of second groom. I took his pet up to the limber lines to look after it there.

For my own mount, I was given a fiery, hard-mouthed little chestnut that took a bit of handling. I had to lead the Major's horse with all of his equipment on board, as well as all my own gear. This consisted of the blankets, oil sheet, spare clothes, overcoat, tin hat, gas mask, haversack, water bottle, bandolier with 50 rounds of ammunition and rifles.

I started out alright, but I no sooner came to the first house in the village when the Huns started shelling it. With a shattering shriek a 5.9" shell burst right inside the mud brick hut not 5 yards from me. I was covered with flying fragments of timber and lumps of mud. My horse went down like a log. I found myself between my fallen horse and the Major's terrified animal.

Amazingly, my own mount had only been knocked out by a lump of earth and was almost unscratched. I got him up, grabbed the Major's horse and, with my tin hat falling over my eyes which completely blinded me, and with all my gear flapping around me, I set off at a wild gallop as more shells fell, leaving the direction to the horses.

We turned a corner, and my horse went down again, tripping into a mass of wounded horses, wrecked vehicles, and a smashed motor ambulance. We got disentangled. Shells were falling everywhere and the village around us was ablaze. My horse was bleeding badly, and I was afraid he was not going to stand much more. Both my hands were fully engaged with the horses. With my tin hat still over my eyes and my gear swinging wildly, we eventually got clear and away.

Major Walker was more concerned about his blasted horse and seemed to think it was my fault. His horse, however, suffered only minor wounds. The vet took over my injured mount and it soon recovered. I felt let down because I had no scars to show for the affair ...

One day Bombardier Anderson, M.M., a battery galloper, came cantering along the riverbank toward us. A German shell burst in the canal beside him. It knocked them over without hurting either man or horse, but they were both thoroughly drenched. When he got to us, he roared with laughter while he felt himself all over. Nothing could upset that chap.

22 August. A big stunt opened up and it was very successful. Several thousand prisoners were walked back past us. The stunt left us out of range of enemy targets. On the 23rd, the attack on Bray was made. Our brigade did not fire in the attack but leap-frogged through the other batteries while they were in action.

Bray is in a deep valley. The surrounding country is high, though comparatively level, like a tableland. As we approached, the Germans were driven out of Bray by our troops, and we could see fighting on both sides of town. The Germans and our own artillery barrage were steadily moving back into German territory. It was a wonderful sight.

This high road into Bray was littered with German skeletons. They must have been there for years. The flesh was gone from their bones, they were just skeletons in rotting uniforms. We could not understand why they had been left there. They were well inside old German territory and had been driven over for ages. Horses hated it and whimpered as there were skeletons of horses too.

On this road, Bray lay at our feet at the bottom of a precipitous chalk cliff over 200 feet high. It was a wonder how we got our guns down that rough track at all. Vehicles tumbled and slipped all over the place. The wheel horses did a wonderful job.

As I was horse handler, I went with Major Walker to look for a new battery position. Bray was not a pretty sight.

However, the Australian dead were few compared to the Germans. They had some good regiments there too, as it was an important railhead, but our artillery barrages must have been terrible. Our new position was through the town and above the railway yard. While we were there, the Major was hit by a shell splinter and rather badly wounded in the right shoulder – a Blighty at least. I thought he had lost an arm. We quickly got him onto a stretcher as there happened to be a First Aid post not far away.

Major Walker was a fine man, and he had the admiration and respect of everyone. He was extraordinarily game in a casual sort of way. I had seen him – to my great fear – when I was with him, walk casually toward a positive hail of shell-fire and usually the shelling would conveniently lift until he had passed. He was more worried about his horse, which was not badly hit. I took it back to our new horse lines on a ridge behind Atenium, across the valley from Chipilly Wood.

This wood was full of English and American dead.

Also on the edge of the wood was an abandoned battery of German 5.9" guns. They had evidently been caught in our barrage while trying to save their guns with disastrous results. The place was a tangle of mangled men and horses. I have never seen such a bloody sight. Two British tanks had been shelled and blown up and their crews were just heaps of ashes. Not a nice place.

That evening, one of our mules (they had replaced some of our extensive horse casualties with mules) in coming back from watering, stepped on the spring of a German mine with the resulting casualties of one man and three mules.

These waggon lines were a long way from the guns which meant that it would take all night for the ammunition teams to make two trips. We would leave the lines about 9 pm in pouring rain, and get back about 6 am, wet, caked with chalk, tired and hungry, just in time to set out on some other job.

I made a couple of trips to the guns in daylight with Tommy Hannah, M.M., 'the water cart king.' Tommy refused medals several times and was finally ordered to take one.

Sometimes these trips were nasty. He had a splendid red silk cushion with gold braid and tassels, which he always sat on, and he cherished it greatly. On one of our trips, we were stopped outside Bray by a military police patrol who said, 'You can't go past here with that thing. It's not safe.'

I inwardly agreed. Tommy quietly told the police where they could go. He nudged his two donks, named *This* and *That*, and went on his way. He said, 'The boys gotta have water.'

When the shelling got bad, (the German balloons were looking right down on us) he would light his pipe and smoke furiously. If only those blasted mules would have galloped.

Sometimes I would sing to stop my teeth from chattering. Several times we were covered in flying splinters, rocks and mud, stones, and the fumes from exploding shells. Tommy's crimson cushion had a corner blown off and one cartwheel was torn by a shell splinter.

Our chaps at the guns on the ridge had been watching us. They cheered Tommy's arrival but left me, who felt rather like a hero, to help with the water. The return trip was just as bad, but we did gallop.

27 August. We moved our guns to a high ridge on the left of Suzanne. The gun position was again an awfully long way from the waggon lines, through difficult country with no roads. We got there with only one chap, called MacLean, and his horse, as casualties.

I was driving wheel on an ammunition cart that night. We were the last waggon in the convoy and got separated by heavy shell-fire in the pitch darkness of some wood. After wandering around for ages, we eventually got our waggon into a valley where we discovered what had once been a road and which we followed. At the junction we came to the remains of a signpost. Dismounting, I finally made out a sign pointing to Suzanne, back along the way we had come. We seemed to be awfully close to German machine-gun fire, but there was no shelling. One of the drivers said, 'God, we could be in German territory,' so we headed away from the noise of the firing line.

A couple of hours later we came upon some of our own chaps who were returning from their second trip, so there was plenty of ammunition at the guns and no need for us to go back that night.

I was doing a lot of driving about this time, usually wheel. This meant that I rode the near-side wheel horse of the six-horse team. They were a pair of splendid greys. Wheelers had the waggon pole between them and took the full brunt of the thrust and the pull of the waggon or gun and controlled the vehicle on hills.

Next day, the waggon lines were moved up to our former battery position at Bray.

Another chap and I were detailed to take rations to the battery. We harnessed up old Polly into the mess cart, a French farm cart with a canvas top on it. Off we went, expecting to be back about midday. We never saw Bray again.

We wandered about for hours looking for our battery, but they had moved during the night. We drove into the village of Suzanne, got chased out of there by shell-fire, went into the next village on its left, unknowingly passing within a few hundred metres of the battery.

Getting chased out of this village too, we decided to try over the next ridge. We soon came back, finding ourselves under direct fire from the enemy and with a goodly piece of the tailboard blown away.

This business of almost walking into enemy territory was occurring far too often.

The trouble was, none of us lesser mortals knew where the front line was. I suppose the Germans were doing the same thing as the position of the line changed sometimes a couple of times a day.

We eventually found the battery on the other ridge, hidden among heaps of German road metal. We also found the rest of our artillery there too; teams, waggons, H.Q., everything.

In our absence orders had come to move up. Someone brought along some of my kit, but most of it was left behind, as usual, at Bray. As we moved forward, I collected new kit from the roadside; someone's overcoat, their bandolier, another water flask and, from an old German dug-out, a supply of blankets.

Unfortunately, our lice were different to German lice and, of course, those blankets were full of German lice. Still, they were a more colourful breed than ours. But lice are the worst trouble, and at roll call we go through our shirts in search of vermin.

That night we camped in some French dug-outs that had been recently vacated by the Germans. We struck camp at 3 am, moving our horse teams up behind the guns while they opened up on an attack…

I shall never forget carting ammunition to the guns in this new and dangerous position. Each team made three trips. Three times we went into that damned gully and every time I thought it would be our last. The Hun was bombarding the dump with 5.9" and 8" shells.

We had to gallop through this inferno into a positive hail of flying shell splinters, coils of barbed wire, planks, and girders. Everything he had in that dump was flying about. Each time we arrived, we gathered in a cutting and the six teams tried to time the series of salvos, taking it in turns to make a wild dash across the gully.[*]

---

[*] This was during the Battle of Picardy on 3 September.

Our casualties were incredibly few. One of my lovely greys got a small shell splinter in her neck. I stuffed a bit of rag in the hole, and she was alright until we could treat the wound that night. All that I got was a nick on the cheek.

Other teams were not so lucky. One man and his horses were obliterated, and a waggon was reduced to matchwood by a flying girder. Han was a bad place. The battery lost several good men including one of our subs, named Kempster, who was killed there.

The next day we changed over gun crews, and I went up to the guns again. Shelling had fortunately stopped. We moved our guns forward near a flattened pile of bricks that had once been the village of Cerisy, in the middle of which were crossroads, a lovely target.

We relieved a battery on the left which reported 80% casualties. It was a rough show we got into. When things finally calmed down, all I could remember was Bombardier Anderson shoving one of those ammonia capsules up my nose while I lay against the bank. The place reeked of gas and everyone else wore their gas masks.

At 4.30 the following morning we opened up our barrage for the coming attack and a nasty accident happened.

During the night, another battery had pulled in front of us higher up on the ridge, much too close for safety. During this stunt, one of our right section's guns miscalculated the angle required to clear the crest and the guns in front, with the result that one of its shells made a direct hit on one of our gun teams in front of us, killing two men and wounding others. This nasty incident indicated how densely packed our artillery was in these attacks.

4 September. Our waggon lines were bombed out of their positions by planes, so we moved behind Suzanne into the reserve. On the 6th, near Han, we rested. The roads were blocked at night with men, munitions, guns, plus horses, lorries and even cavalry, all moving forward. The presence of cavalry meant they were going to try a breakthrough. Obviously, something big was afoot. It turned out to be the capture of Peronne and Mont St. Quentin.

On the 9th of September we moved up through Peronne and made reserve lines about a mile in front of Doingt. Peronne showed signs of having been a fine town but, when we passed through, it was little more than a heap of rubble.

Another *big push* seemed imminent. We suspected that we weren't being rested for no good reason. Great efforts were made to prevent observation of our back areas in the build up of our stores. By now the Hun was getting a bit timid about flying over our lines in daylight but kept up heavy bombing raids at night.

13 *September.* That night, about a dozen enemy bombers came over low. Immediately the sky was alighted with search lights. The planes were subjected to a withering fire from machine guns, including ours, and several batteries of anti-aircraft guns. The planes did not last long. Many of them crashed in flames, their bombs exploding when they hit the ground. I doubt there were any survivors.

A bomb crashed uncomfortably close to us. It was a terrific sight, but what went up had to come down. One could hear those thousands of machine-gun bullets and shell splinters swishing past us.

At that time, one of our men was killed by a piece of shrapnel that went right through his tin hat, so I didn't mention the shrapnel wound to my left knee. Later, I was patched up with a sort of splint and carried on with a stiff leg for about a month. This was the only war wound to cause me trouble in later years.

About this time the idea was conceived whereby a particular section of the front line would contact a particular aerodrome when bombers flew over them at night. Night fighters were sent out but kept in the background until searchlights picked up the bombers.

The fighters came from behind, dropping *ceasefire* signal rockets as they moved in for the kill, so we immediately ceased our firing. We saw five bombers shot down in one night but felt that the British pilots took a great risk of being shot down by our *friendly* fire.

A moving verse

A copy of the following verse by David McNicoll was found in Jim's papers. His niece said *Epitaph for a Soldier*, published 1944, was Jim's favourite poem.

EPITAPH FOR A SOLDIER[173]

Build me no monument should my turn come.
Please do not weep for me and waste your tears.
Write not my name on honour rolls of fame.
to crumble with man's memory through the years.
Wear no dark clothes, speak in no saddened voice,
seeking rare virtues which did not exist.
Just let me lie under the cool, sweet earth
and sleep in peace, where I will not be missed.

I ask one thing, that in still far-off days
someone who knew me should, in daily round,
suddenly pause, caught by some sight or sound,
some glance, some phrase, some trick of memory's ways
which brings me to his mind. Then I shall wait,
eager with hope; perhaps to hear, 'How great
if he were with us still.' Then, at the end,
all that I wish for – just: 'He was my friend.'
—David McNicoll

CHAPTER 36

BEHIND THE HINDENBURG LINE

'We slept while riding, and we slept whilst walking, and we slept while standing up.'
Jim Armitage[174]

During the Hundred Days Offensive following the Battle of Hamel, Field-Marshal Haig visited the area frequently and was present when Lieutenant-General Sir John Monash held the great battle conference at the Australian Army Corps headquarters. Working with two of the Canadian divisions, the Australian Corps overwhelmed the Hindenburg Line.

In his diary entries, Jim describes being behind the Hindenburg Line and contrasts the tactics of the British and American troops, after finding an ominous tunnel with a great many dead bodies.

Jim Armitage's diary[175]

17 September 1918. We moved forward through Courcelles, passing by a demolished hospital, through open country to a gully running roughly parallel to the front lines, which we travelled up.

The night was still, ominously still. Even the horses were nervous and jumpy.

Suddenly, a gas shell whizzed over us with its peculiar noise, exploding three quarters of a mile away, followed by a high explosive shell, bursting 100 yards nearer.

The Hun was sweeping this gully with gas and high explosives at 30 second intervals with 100-yard sweeps. We were going toward the shelling, and it was coming towards us, so we increased the distance between vehicles to 150 yards. As we quickly proceeded, a large shell exploded between the first- and second-gun teams. Another exploded in a heap of blue metal. I think every man and horse within 100 yards was gashed by flying debris.

We were close to the enemy lines. Finally, the moon came out, revealing 'C' sub's six grey horses in their gun team, plus a bomber cruising low overhead. The bomber swooped. As bombs exploded, we cursed the greys, and we cursed the moon.

A telegraph post, struck by one bomb, fell onto the greys, tangling the horses and men in wires.

Mercifully, the moon went into heavy cloud again and the bombing stopped. We finally established waggon lines in peace, in front of Hamlet, and to the right of Roisel.

That night was cold and raining. Our greatcoats were sodden with water. We couldn't smoke, being under direct observation from the enemy. We lay on the ground beneath the waggons and tarpaulins. When the moon came out again, two enemy planes spotted us and dropped an aerial torpedo, which fortunately exploded on the bank above us, leaving a crater about 12 foot deep and 20 foot wide. Other bombs fell nearby, damaging our waggons and the tarpaulins under which we lay. Several men were hit.

A dog, from heaven knows where, found its way under my tin cover, and tried to lie on my face. Badly injured, it bled all over my gas mask, much to my annoyance.

Our guns went into action before Jeancourt, on the edge of Bois de Hervilly. Thunderous attacks opened at dawn and four times that day our guns were advanced. Talk about work! Thousands of prisoners were brought back past us, a sign of how the fight was going.

That day and the following night, the Germans were driven back to the first defences of the Hindenburg Line. It must have been a magnificently controlled advance ...

We slept while riding, and we slept whilst walking, and we slept while standing up. We moved forward on the 19th through Jeancourt, taking up positions on top of the chalk pit looking into Le Bois du Grand Prieul.

One of our chaps, Stevens, was unlucky. Firing a Lewis gun at an enemy aeroplane, the rear gunner got him with a well-directed burst. There was nothing we could do for Stevens. Also, we had a busy time when the camouflage netting over our gun was ignited by that shell fire.

Assembled tanks gave some security by deterring the occasional strafing while we were watering our horses at large troughs in a disused sugar factory nearby.

29 September. Pulling our guns out, we moved northward, back along the same gully past Roisel, camping in an open field near Hebecourt. Before daylight we moved back into the line, equipped as Horse Artillery. Blankets and gear were left behind, but necessary rations were strapped to each gun limber.

We passed through Hargicourt and the whole 8th Artillery Brigade assembled in a big gully, waiting for the attack to develop. We were to leapfrog and pass through the American brigade who were attacking this time (our first experience of actively supporting the Yanks).

The line was over the rise in front of us. We were to dash into action before the Hun could recover from their first onslaught.[*]

---

[*] The Battle of St. Quentin Canal.

The Yanks went over but we still waited. A Hun plane swooped and spotted the whole brigade assembled, dropping a signal flare for its artillery. Luckily, the air was so thick with smoke, bursting shells, tank exhaust smoke and smoke screens, that the signal was not seen. Machine-gun fire brought the plane down.

At last, we got the order to advance, and went over the ridge, in the midst of the most wonderful, impressive battlefield scene imaginable, a scene never to be forgotten. Infantry tanks, guns, everything was in action in an inferno of smoke and shells.

We immediately encountered a hail of machine-gun fire, which cut short our ideas of any further contemplation of the scene. Our horses were getting hit and we retired hastily.

Amazingly, the Americans advanced through the German's first defences without even stopping to clear dug-outs and machine-gun pockets. They went onwards to their second line of defence, sending prisoners unescorted to the rear. Those prisoners, on finding their first line defences still occupied by several German soldiers, rallied, and reinforced their comrades.

The Americans found themselves between two lines of German trenches, cut off from both retreat and reinforcements by a barrage from the re-formed German machine-gunners.

This terrible example of bad field discipline cost a lot of lives. We could not give them any support. Firing so close to cover, we would have been literally mown down trying to sight our guns on top of the ridge. We camped that night in some old trenches.

1 *October*. We went into action to the right of another totally destroyed village, the centre of terrific fighting in the previous day's battle. The adjacent wood lay thick with American bodies, derelict tanks, and large numbers of German dead.

Our position was amongst the trenches of Germany's Hindenburg Line. We cleared away their dead, so that we could make camp. Here we stayed for two or three days getting heavy

German artillery fire directed at the barb-wire entanglements about 30 yards from our guns. Although the German's fire was extraordinarily accurate, we were not touched.

I slept in a shallow trench that night. Unfortunately, a mate and I ate chocolates received from England, and my tummy was not feeling very happy.

Twice during the night, a man who had camped further along, dashed wildly over me, trampling on my face and body. Shivering, he swore that he had heard groans coming from a decapitated German body. Shell-shock! Next day, the poor chap was sent back behind the lines. This bloke's gruesome descriptions did nothing to improve my digestion.

Along the Hindenburg Line the Huns had placed a machine gun every twenty yards. We moved up into Bellicourt. This town was not badly knocked about and was built high above a canal, which ran under a considerable part of town through a tunnel.

In this tunnel the Germans had boiling-down works, where they extracted fat from their own dead. The tunnel certainly contained great boilers and a good many dead, but these latter were obviously killed in the fighting. Since most of those boiling work's fittings had been removed some time ago, it was impossible to guess to what purpose the boilers had been put.

Strange stories are current regarding a plant found in the Canal d'Escant* for the reduction of human bodies (to obtain glycerine) and other purposes than decent burial. There a dreadful scene occurred when a British shell exploded amidst a number of men collected around a big boiler. It was found that the boiler was surrounded by portions of humanity; there were heads and pieces of mutilated bodies. Eye witnesses declare that the spectacle was horrid beyond description.

---

*   Canal de l'Escaut.

Doctors who visited the spot state that some fragmentary bodies had not been blown apart by shells but had been scientifically severed by proper surgical instruments ...

Still in Bellicourt, we put our guns into action in front of Wiencourt, establishing limber lines in a valley behind the guns, in case we had to get out quickly. The night before the next attack we were to take part in, our limber lines were heavily shelled. I arrived about 2 am to find our men evacuating for all they were worth, trying to save their horses.

The night was pitch black; the valley full of gas. In the confusion, I charged over a steep embankment some thirty feet high. My horse fell. We rolled to the bottom in a cloud of dust and gas but, thankfully, neither of us were any the worse for wear.

It was impossible to see properly through the fogged-up eyeholes of one's gas mask. So many gun layers risked their lives during an attack by taking off their mask, leaving only the nose and mouth pieces in position.

The 49th Battery was near us. I finally caught up with Brunton, Phippard and Wilkinson, and for a brief time, heard about their wartime experiences.

At 4 am our waggon lines moved up to our temporarily evacuated limber lines. Again this happened while I was on another job. My kit, of course, was left behind once more.

Vast numbers of cavalry were used in this attack, together with the new fast Whippet tanks. It was a tremendous success. The enemy evacuated a large area, while burning stores and villages as they went, mining roads and booby-trapping abandoned guns and equipment. We took greater slices of territory at each successive attack.

A tank drome was established near us after the show. Crews told their great tales of far penetrating attacks that sometimes developed into a chase. According to them, three divisions of German cavalry had been taken as prisoners.

15 October. We moved forward through Remicourt to Montbrehain. Civilians began emerging from the caves, woods, and deserted houses. They were mostly old men and women, and some crippled young Frenchmen who greeted the Allied soldiers with pathetic enthusiasm. They told of a great bombardment ten days ago, which gradually came nearer. Three days ago, shells were bursting in the neighbouring ridges. The Germans had rounded up all of the able-bodied persons, despatching them to the rear. One old man, a woman and a girl had hidden in a cave. They had looked out anxiously each morning, seeing German troops still in the vicinity. This morning the girl had peeped out and cried, 'Les Anglais.'

Montbrehain

John Roxburgh was Jim's best friend at Sydney Grammar School and during the war years they shared many adventures. John was born in Burwood, NSW, in 1898, and enlisted with Jim in May 1917. He toured England with Jim's family before returning to Australia. Roxburgh would become the Honorary Treasurer for the Australian Red Cross Society, visiting the Malayan Army Command in 1941 and helping to organise convalescent hospitals for officers and men there.

Here Jim describes their arrival at Montbrehain days after the main battle.

Jim Armitage's diary[176]

15 October. They emerged to welcome us. It was indeed strange to see the old women wearing our steel helmets, which we willingly gave up, in walking them back through the heavy shell-fire to a point of safety. We helped to reassure all of the frightened refugees whose nerves were shattered by the terrible shelling, while the old men coming back halted at every shell hole, listening for the shells, ready to take cover. Through Brancourt and on to Primont, where we established our waggon lines, we waited in reserve, prior to taking part in another big stunt. We came in for heavy enemy shelling in which several men and horses were killed. We all felt the loss.

Battle of St. Quentin Canal: 29 September to 23 October 1918

The Battle of St. Quentin Canal involved British, Australian and American forces operating as part of the British Fourth Army under General Sir Henry Rawlinson. Sections of the British Third Army also supported the attack further north.

One of the most heavily defended stretches of the German *Siegfriedstellung* (Hindenburg Line) in this sector used the St. Quentin Canal as part of its defences. The assault achieved its objectives in the first full breach of the Hindenburg Line, convincing the German high command that there was little hope for an ultimate German victory.

Jim Armitage's diary[177]

I had a couple of close escapes. I was in a party of six (about 70 yards in front of our guns we were each *laying out* our respective gun aiming posts) when a veritable hail of shells burst on us. There was absolutely no cover, but we saw gun flashes and fell flat on our faces. My night lighting equipment got knocked about badly.

In falling, I lost my torch and groped about endlessly in the dark looking for it. Thanks to that evening's rum rations, and to four friends who did not drink, the whole business amused me considerably.

Finally locating my torch and the aiming equipment, I found it impossible to see what was wrong, so tried to risk a quick light shielding it with my body, but I immediately became the centre of concentrated machine-gun fire. From then on, I worked in pitch darkness between bursts of fire, taking ages to get the apparatus set up, before finally getting back to my gun. The others were not amused.

We opened up in the early morning hours. Things looked bad as the crew of 'E' sub guns were wiped out. A lot of our ammunition was burning. Several men in 'D' sub were wounded and six horses in one team waiting behind the guns were killed. The bracing effect of rum had long since worn off, and I was feeling edgy, in fact we all were.

Suddenly, with a shattering shriek, a shell tore through our gun shield, burying itself right beside the gun trail. In that split second, we knew we could not possibly survive.

We held our breath, but nothing happened. We started to breathe again and realised that the shell was a dud. After that, we all felt much better, as though some long-awaited disaster was averted. Then we manned our guns like a quartet of demons, yelling and cursing and generally letting off steam.

Many prisoners were taken in that stunt. Heaven only knows where they put them all. Some American detachments got lost in the confusion, coming back upon us, ready to fire, but they hesitated, half thinking we were German gunners. We soon told them!

The Germans put up a fierce fight, their counter-artillery fire on our section being severe. We had a hot time as we followed on the advance, immediately moving along a road littered with the debris of war. There were hundreds of German and American dead amid horses, waggons, tanks, and supplies.

It worried me that the Americans had still not learned the art of strategy or initiative. There were lines of American dead in front of machine-gun nests. Gamely they rushed headlong at entrenched machine guns, never outflanking them. Other troops would go around them, attacking the posts from the rear, where the Hun could not bring his machine guns to bear.

As we approached our new position, we came under shell-fire. Speeding up, we galloped through Saint Martin, with bricks and mortar flying everywhere.

There, a man casually stood amongst it, taking a moving picture of us.[*] We decided he was a bit light in the head.

Owing to some mistake, it was impossible for us to fire from our new position. We were too close to the enemy lines. We would have been blown out of existence if we had broken cover to sight our guns.

It transpired that the Americans in front of us had been unable to drive the Germans out of a strongly held position in a deep railway cutting, leaving a salient in which, unfortunately, we were in the middle.

To remedy this, English troops made a daylight attack with little artillery support. Close behind, we lay on our stomachs and watched. They were magnificent as were their tactics. They drove the enemy out of his stronghold and into the distance. The scene was surreal, it was so ordered. Grey and khaki figures were running, fighting and falling, amid grey puffs of bursting shells.

Battle of Montbrehain: 5 October 1918

Early in the morning on 5 October 1918, the 6th Brigade A.I.F. succeeded in occupying Montbrehain village and capturing over 400 German prisoners, but at the loss of 430 Australian casualties.

This was the final major battle in which Australian troops would take part toward the end of the war. After the last brigade fought and took Montbrehain village, the Hindenburg Line was completely broken. American troops now defended this sector, while exhausted

---

[*]   Captain Frank Hurley, official A.I.F. war photographer.

and depleted Australian soldiers were withdrawn for a badly needed rest, having fought for over six months without a break.

The following extracts show General Monash and the London War Office's appreciation of the soldiers' efforts during the war.

Monash letters, *The Newcastle Sun*[178]

Letters from England, which I have seen, go to show that the War Office people are talking about the work of our three divisions astride of the Somme, and covering Amiens, as a feat finer than the retreat from Mons. Thus, the division carried out a long series of daring raids during the winter of 1916–17; fought in and helped to win the battle of Messines on June 7, 1917, and the battle of Warneton on July 31, and the two phases of the third battle of Ypres on October 4 and October 12. Since then we have been more or less at rest, waiting for the present emergency, and the chief's confidence in the division has not been misplaced; for its entry upon the stage has had a decisive and far-reaching effect on the whole situation. We are none the less proud, too, of our sister Australian divisions, all of whom have a fine record.

CHAPTER 37

LULLABY OF THE GUNS

'Perhaps, at first, they will be unable to sleep on
account of the quiet of the night. They are sure to miss
the lullaby of the guns.'
Margaret Bell[179]

Margaret Bell

Most of this book covers the soldiers and nurses, the men and women involved in the war, but stories about the children also need to be told. Fortunately, I discovered Margaret Bell, British journalist and aviatrix, and her amazing articles published in 1919.

The following are extracts from some of those tales about the children, orphans and refugees whose lives were impacted forever by the insanity of war and by the lullaby of the guns.

The children of the Yser
Margaret Bell, *The Catholic Press*[180]

Belgium. 1915. The smallest tots carried three flags: Belgian, French, and English.

Presently they came within sight of the grey stone chateau, with Norman turrets looking up to the sky; its grilled windows breathing of secrets and old-time feuds. Small wonder the children's wide eyes grew a little wider! In front of the great door, and midway between the turrets, stood four nuns and an Englishwoman who had helped to get the children there.

At the sight of her, a hundred and twenty voices, carefully trained along the way, shouted with enthusiasm, 'Vive l'Angleterre! Vive les Anglais!' Les Anglais had been a magic word with them for days. They knew that in some tangible way their lives would be greatly influenced by it. So, the cheers were followed by the Brabanconne sung in both Flemish and French, and a kind of Flemish Tipperary, which all the Allied soldiers were singing.

They marched through the big doors of the chateau into a large room, where one had an opportunity of seeing them as they were in all of their tired tawdriness. Mother Superieure Gertrude looked at those masses of tangled locks, mentally visualising a next morning scene in the washroom, with scissors and comb.

There were the Verkoven twins, who had known no home but the trenches for four months. Their grimy, grey dresses had also known the trenches for the same length of time, without being changed. The twins clung to each other as if fearful of this strange, quiet land. So long had they been accustomed to the noise of bursting shells that a rational order of things seemed untrustworthy.

Many children were barefooted, and sore and tired little feet they were. There was a big surprise for them in the next room. Long tables of food, with plates and knives and forks. But not least important was the food itself.

At first, some of the children were afraid to touch it. The fear of unusualness clutched them, so that they even forgot that they were hungry. Sister Agnes explained that it was an English food called *oatmeal*, and that the English were very fond of it, so the day was won.

Bedtime was an orgy of childish luxury. Rows and rows of iron cots, with clean sheets, pillows, and blankets, stood silently soliciting tired, tussled heads. Two hundred and forty eyes opened wider. Would they dare to soil these beautiful beds? They had nothing to wear but what they had worn for many weeks.

There was another surprise. Neatly folded on the top sheet of each bed was a new nightgown. Perhaps there would be a little difficulty as to the adjustments of size, but that would arrange itself in due time. Such dreams there were that night!

When the morning sun peeped in through the long windows of the chateau, a hundred and twenty pairs of eyes suddenly opened upon a reality no less satisfying. The whole world was a great Pandora's box, bursting open to fling surprises at them. After breakfast, there was an assembling in one of the larger rooms, in which was another long table piled with mysteries.

The mysteries were English too, like the oatmeal and blankets. There were all sorts of clothing in all sorts of colours. The white mysteries beneath were worn under the coloured ones. A new outfit for every child!

In one corner of the room were dozens of boots, *sabots* in the Flemish tongue, which would offer a later problem of adjustment, just as the nighties had done.

After a few days, the children grew accustomed to the new order of things. Gradually this life became normal, until the old days spent in the hell of shell and shrapnel were now only an unpleasant memory. Lessons and play made the days fade into weeks, but no day was ever complete without a prayer of thanksgiving to Les Anglais.

To accommodate over 800 children gathered in this town just behind the firing line, large wooden huts were erected at the edge, a quarter of a mile beyond the range of the Teutonic guns. The town itself was often shelled. The children came to the convent early each morning before any bombardment commenced, and returned in the evening, after it was finished.

Fringing the huts were trenches and dug-outs, to which the children sometimes were obliged to run, for the graceful dove of Teutonic frightfulness often came swooping along with a burden of bombs.

The children are being kept in school, as though the present days of bombs and hell are rational days. The nuns are teaching them; silent, self-sacrificing nuns who, until two years ago, had never experienced any of the problems of life but such simple ones at existed within the cloister walls.

It is the duty of three volunteers to provide a meal for those children in the middle of the day. Preparations begin at 9 o'clock and include cutting up bread – huge loaves manufactured from Canadian flour by the local baker in his subterranean shop; and the spreading of it with some satisfactory *spreadable*, either jam, marmalade, or margarine.

The piece-de-resistance is entrusted to Natalie, a capable Flemish cook. Often her chief dish is a marvellous concoction including tinned mutton from Australia, with potatoes, some turnips, and onions. This is called Flemish hutze-pot. The children are fond of this because, until lately, their palates were unaccustomed to the taste of meat.

In the bread line in Belgium
Margaret Bell, *The Catholic Press*[181]

1916. Through the thick Flemish mist, I could discern a line of figures, stretching from the door of our supply depot to the road. The hour was early. The distribution of clothing and food was not until 2 o'clock. Yet here were all these pitiful refugees lined up in the mud and damp of a drizzling autumn morning, prepared to wait seven hours for their share of warmth and sustenance! By the time that the distant clock on the shattered Hotel de Ville sounded out a weary nine, the queue lengthened across the ditch and down the cobbles, past the *magasin* of Baptiste, the one-eyed mender of shoes.

I did not see them again until 1.30 pm, half an hour before the big, creaking doors of the depot would open to receive them.

All that morning a drizzling rain had drifted down. The queue seemed to huddle closer, as if the damp proximity of other tattered skirts and shawls might add protection. They talked in hopeful, guttural monosyllables, of homes that once were, of the savings of years suddenly evaporated, of the necessity for making a new beginning.

As they talked of life, from across the desolate fields came an incessant accompaniment, now rumbling and monotonous, now interrupted by short, sharp crackling, as of a warning from a frenzied soul.

Scarcely five miles away, many of their sons, husbands and brothers kept watch from a subterranean look-out in the heart of a once thrifty homeland, now smarting under the lash of the tyrant. The daughters, wives and sisters clung desperately to life in that small corner of the country which remained shielded in pathos from the enemy's guns.

How wretched they were! Many were without shoes, scarcely any had hats; sometimes old sacks took the place of shawls.

Leonie, the first in line, had seen 92 Flemish Christmases and watched 92 green summers fade into brown. She too had faded. Her little body curved more and more with the passing years, until she was scarcely five feet of warped vitality.

Everyone knew Leonie. That is how she did not have to stand in line but had a small packing-case on which to sit. She had been a servant, but the enemy shells had turned the home of her mistress into stones and rubble. She had to go and look for another lodging, and found one in a loft, with straw for a pillow and two canvas sacks for a coverlet.

On that dull, drizzling morning, with the never-ceasing rumble of guns in her ears, she sat on her packing-case crooning snatches of songs she used to know when she pattered about the little, white-washed cottage in barefooted, peasant glee. She crooned another song of more recent learning. If her pronunciation was not always perfect, what did it matter? For the melody was there, and there was only one melody to 'Tipperary', no matter how contorted the accompanying words might be.

A pitiful story
Margaret Bell, *The Journal Adelaide*[182]

1917. The refectory seats one hundred and eighty children at a time. First come girls, bowing majestically, curtly, or self-capaciously. Of those, Paula is a great favourite, with her brown curls, dimples and long, sweeping lashes veiling deep blue eyes. She is blessed with a shyness which is no less becoming than it is rare. There is Juliette of the flaxen hair and oval face, with her clogs and blue bonnet; an absolute picture of Flanders, the kind which everyone knows – windmill, long low cottage, an inimitable stretch of lowland.

After the girls have finished their meal the boys come, a great army of them, trooping noisily along, swiftly taking their places behind the steaming plates. The boyish appetite is a thing of beautiful satisfaction, an absolute joy to the dispensers of soup and hutze-pot. This portion of the Lilliputian colony shows its appreciation by learning a few words of English, to which everyone gives prominence at every possible opportunity. They come with pockets brimming full of souvenirs; military buttons, cartridge cases, and heads of shells.

Four little children wait beside the door – four little sisters from nearby Malines. Hand in hand they come to school, their *sabots* clicking on the cobbles, their little hearts beating a happy accompaniment, for they love the school hours and the kind, quiet nuns.

With them always came their mother, terrified to let them leave the crude shack called home, without watching their journey across the Plage, through the shell-riddled streets.

One day we missed them, one day when the great shells were whistling overhead and fell in the town where the little shacks were huddled together.

After the bombardment ceased and heaps of bricks and contorted earth told the story of it, we went into town to find them. They were standing in a corner of the house, eyes wide with terror, unable to understand why they were deserted so long by the little mother who had left them, only for a moment, she said, and had not returned.

The mother? She was crossing the Plage when a shell came, crossing to the food depot to get a loaf of bread for the children's breakfast.

Eventide in Flanders
Margaret Bell, *The Register Adelaide*[183]

1917. When afternoon slips into evening, there sounds across the silence the deep, clanging notes of a bell. From the orphanage, a procession of black-robed nuns appears, slowly and solemnly treading along the narrow street to a large building with great iron-bound shutters. A woman opens the door, bows before the nuns and when they have entered, shuts it. The priest comes next, a tall, bronzed man, wearing a long, khaki overcoat. He speaks a cheery word to the old woman and enters the great convent door, ready for this evening's salut.

It is a beautiful service, the salut; nor does it seem less beautiful in the small room with the obstinate piano and a dozen voices singing in almost as many different keys. The priest is no longer in the army uniform that he wears amongst men; the acolyte is there as in normal times.

If you understand Flemish, you learn from the old woman that it is a miracle the whole convent is not a heap of ruins, like the church a few yards away. A shell fell one afternoon, fortunately when the nuns were visiting some poor refugees who had just arrived.

It might so easily have fallen through the roof, but the Holy Virgin was listening, the old woman says, while she knelt praying in her room in the cellar, and allowed only windows to be smashed and the ceiling pierced by the shell piece which came hurtling in.

The Good Englishwoman
Margaret Bell, *Freeman's Journal*[184]

1917. In the narrow streets there are many hurrying figures. One is distinguished by the small, red gleam from a lantern the woman carries in her right hand. In her left hand is a black leather bag, such as doctors carry. In it are dressings, a few bottles of antiseptics, such old-fashioned medicines as liquorice powder, fruit salts and aspirin. She may be a stranger among the little populace – a stranger in nationality, but a friend in motive.

She is English, '*la bonne est noble dame*' the villagers call her. Every evening, when her more arduous work is done, she goes the rounds of the cottages and shacks which house the refugee population, seeing to manifold ailments that are too severe to allow their victims to come to her small dispensary at the dressing hour.

She stops for a minute at a large building overlooking the canal. Inside, in a small room apart from the general one, sits an elderly man. The white shelves in his office are lined with bottles, his desk littered with glass needles, some microscopes, and an indiscriminate deluge of papers. With him the Englishwoman confers. He supplies some antiseptics she needs in her dispensary, and advice.

Of course, such professionals as have at their disposal a varied selection of antiseptics, and whose dispensaries are lined with mahogany cabinets containing all of the latest devices in liquid and powder, might scoff at his white cupboards. His pride is those shelves with their simple burdens of boracic powder, liquorice powder, potassium permanganate, hydrogen peroxide, and Epsom salts. The latest jealously guarded acquisition is a one litre bottle of ether, secured through the kindness of the village chemist, who refused to leave his laboratory even after its roof had been removed by a shell.

There are bandages, happily in greater numbers than before, and swabs manufactured in the Poste de Secours, from packets of absorbent wool generously donated by kind friends in England. This dispensary is really an offshoot. Caring for several hundred refugee children was intended to include only such weapons of necessity as would ward off cold and hunger.

The nuns
Margaret Bell, *Bendigo Advisor*[185]

1918. During the past four years, Sister Marie-Therese has been living with seven other nuns in the cellar of their convent, ministering to the flock of homeless refugees, huddling in shacks and hovels in this small corner of Belgium.

Only recently they were obliged to leave. One morning, during Mass, the old Curè warned his flock that they must not stray far from their cellars and dug-outs. Rumours were abroad that the enemy contemplated strange new horrors against the civilian population.

Next day, long before the sun had snatched dew from the stunted shrubbery, the nuns awoke, coughing and choking.

'We must have taken cold during the night,' said Sister Marie-Therese, as a gendarme knocked on the cellar door.

'Get your gas masks and hurry to the chateau,' he shouted. They hurried through the crooked streets, their long rosaries swaying. At last, they reached the chateau, situated at the edge of town in a clump of pine trees. Across the grey dawn an ominous cloud was rolling from the direction of the enemy trenches. Up climbed the nuns, three flights of cold stone stairs, followed by a terror-stricken populace. When they reached the top room, the nuns knelt in a corner and prayed. Nearer rolled the sickening cloud.

It was almost at the canal. The terrified populace watched from the chateau windows. Over the town fell a portentous silence as the gas cloud reached the canal. The barges were lost from sight. Then a miracle happened. It hesitated, wavered a little, and turned, for the wind had veered suddenly.

Down trooped the populace and the eight nuns, everyone talking excitedly.

Scarcely had they reached the shelter of the woods when there sounded a whistling above their heads – then an explosion – then the beating of great engines in the air. It was a double bombardment. The planes seemed to come down and sit on the housetops, which they then peppered with machine-gun fire. It went on for over an hour. At length, the warning tocsin sounded again and the shelterers crept out from amongst the trees. The chateau was a pile of bricks and masonry.

The nuns filed back toward their convent, but before reaching the great stone wall which surrounded it, they knew the worst. Flames leaped up into the air and hissed and crackled. An incendiary bomb had fallen on it.

They stood watching the flames until all that remained was the charred bronze figure of the Madonna which had stood in their chapel. Sadly, they turned away to help other homeless ones whose shacks and cellars were also unliveable.

Shelling went on every day in Flanders. One after another of the clustering cottages fell into ruins. The nuns found a place of shelter in a barn, surrounded by troops of soldiers, an atmosphere unsuited to the protected ears and senses of the cloister.

Silence
Margaret Bell, *The Journal Adelaide*[186]

11 November 1918. Silence. The guns have ceased. Silence across the flat plains, where the wind-mills wave their giddy arms. Silence in the old town, whose towering belfry daily sounded the tocsin of warning that great air birds were on the wing! Silence over the yellow roofs of the cottages and the crests of the gaunt, old poplars which fringed the road to Ypres.

I am thinking of old Sophie, who has watched 87 summers come dancing across the Flemish plains. Old Sophie carries a score of wounds. Her war habitation has been the loft of a disused stable near Steenwerke [sic]. I met her during an air raid. What must old Sophie think of the sudden silence?

It must seem strange to little children who came into a world of incessant thunder, to hear nothing all day but their own laughter, and the music of happy voices. Strange to be able to play all day without ominous whistling or the click-clack of the mitrailleuse to send them scuttling back to their cellars.

They are all well-trained in the sounds of war and will not soon forget this knowledge. Perhaps, at first, they will be unable to sleep on account of the quiet of the night. They are sure to miss the lullaby of the guns.

CHAPTER 38

MADEMOISELLE FROM AMIENS

> 'The creamy throat that came up through a Digger tunic collar supported a stately little head whose windows were the loveliest grey eyes I had ever looked into.'
> The Digger[187]

Every good book needs a great love story, and that was one aspect still amiss in this adventure for me. While Jim would meet and marry Lurline Buchanan after his return to Australia, there was no romance mentioned in his diary. The article about 'Mademoiselle from Armentières' spoke of love and sex on, or rather off, the battlefield, but that writer spoke in generalities and did not come close to the human element of love that was needed to complete this saga.

Then I discovered the following story in *The Sun*, Sydney, written by an anonymous digger and printed under the title 'Hidden Treasure'.

Assuming it to be a true love story, all the missing elements were there, including some major coincidences. The setting was in the Somme region of Ribemont, a location Jim had mentioned in one of his diary entries. Plus, there were references to helping a digger, a pun in the title of 'Mademoiselle from Amiens', and a happy ending situated at Circular Quay, Sydney. It all fitted perfectly. I have included the article verbatim as it was in the original.

Hidden treasure indeed!

The Sun[188]

The old Somme town of Ribemont was being badly battered by Fritz's guns on the day I took possession of a temporary wartime residence in the cellar of a shell-shocked house.

On the second day of our occupation of Ribemont I was clearing away some fallen debris which was trying to shut me away from the outside world. As I was struggling to raise a heavy beam from the cellar entrance I found a pair of friendly hands assisting me from outside. I thanked the Digger, and as we heaved together, I was struck by the beauty of his hands. The long, tapering fingers; the well-cared for nails; and the creamy skin, slightly soiled by dust, made them look like the hands of a carefully-nurtured woman.

However, I was too busily employed by the troublesome beam to pay the obliging hands any further attention.

In a few minutes time, the doorway was cleared, and the Digger came underground at my invitation. I had salvaged a bottle of wine and intended to reward him for his help. But when I placed the bottle on a box which served as a table he declined the refreshment.

'No, thank you. I am not vur-ee thirsty,' he said.

GREY EYES AS WINDOWS

The voice was so unlike that of the average Aussie that my eye commenced to make a closer inspection of my guest. The word 'War-baby' begun to form in my mind (for his face was almost childlike), when my suspicions were aroused. Surely I was looking into the face of an exceptionally pretty girl! The creamy throat that came up through a Digger tunic collar supported a stately little head whose windows were the loveliest grey eyes I had ever looked into. The sweet, oval face was slightly soiled by dirt, which strove to conceal its roses. But it was the gentle rounding of the tunic, not far below its collar that finally decided my suspicions.

'Who are you?' I demanded. 'You are not a Digger!'

'No, m'sieur'; and the brim of a steel hat dipped forward as its pretty support slightly bowed.

'M'sieur. This ees mine old home. I am Mademoiselle Madelene Decayeux. See! There ees mine family name on that box. I was in Amiens living with relations when mine mother and leetle sister fled from zis house when ze enemy bombardment come, and zere zey joined me. At Amiens I have been at an Academy des Arts for two years. Zere, zere was an English mademoiselle who taught me to spik her language.' Mademoiselle Digger paused.

'Then what are you doing in an Australian uniform, mam'zelle?' I asked.

'M'sieur. Eet ees said by zee French mademoiselles that the messieurs from Australie are gentlemans. M'sieur, you look so. Can I trust you for to help me; for your kindness will mean so much for Madelene Decayeux?' The earnest look in Mademoiselle's eyes convinced me that here was no spy. But her presence still puzzled me.

HAZARDOUS JOURNEY

'Yes. Mam'zelle. You can trust me; and if I can help you I shall be glad. But how did you manage to get to Ribemont undetected by the soldiers you must have met?'

She smiled. 'Do I not look like one Deegar?' she asked with a brightening face, and then added: 'Zere ees plenty old Deegar uniforms at Amiens. I have find zis one een an old house.

Well, when anyone ees spik wiz me, I am deaf by one beeg cannon; and so I walk along wiz mineself, and no one ees stop me, M'sieur! When mine mother arrive at Amiens she ees nearly frantic. Always she was nervous, and when zee first cannon come to Ribemont she ees fly wis mine leetle sister. And in her fear she ees forgot one important theeng. I have come back for zis theeng, and if I do not get it there ees much misery and poverty for us. No longer can mine mother afford to send me to the academy, if I do not get it.'

Here mademoiselle paused, and her eyes looked up at the low ceiling.

'Zee kitchen was above zis place,' she went on. 'And in its floor which ess zis ceiling, mine mother ees always hide her money in zee way many French people do. In her fright she run away and leave it here. And so I came from Amiens to get it if M'sieur will be so kind for to help me.'

SHOWER OF GOLD

I began to question mademoiselle about the ceiling; and when she had decided the exact position of the small, treasure storehouse, I turned my box-table on end, and set to work with my entrenching tool on the bricks lying in between two ceiling beams. For two hours I attacked the stubborn cellar roof with bayonet and entrenching tool. It was when I was forcing out a piece of broken brick that a stream of gold coins showered over me and down to the floor. Madelene went feverishly to work and gathered them up, while I made a breach big enough to admit my hand and arm. In ten minutes' time we were satisfied that the ceiling had yielded up all the treasure it had contained. This we put into an old woollen sock, and into the haversack carried by mademoiselle. And then I gave some attention to my companion's make-up. By the time I had finished with her she was a 'dinkum Digger.'

I gave her many instructions regarding her bearing, and finally stuck my knife and fork in her puttees. I reckoned that this sign of 'Diggerism' would be sufficient passport through our lines.

Nine months later I had the pleasure of calling on mademoiselle in Amiens, where we spent many happy times together. For the service I rendered mademoiselle at Ribemont, I was rewarded, for not long ago, I found her smiling down at me from the deck of a big liner mooring at Circular Quay.

CHAPTER 39

ARMISTICE DAY

'The war was dying, and dying, it still gasped sudden death and fearful hurt.'
Jim Armitage[189]

The Australian Corps suffered 34,000 casualties under Lieutenant-General Monash's command during the critical Hundred Days Offensive. In the last days of the war men were still dying, even though the Hindenburg Line had been broken. After a brief encounter with some famous Scottish regiments billeted nearby, Jim Armitage's battalion once again came under fire and several men were gassed. Rumours of an armistice held some hope for the cessation of hostilities before Christmas.

Jim Armitage's diary[190]

November 1918. Part of the Hindenburg line was formed by a railway cutting. Here I met Rex Chambers, an officer in a battery of the 7th Brigade. He spent the last 24 hours in a shell hole on observation duty and looked like one of Bairnsfather's sketches. We moved forward to a position behind Ribeauville, a place with lots of shelling and gas. I stopped a small piece of splinter in the neck, a slight wound; a dose of iodine did the trick. The 29th Battery, 100 yards to our left, sustained heavy casualties.

We moved to a position in the open fields near Le Gateau. From there we were to fire part of the next stunt, then move with the advance a couple of thousand yards and go into action wherever a target presented itself.

Because of our 18 pounder's short range, we often moved forward in the middle of battle to keep within striking distance of the retreating Germans. Our infantry never seemed to miss a trick, and our boys seldom held us up.

As we moved forward again, a German shell landed under 'C' sub gun team and blew men and horses to bits. Fortunately, none of our own shells in the gun limber exploded or things would have been even worse. When the rest of our battery reached our new position, it was up in support lines and our machine guns were putting down a barrage. We had to wait while a hail of shells and enemy machine-gun bullets hissed harmlessly overhead. One of 'E' sub's waggons was knocked out, all of the horses killed, and their men wounded.

We stayed several nights, firing a stunt, then pulled out and went to Wiencourt. We lost all idea of days or dates as we tramped a day's march to Ville Malabri for a brief rest. In this village some famous Scottish regiments were billeted; the Black Watch, the Gordon Highlanders and the Camerons. They were the finest looking men I have ever seen, and they put our ragged shell-torn lot to shame.

With our guns in front of our waggon lines at our next position, we got a bit of strafing, and an English observation balloon was destroyed alongside us as it was being inflated.

The road to the guns was treacherous, always under fire and some of our chaps were gassed. When we pulled out from there, we headed again for Wiencourt. Horrible weather, raining in torrents! I took over Terry's horses when he was hit and taken to hospital.

We had just ridden through Brancourt when the leading column suddenly turned about, so we concluded we were being called into action. However, the whole brigade stayed at Brancourt, and we made ourselves comfortable in the deserted and partially destroyed village. This must have been the 10th of November.

Last Battle of Mons: 11 November 1918

Typical of the open warfare following the battles of Hamel and Amiens, a battle plan was put together at relatively short notice. However, this plan applied many of the successful tactics that had been learned since Hamel.

The Belgian town of Mons had been held by the Germans since August 1914, since the First Battle of Mons. On 11 November 1918, World War I's final day, Canadian Corps recaptured Mons after fierce street fighting. The early-morning offensive happened just hours before troops learned that Germany has agreed to an armistice at 11 am.

The Telegraph[191]

It was early morning on the first Armistice day. All was nearly quiet on the Western Front. A kilometre ahead lay the Line. A sullen November sun sent a few struggling rays through the scurrying clouds, lighting up the shell-scarred face of what was once a placid smiling plain of Picardy. Intermittently there came a muffled reverberation, the echoes of some shelling on a distant sector. The whirr of a lone 5.9" split the still air that was suddenly shattered as it burst in a crash of sound, its hurtling splinters questing the human billet.

The war was dying, and dying, it still gasped sudden death and fearful hurt. Overhead two of Hell's Angels fought their last duel with mortal chance, defiant to the end. The blue sky was splashed with snowballs that pitted themselves around the diving and twisting planes. They looked innocently picturesque, these white snowballs – but they were as venomous as exploding dynamite.

A clash of iron on iron gave a dreaded alarm. The Hun, vengeful to the last, had sent the breath of choking death upon the slight breeze, which was now laden with whitish vapour, smarting stuff that, one inhaled, shrivelled the men's lungs so that in a ghastly contortion of agony, they died. Death by gas was not the most pleasant way of saying farewell to life. With their goggle masks and other impedimenta, the khaki inhabitants of that particular stretch of the reserve trench of which I speak looked like human gargoyles.

To teach Fritz to be cautious, one or two bursts of shrapnel were sent his way as a forcible reminder that this was a game two could play.

Everyone knew that this might be the last day of the war, but such a long looked for eventuality seemed so inconceivable no one believed it. With 10 o'clock there came a sudden stillness.

Two or three high officers of field rank appeared – a significant portent so far up. They were usually at headquarters, many kilometres back.

Men who were war-weary looked at each other in an unspoken query. Was it true that Fritz would sign?

We have repressed hope for so long and so sternly that we would not admit that this most improbable of possibilities might come to pass – that this welter of noisome trouble in which we are embroiled – sudden death; the horrid stench of dead mules (and of other things too unmentionable) swollen like balloons; mud, slush, lice, forced marches, blasted trees; an eternal vista of pillaged towns and villages that are a chaos of stark ruin; sudden alarms and excursions through barb-wire which rend and tear mud-caked clothes and sodden limbs; air raids and bombs from the murky mists of night; gas, shot, shell, shrapnel, orders, counter-orders, petty tyrannies innumerable; mud baths; poor tucker, or no tucker at all; diving into muddy shell holes as the whining 5.9" or vicious whizzbang suddenly arrives, turning the world to pandemonium and your mates into unspeakable fragments; mustard gas that splashes from the pools at unsuspecting feet and burns to the bone; the devil's pyrotechnics that are the nightly display of fearful fireworks; the flaming onions that send unfortunate airmen to a hideous incineration in an inferno of flame; the blazing ammunition dumps; the sudden domelike upheaval of earth that literally hurls thousands to eternity, that bespeaks the sprung mine; the bullet that catches you unawares (one moment you are alive, the next kaput); the swelling roar that is the guns' vocal voice with lethal hate that dins unceasingly upon your affrighted ears; all these things and more that even Dante with all his macabre imagination could not glimpse, that one has endured for years, are they to stop, and the blessed silence of Peace come upon the earth again? Impossible!

The tall lieutenant, his voice flat and emotionless as if passing the time of day instead of officially chronicling the miracle of the impossible, said, 'Well, boys, that's the finish!'

The unnatural stillness held!

The Sydney Morning Herald[192]

'The Germans must sign, and they know it,' General Grimwade replied to a remark about the peace treaty. 'If they don't sign now, they will very soon have to sign in Berlin.'

CHAPTER 40

A VILLAINOUS-LOOKING LOT

'We paraded and were inspected by the Prince of Wales, most unwillingly on our part because we still had not been issued with new uniforms.'
Jim Armitage[193]

The war had ended. Despite this, soldiers were not permitted to relax but were kept extremely busy on often unnecessary tasks. Fed up with the situation, Jim Armitage's whole division staged a protest parade, although kept an orderly manner. Fortunately, the General agreed that their grievances were genuine and granted their reasonable requests. Then the Prince of Wales – later briefly King Edward VIII – arrived.

Jim Armitage's diary[194]

11 *November* 1918. Armistice. News that the war was over. That night we celebrated by blowing up old charges of cordite and stacks of German Verey lights, but it took a day or two for the implications of the Armistice to sink in. Everyone became very quiet and relaxed.

Unfortunately, some top brass decided the Australians must be smartened up. This did not mean replacing our terribly ragged, gun-oily clothes, but polishing our guns. Bits of brass had to have paint scraped off, we even had to polish the steel wheel rims.

We had constant review type parades until finally, some weeks later, the entire division staged a protest parade as we were all very weary and wanted a little time to relax. We still had all of the usual horse work to do, like cleaning lines, watering, feeding, grooming, and exercising horses, plus guard and picket duties. This protest parade was a model of order and discipline, but officers and N.C.O.'s were excluded. Temporary section and battery leaders were appointed. On the day, the General agreed to hear our plea.

We paraded in a large paddock, an excellent, well-disciplined parade. A trumpet fanfare greeted the General's arrival. A short, written request was presented to him. We marched off in our units after these requests were immediately granted as being sensible and reasonable.

It was the smartest parade I had ever seen, taking into account the ragged condition of our clothing. Most of us blamed the Railway Union leader in Australia for all this. Chifley had called a nationwide strike and had blocked all sorts of stores from getting to us in France.

In early December we made a three-day march from Brancourt to Hautmont. The whole brigade's horse strength was stabled in a huge salt factory there. The men were comfortably billeted in private homes. People waited on us hand and foot. After early morning stables, the parade was not until 9.30 am. In the afternoon there was a variety of classes one could attend.

We were close to Maubeuge, a big mining town south of Brussels. This place still had a civilian population and was not badly knocked about, except for some large mines the Huns had exploded. The population consisted entirely of old men and women; the young were in forced labour camps in Germany. The capture of Maubeuge severed the last German artery on that section of the Western front, making it impossible for the enemy to shift his forces to meet any new attack.

The shops were empty, but the estaminets dug up a lot of champagne from extraordinary places. Some of us breakfasted on this fare one morning. We finished up driving an abandoned Jerry lorrie into a huge mine crater in the middle of the town square.

We paraded and were inspected by the Prince of Wales, most unwillingly on our part because we still had not been issued with new uniforms. He must have been equally reluctant to walk down the lines of a ragged, villainous looking lot. We were ordered to wear greatcoats to hide our uniforms, but when the C.O. saw the state of our greatcoats, he said, 'For God's sake, take them off.'

Because I could speak French, I was given the job of advertising the pending auction sale of some of our livestock. The horses graded first class were to return to England. Second class horses (some a bit the worse for wear) and our mules were to be sold to French farmers. They desperately needed horses as the Huns had seized their livestock.

My job entailed riding out every day with a mate, visiting local mayors in the villages in a wide radius around Maubeuge, giving them posters and telling them what type of horses and mules were available for sale.

We had a whale of a time. Every child and all of the girls had to try on our hats and learn a few words of Australian, mainly *Good Oh*. Meanwhile, we consumed large quantities of food and wine pressed on us by their gleeful families. We always arrived home feeling very happy. It's just as well that our mounts knew the way.

There are two little pack ponies at the depot, having come down from the line a few days ago, called 'Dilly' and 'Dally.' They have been out practically since the beginning of the war. They are a beautifully matched pair, standing barely 13 hands, and as hard as nails. They can go like the wind. It would be a shame to sell them separately, as they have, according to their papers, always been together.

It was funny at the auction, the auctioneer wanting to know 'who the "b" hell Monsieur Jim was?' The C.O. wanted to know what tales I had been telling.

For several days after the auction, mules and horses kept arriving back at the battery, after having slipped away from their new owners. They must have missed their mates.

I could have made a packet selling odd horses under the table. My two fine wheel horses went back in England, despite the fact that they both had minor wounds.

The war horse

The artillery and cavalry units could not have functioned without horses, though each had needed a different type of training. After the war ended, disposing of thousands of horses became a major issue. They could not be brought back to Australia in such vast numbers and priority had to be given to returning sick and wounded soldiers. A brief look at training a war horse follows.

Daily Mercury[195]

2 November 1918. The real war horse has quite a long education before he is proficient, and an education as severe and comprehensive as that of the recruit who ultimately rides him into battle.

It was in no small way due to the mettle of the horses they rode that Lord French was able to say of the British cavalry at the first battle of the Marne, that they were able to do as they liked with the enemy. The well-bred cavalry horse possesses a highly-strung nervous system, but when properly trained, he will face barbed wire and even rush an entanglement when put to it, regardless of lacerated legs and flanks. But his education is begun carefully, or he may be ruined by a few careless lessons.

His education must not begin too soon after being brought to camp or his legs will not stand the strain. The first step is the most important. If he is terror-stricken, or his temper aroused, he may never get over the incident. He is walked around free from the leading rein. After he has been accustomed to having a man mount rapidly onto his sensitive back, he is taught to kneel with his rider.

This is an elaborate lesson. The first stage consists in getting him to bend his forelegs slightly before he gets to the stage of lying down on his side. He must be taught to pull up in his own length from a gallop, to stand steady while his rider fires from his back and to lie still on the ground while he is being used as cover for his rider, who snipes over his side.

One of the difficult things required of a war horse is to get familiarised with weapons fighting on his back. Here the greatest care is taken, or he may be frightened at first and never recover his nerve. In real warfare it is a common trick for a cavalryman to aim his first blow at the opponent's horse. This is especially the case with lancers, for no horse can stand being pricked on the nostril or lip.

It is a peculiar fact, however, that when a horse knows his rider well, he will face blows if properly handled, such as would not usually be expected of him. A brigade has been known to go through three lines of bayonets or through a barbed-wire entanglement and trampling everything underfoot as if it were straw.

A horseman finds the death of so many animals heartbreaking. These horses are another responsibility as gunners have to save not only themselves but their mounts while bombs or German artillery barrages rain down upon them. Wounded horses need attention from the field vets, stationed behind the lines. Once recovered, the remounts are sent to any battery needing replacements, which proved a problem in earlier years as horses tried to return to their former owners. Later photographs show details painted on their hindquarters in an effort to reunite them with riders to whom they have formed strong attachments.

Hundreds of wounded horses are tended day after day by the Army Veterinary Corps. The wounds of animals are as carefully treated as those of the soldiers. Base hospitals and homes are utilised to nurse the injured chargers back to health.

The veterinary surgeon at the front needs to be a brave soldier, for he has to round up panic-stricken horses whilst shells are whistling over his head. Unless a horse is too badly mutilated to stand, it rushes blindly about the battlefield, maddened by the pain of its wound. It is these animals which the vets capture and place in special horse-ambulances. A soldier-attendant generally sits on the animal to keep it tranquil.

CHAPTER 41

LEAVING THE BATTLEFIELD

*'Shall I look forth on some new greater sky
Where stiller galaxies of stars unfold?'*
N.J. Cocks[196]

Photographs in the Australian War Memorial show the 8th Field Artillery Brigade amassed in a Flanders field, awaiting orders. Soldiers crouched around smoky fires burning in empty petrol containers. Many pictures depict the devastation of surrounding towns such as Péronne, Corbie and Amiens. A recurring image is long lines of limbers, drawn by stalwart horses.

Jim's artillery war was finally over, but he would soon fight a different one in the form of the Spanish influenza.

Jim Armitage's diary[197]

I applied for early repatriation to Australia on the grounds of being a student, then got word that Father and Mother were coming to England to meet me, so I applied for discharge in England. Both applications were granted, and this caused some confusion. The army was happy to give me my discharge. I had to sign away all claims on the Australian government, such as the cost of returning to Australia and repatriation benefits of any kind.

Before I left France, Europe and England were smitten with a terrible type of flu which killed hundreds of thousands of people. We all got it in our billet and, of those who went to hospital, nearly all of them died.

Snowy Hamilton, John Roxburgh and I were treated by the old woman who owned our billet. She was so good to us. She dosed us up on herbs that she collected from the countryside, and we made a remarkable recovery.

After spending weeks in an English holding camp, I became a guinea pig for testing all sorts of injected anti-flu drugs. I got my discharge in time for a joyful family reunion.

We bought an old Sunbeam car and toured England, very pleasantly accompanied by my friend, John Roxburgh. When we finally boarded the steamer to return home, I was in civilian clothes and my war was over.

Eternal remembrance
Queensland Figaro[198]

ETERNITY
Shall I look forth on some new greater sky
Where stiller galaxies of stars unfold?
Or by some fireside nook shall tales be told
Of how we fared and fought, my friend and I?
—*N. J. Cocks*

CHAPTER 42

ALWAYS THERE ARE POPPIES

'Their blood-red beauty the only spot of colour in this hallowed place.'
Lucy Morris[199]

Red poppies

The journalist Lucy Morris visited the war graveyards in 1921. Her report below makes sombre but necessary reading as she comments on the meaning of the red poppies.

The Daily Mail[200]

Flanders. 1921. We come to Pozieres with its simple Column of Commemoration to the Australian and New Zealand soldiers who sleep in this land so far from home.

Pozieres Cemetery, with row upon row, and row upon row of simple, rough wooden crosses so close together, each with the short inscription, which one must bend low to read. Row upon row, row upon row; standing in their serried ranks like soldiers whose memories they perpetuate were wont to do, and who now lie awaiting the final call of the Resurrection.

Here and there are slightly larger crosses painted white, in which case the inscription is in plain black letters, with the addition maybe of a tiny painted kangaroo or boomerang appearing strangely in this foreign God's Acre.

One passes between the rows, for there are no mounds, and reads a few names. Then come more rows where each cross bears the title, saddest of all, 'Unknown British Soldier,' or 'Unknown Soldier A.I.F.' It appears with painful monotony upon graves where no mother comes to weep and pray, knowing it to be her son's last resting place. Wild grasses do not trespass here, for the surface of the ground has been prepared for turf. But poppies, not to be displaced, cluster tenaciously about the shafts of crosses, their blood-red beauty the only spot of colour in this hallowed place. Always there are poppies.

The Diggers know every inch of the Somme valleys from the sea at Abbeville to Peronne; they know every town, village, and farm. Five of their splendid memorial obelisks stand in the Somme country, where they can be seen for miles around. Not a man of those who returned will ever forget the poppies of that countryside or its resolute warm-hearted people. It is a broad, rolling country. The main uplands and valleys lie east and west, but near the river undulations are much more confused.

From Amiens centre, five straight main roads – Roman roads – run out to all points of the compass. Amiens is the centre of a spider-web of roads. On the eastern side of the township especially, crossing roads run like the outer filaments of a web. At every road crossing, at every knot in the web, stands a farming hamlet or small village. Trees bedeck the winding riverbed with woods and copses atop most of the hills. Here and there are, or were, larger towns like Villers-Bretonneux, Corbie, Albert, Bray, and Peronne. These were the market centres. Smaller places were collections of farmers' homes, for in the Somme district, unlike Belgium, there are few farmhouses built on farmlands to which they belong.

The lands, unfenced and unhedged, surround the village. The villages are located three or four kilometres from each other upon almost a mathematical plan, and indicative of an even distribution of the farmlands among the inhabitants. The farmers' families are out at sun-up and remain out till dark, men and women alike. When the war called away the menfolk, women heroically continued their time-old working system.

Australian soldiers, billeted upon these families, came near to replacing the absent sons and brothers. They did odd jobs about the homes, helped drive the cows in, often had hot baths and washing done at Madame's. They clustered in every open doorway in the evening's leisure to yarn with the family in the *compree* language. What wonder that French people said of the Diggers that they fought in the defence of this country as if it were their own! ...

Flowers grow from poppy seeds, reviving grateful memories for the living, and poignant grief for the dead. They would be in intimate association with the graves where the hopes of countless Australian families of this generation are buried; but they would speak also of the restoration of that countryside which followed our soldiers' heroic efforts, and of the rich reputation won there for the name of Australia ...

Poppies spring so thickly and unbidden in these hallowed grounds. There amongst the graves of my countrymen I stood silent. Over the cemetery lay a brooding peacefulness; not a sound to be heard save the twittering of birds; nothing to be seen but the mute rows of crosses; the wilderness of grass and flowers stretching across the plain to the bare trees outlined against the sky.

A memorial wall has been commenced. In time there will be erected, as is the old French custom, a figure of the suffering Saviour. We take a last lingering look, for we may never pass this way again.

Summer grass and flowers will wither and fade with autumn's chilly blasts. The snows of winter will mantle the ground and drift against the crosses. We shall not be here to see it; but can we ever forget the crosses of Pozieres and our men and women who fought and died in freedom's cause?

Back among the ruins

As the soldiers farewelled the land of Flanders, they also farewelled friends they had made. Local children promised to tend the graves of the fallen, and to never forget what Australians had done for them and their future security. The following is a report from a correspondent visiting the area in 1921.

The Herald[201]

Here in Picardy, two of the greatest battles in history were fought. People of the devastated zone, whom the blasting breath of the fiery furnace could scarcely drive from their homes, are back among the ruins, clinging to the site of old habitations with a zeal pathetic but sublime.

'Villers-Bretonneux, a name to which Australian hearts will ever respond with a thrill of pride,' we are told by a girl who could have been no older than seven when the war broke out. Though these children could not remember all that occurred, their parents spoke warmly of the Australians. Children loved those brave soldiers who came from so far, far away.

The youngster looked sadly into the distance. Suddenly her eyes lit upon one prominent sign in the village, and her face brightened up. Painted in huge black letters on the front of the only house left standing were two words: *VIVE MELBOURNE.*

The little girl, joined by others younger than herself, told how the Corona School in Melbourne had sent them Christmas trees in 1919 and 1920. One little urchin, who typified life among the ruins, asked me wistfully if they would get another this year. Of course I said yes, for who had the heart to dampen what little enthusiasm remains amongst all the desolation?

'Will you children look after these graves when we have gone?' I asked.

'Oh, yes, M'sieur!' was her reply. 'We shall honour and reverence your dead when we have grown up and our parents have passed away. We feel so sad when we think of their dear ones who live so far beyond the sea.'

Our glorious dead

A bereaved Australian mother, visiting her son's grave in France, wrote the below to a friend in Brisbane.

Armidale Express[202]

His grave is at present covered with beautiful crimson poppies; in fact, the whole of the cemetery is one vast blaze of blooming crimson poppies, a vivid reminder of what has been done by the brave men who are sleeping their last sleep in this quiet section of God's Acre. It is very pathetic to see the tiny French kiddies, who are constant visitors to this spot, where rest some of Australia's bravest and best sons, gather the poppy and make them into wreaths and crosses to put on the graves of our glorious dead.

CHAPTER 43

TURMOIL AFTER THE WAR

'As the hospital came into sight, Leo asked me if he could say goodbye properly, but I wouldn't let him – for which I was to break my heart within three weeks.'
Jean Curlewis[203]

The Spanish influenza

The Spanish Flu epidemic had begun during the war and reached Australia in early 1919. Two thousand beds were available in NSW hospitals, but over 25,000 patients needed hospitalisation. Hundreds of temporary emergency wards were established in schools, large halls, factories or other places containing sufficient amenities for such overwhelming numbers. Fifteen thousand Australians died in under one year. Man, woman or child, young or old, rich or poor; the virus did not discriminate.

Soldiers, nurses and medical staff had returned to their homes and families after the war. Doctor Davenport was supervising an emergency hospital in Concord West, NSW, when Jean Curlewis began working as a voluntary aide in 1919. Jean's fiancé, Doctor Leo Charlton, contracted influenza, and she wept bitterly on hearing that news.

As the daughter of Ethel Turner, the famed Australian author of *Seven Little Australians*, Jean inherited her mother's gift for writing wonderful prose. Jean penned numerous letters to her family during late-night shifts when the wards were quiet. Those letters, preserved in her family archives for almost one hundred years, have now been transcribed by me and finally reveal the reality of life for Jean, her fellow workers, and the patients during the 1919 Spanish Flu epidemic.

Letters from Jean Curlewis[204]

Sydney. April 1919. Influenza broke through the quarantine barrier in February. At the beginning of April things were so serious, and the shortage of nurses so great, that my family sportingly allowed me to enlist.

8 April. Mother and I went to the Red Cross Head Office where they enrolled me as a Voluntary Aide probationer for the Walker Emergency Hospital on the Parramatta River. We were to actually nurse the patients but actually to be exempt from any responsibility.

It was significant of the shortage, I think, that they took any girl as young and as entirely untrained as I (and so useless looking) on first sight …

9 April. Leo Charlton[*] came for lunch to take me up there (I had rung him up the night before) … He himself was rather worried. Incidentally, he thought I didn't know the duties of a probationer and was extremely doubtful of how I should get on, I suspect.

We went down to Milson's Point where my brother, Adrian,[†] who was curiously impressed by my going, had cut school to say

---

*   Fiancé of Jean Curlewis.
†   Adrian Curlewis.

goodbye to me. He presented me with his wristlet watch for the duration. Enjoyed the interested glance that the man at the ticket window gave me when Leo bought my ticket for Walker Wharf and told the boat to stop at that shunned and quarantined ground.

So then I landed at the wharf with the lower bridge over it, that was afterwards to have such terrible memories and walked up the paved path to the huge building.

A slim girl in white, with her mask thrown back, took me into the big, big hall with the polished floor and the glass doors at the end, then into a sitting room where she began to take down my particulars. 'Name? Oh, are you Ethel Turner's daughter? How exciting! Health? You look frail, Miss Curlewis.'

Me – frail? I soon discovered that she wasn't an aide but the Matron and felt slightly upset but she was very kind. She gave me a clean gown to wear, a shapeless thing of unbleached calico from neck to ankle and to the wrist, and an overhead mask and a toothbrush.

She led me through the hall and along a corridor into a grassy quadrangle, with a fountain in it, in the cloisters around which were rows of beds and suggestive white screens with red crosses on them. I had a glimpse of the first flu patient I have ever seen, a flushed face and a tangle of black hair on a white pillow …

I put on my gown and mask as artistically as possible, too artistically to be hygienic as I left exposed a fraction of hair and caused an aide who saw me to think that, though the new arrival made an ornament for the front hall, she would not have sense enough for the wards.

Found my way down to afternoon tea in Matron's dining room, protested that tea was an unnecessary luxury but was squashed with 'Aides eat when they are told. You are expected to keep your strength up.' The hospital had been open eight days, and they have had nine deaths, eight men and one woman.

I was then put on as Matron's orderly to answer the telephone, mostly enquiries as to the conditions of patients, which I got from a list on the wall marked with code letters. D.I. was dangerously ill; N.W. not so well; N.C. no change; C. convalescent. It was hard at first to give shocking news, but it was curious how quietly the voices at the other end took even the worst reports – scarcely a further question, except once or twice, 'Is he conscious?'

Much coming and going of masked and bewildering figures among which was the tall, straight, young doctor (a returned soldier) named Percival Davenport who stood out clearly. He spoke to me curtly once and later unexpectedly apologized.

Once, a man in a black mask and gloves came to enquire for 'the keys of the mortuary, the death certificates and a tape measure to measure the bodies.' He was from Wood and Coffill Undertakers. It made things rather real.

Doctor Davenport, as I mentioned previously, is a returned soldier, brief spoken, sharp-eyed, and decidedly kind. Jerks out sentences like 'Aide, you needn't stand, sit down. Aide, you can save yourself by doing so and so,' which, considering the number of sisters, nurses and aides flitting round here, shows a capacity for detail that is rather remarkable.

The fate of Jeanne Plouvier

I searched for information on Doctor Percy Davenport. In the Trove archives, I found several references to his name, including the birth notice for a son born in October 1918. Notably, I discovered the following request to the *Singleton Argus*, asking them to print his letter below about a young woman he knew whilst with the 2nd Australian Division in Steenwerck, Flanders.

Singleton Argus[205]

Doctor Percival Davenport, of Singleton, in forwarding the following letter just received by him from France, says:

> 'In translating it from the French I am afraid I have not been able to adequately convey the sense of pathos which permeates the original. Letters such as this help one to realise a little the way in which the people of France are suffering, and yet we have in our midst so-called men clamouring for an immediate peace, i.e., defeat. I might add that the writer of the enclosed letter, a girl in northern France, has lost in this war all the male members of her family, her father and three brothers.
> Doctor Percival Davenport'

To recap, Jeanne Plouvier, identified previously by Sir John Monash in one diary entry, had written to both Monash and Davenport about losing her mother in the panic when fleeing Steenwerck during the town's bombing. She had reached comparative safety in Normandy. The first part of her letter is on pages 17–18 and the remainder follows here:

The Sydney Morning Herald[206]

> One day your comrades will tell you what the retreat from Flanders has been like and, at Steenwerck, the Boches were there. We had to go and now I have nothing. I do not know where my mother is, and I have lost my sisters and so you understand my grief. We poor women of France know what

war is. One day we are happy and contented, the next day – nothing. But when the day comes when we are victorious, we shall forget that we have ever been unhappy.

I do so hope that you will write to me and sometimes think of the happy times passed at Steenwerck with the officers of the 2nd Australian Division.

What misery when we had to go, leaving there the Boches.

Jeanne Plouvier

•

During a final search for the surname 'Plouvier', I found a one-line reference in a February 1928 edition of the *Catholic Advocate* newspaper: 'Madame Louise Plouvier, of St. Catherine-les-Arras, France, has been awarded a Vermeil Cross with silver bar in recognition of 52 years' service to the parish.'[207]

The article had been published over nine years after the war ended. Such prestigious awards were endorsed by the Vatican, so were newsworthy across the Catholic world. This snippet gave me the clue to concluding the Plouvier story.

After the Armistice, Jeanne returned to Calais, and received news through her church network that her mother was alive. I can only imagine their tearful, yet joyous, reunion.

Photographs of Steenwerck church and their chateau depict a mass of stone and rubble. They did not return to live in Steenwerck.

The chateau

The following article was published a month after the end of WWI and captures visions of the town and the chateau at Steenwerck in the month after the armistice. Steenwerck was forever changed by the war.

The Urana Independent[208]

December 1918. A chilling nothingness. Substance – yes, but substance that has no shape, no meaning. Great, white-bleeding trunks of trees; a countryside gaping with wounds; raw earth laid bare to a protesting sky; a crumbled ruin of a house.

Inside a litter, knee-deep, of unrecognisable things, of strips, and bits and pieces; an iron stanchion that shows where a gate has been and, beside it, a spare yard of brick wall that is all of the lodge. Crows and carrion birds are croaking over the ruins …

Desolation, oh such utter, utter desolation. Only the sky has not changed, for the Germans cannot change that.

EPILOGUE

TIME AND ETERNITY

> 'Rank, fortune, love, earth's highest bliss,
> All life can yield, of sweet or splendid,
> Are but a thing that scarcely is,
> When, lo! its mortal date is ended!'
> Gerald Griffin[209]

The voices in this book have spoken about both the horrors of war and the endurance of the human spirit. Jim Armitage's wartime diary has shown us despair and atrocity, but also moments of humour and friendship. Sir John Monash's words and deeds have demonstrated the power of strong leadership and decisive strategy. The numerous soldiers, nurses, doctors and gunners illuminated the shades and subtleties of wartime experiences.

I have set out to share tales that had previously been untold, and to share voices that had previously been unheard. My journey has involved many coincidences and unveiled many unexpected connections.

After having the privilege of reading Jim Armitage's wartime diary, life delivered me the letter from that refugee fleeing Steenwerck. I then discovered Jim Armitage's link to the Snow Ghost commando, Lieutenant Dalton Thomas Walker Neville. This led to me uncovering Dalton's ties to Sir William Birdwood, whose connection to Sir John Monash led to young Jeanne Plouvier and Major Walker. Ultimately, that letter connected me, through Steenwerck, to Jim Armitage, and to you, my readers. This has indeed proven to be six degrees of separation.

Anzac voices continue to speak to us, through time and through memory.

I leave the final words to Sir John Monash, whose dedication, brilliance and perseverance have helped to keep the Anzac spirit alive here in Australia.

John Monash's Anzac Day address, 25 April 1930
Northern Territory Times[210]

> Engraved on the heart of every true Australian is the memory of those brave men who on far-off fields of battle put the seal on Australia's honour and nationhood with their lives.
>
> With a common impulse, therefore, the people as a nation pause each year to pay their tribute of remembrance and to commemorate in a spirit of love and gratitude the heroism and sacrifice of those who did not return. Each year finds this sentiment deeper and more abiding because time, which proves all things, is confirming the debt we owe to those who fought so valiantly and died so nobly in their country's cause.
>
> Deep as may be the sorrow, there is also the feeling of pride that, on Anzac Day, Australians faced their grim baptism of fire in one of the most hazardous adventures in history with a clash and daring, an abandon of courage that earned them enduring fame. Against the background of years, the message of Anzac Day stands out in shining letters. It is 'courage and fortitude.'

Today, when the problems of peace, some of them the aftermath of war, press so heavily upon us as a people, it should be our inspiration. Not only should we follow the precept, but also the example set by our soldiers, who never wavered.

The fundamental lesson taught by the Great War was co-ordination and solid undivided efforts by millions of men and women united in a common objective to make the world safe for democracy.

The soldiers of Australia and the rest of the British Empire, though composing all shades of religious and political opinion, submerged their individual beliefs in that of patriotism and love of liberty; they united in this common objective. Can we not do the same today? Are we going to let down the Australians who gave their all – their lives – in the one hope of making this fair land safe for the principles which the previous speaker has enunciated?

We find Australia today torn asunder within! The vast majority of her people are eaten up with selfishness! Is this the spirit of Anzac? Can we not say instead that we will take the great lesson to heart and cure the disease which is spreading its octopus-like grip over our whole national life?

In Australia we have a most wonderful heritage. From Tasmania in the South to our own Darwin in the North we cover a vast area. Practically all of the world's great sources of wealth are here. We are not afflicted by earthquakes, blizzards, and other similar agencies of destruction so common in many other countries. Yet we find we are still content bowing to the unfortunate prevalence of the lack of patriotism in our midst which has been usurped, for the present at any rate, by that evil agent 'self.'

In this demonstration of love of country, the grinning monster 'self' has no place, and the result is the point of view.

Let us do as the Anzacs did. Get together. Let us learn to be tolerant and not intolerant of the views of others. Let us have construction, not destruction; harmony, not discord; a little faith in one another. If we can only do this and learn the lessons of Anzac, then this country will leap ahead and, in a short space of time, have millions in both people and wealth.

BIOGRAPHY OF

James (Jim) Armitage

by Jane Suranyi, Jim's niece

James Ramsay Armitage was born in Camden on 5 May 1899 to James Robertson Armitage and Margaret Alston Armitage, née Smith. He attended Sydney Grammar School on College Street in Sydney, where his name is listed on the Great War honour roll.

'Uncle Jim', as all his family knew him, was a gentleman in every sense of the word. I had the privilege of visiting him with my young son during his last years. Whether it was morning or afternoon tea, he would always have biscuits and orange juice ready, a story to tell and a game to play, much to my son's delight.

In his childhood, he often visited his grandparents in Marrickville, considering it a real treat to ride in their Coach and Four through the woodblock-paved streets of Sydney City.

Later, when travelling in his family's tourer, Jim's father would have to reverse up the hill to their house with Jim in the front seat and his wife in the back, since it did not have the power to go up forward.

When Jim turned eighteen, he enlisted for general service in the Australian Imperial Force at Victoria Barracks in Sydney. Gunner Armitage served in the 8th Field Artillery Brigade throughout the battlefields of France, from Villers-Bretonneux to Peronne and Montbrehain in 1918. Here, he engaged in some of the fiercest fighting of the war.

After the war, Jim eventually made his way back to Australia to live with his parents at Sutton Forest where he farmed the land adjoining their house.

He re-enlisted in the A.I.F. from 1922 to 1924. During this time, he met a Miss Lurline Buchanan, who was living at Moss Vale with her mother, older sister and younger brother. Lurl and Jim were married in 1925 and went on to manage Killarney Station at Narrabri.

In 1932, they bought their own property of about 5,000 acres on the Namoi River near Boggabri, which they named Kurra Wombi. Jim started a neighbourhood cooperative for the purchase of machinery and supported the local agricultural show and picnic races.

When WWII loomed, Jim re-enlisted in the A.I.F. again where he served in the Boggabri Troop of the 24th Light Horse Regiment, including a promotion to Lieutenant in 1940.

After the unit disbanded in late 1944, Jim decided to return home after a particularly severe flood devastated the farm. Lurl had been left rescuing sheep from the floodwaters on her own after their hired man decided it was too dangerous!

Jim and Lurl retired to Mt Wilson in the 1950s, building a house and creating a beautiful garden. In the 1970s they moved to Armidale, where they again built a house and cultivated a garden. Wherever they lived, Lurl and Jim enjoyed entertaining, camping and picnics.

As Lurl's health declined, they moved to a retirement village at Kincumber on the NSW Central Coast, where Jim helped care for her until she passed away in 1996.

On 2 November 1998, Jim was presented with the Chevalier Legion of Honour Medal by the French Consul-General to Australia, Mr Jean-Claude Poimboeuf. On Anzac Day 1999, the

Australian government awarded Jim a medal at a ceremony at Heazlett Park, Avoca Beach.

In May of the same year, Jim celebrated his 100th birthday surrounded by his family and friends. When everyone else had gone, it was time for biscuits and orange juice.

In a rare interview several months before his death, Jim spoke to journalist Joanne McCarthy, from the *Newcastle Herald*, who wrote an article titled 'Silent Memories' in 1998.

Newcastle Herald[211]

> War veterans tend to settle into one of two camps. The smaller camp is of men who are willing to talk to their families, friends, and the occasional journalist about their war years.
>
> The larger camp, by far, includes men such as World War I veteran Jim Armitage of Kincumber, who won't talk about it.
>
> Out of politeness, Mr Armitage will tell you how his money belt, filled with the proceeds from two-up games, came between him and an exploding shell. He will even laugh when you joke that two-up saved his life.
>
> He will talk about the work of artillery and infantry on the battlefield and their respective jobs.
>
> He will even talk about how he got the job of selling the infantry's horses in France after the war because he was about the only Australian who could speak French. But Mr Armitage will not speak about the horrors he saw and experienced in the French Villers-Bretonneux area, the detail of which is kept in a diary that he wrote in 1918 …
>
> 'I don't know how many people have quoted me the line that war is 90 per cent boredom and 10 per cent excitement …

'That's not boredom. It is something else that only someone who has been there can relate to but it's not boredom.'

Mr Armitage has never been keen on Anzac Day events, for no other reason than he feels 'notorious' as one of the few surviving WWI veterans ... He does not like the label ...

He turns 100 in May ... He appreciates the feeling behind the fuss that will be made of him on his birthday but remains removed from it ...

•

On his 100th birthday, he was surrounded by his family, friends, and acquaintances. He remembered earlier days, as in a photograph of himself and his wife, Lurline, at Killarney, seated on horseback. Jim died on 16 November 1999. His ashes were scattered at Northern Suburbs Crematorium with those of his wife. As a relative stated at his funeral, 'Uncle Jim was indeed one in a million.'

Timeline of the battles

Battle of the Somme, 1 July–18 November 1916

The Battle of the Somme was one of the largest and deadliest battles of World War I and involved millions of soldiers from the Allied and Central Powers.

Battle of Messines, 7–14 June 1917

The Battle of Messines was a significant engagement during World War I on the Western Front when German forces held the Messines Ridge. Allied tunnellers had secretly dug deep tunnels and successfully detonated nineteen mines under the German trenches. The explosions created enormous craters and demoralised the German troops, who surrendered.

Battle of Hamel, 4 July 1917

The Battle of Hamel was the first operation planned by Lieutenant-General John Monash since taking command of the Australian Corps. Regarded as a small-scale but brilliant attack involving Australian and American soldiers fighting together on the battlefield for the first time, around 1600 enemy soldiers were captured in just over 90 minutes. However, the number killed or wounded in the battle amounted to 1380 Australian and US personnel.

Battle of Passchendaele, 31 July–10 November 1917

Passchendaele, on the last ridge east of Ypres, 8 kilometres from Roulers, was a junction of the Bruges railway. Roulers Station was on the main supply route for the German 4th Army. Once Passchendaele Ridge had been taken, the Allied advance could continue. Canadian Corps captured Passchendaele in November.

Battle of Polygon Wood, 20 September 1917

In 1917, Australian soldiers added to their already magnificent reputation with the part they played in the third battle of Ypres. Destroyed by the huge quantity of shellfire from both sides, much of the woodland area changed hands several times during the course of the war. In 1918, General Birdwood spoke with pride about the Australian soldiers accomplishing victory at Polygon and on the Menin Road.

Battle of Hellfire Corner, 1915–1918

During World War I, Hellfire Corner was a significant landmark in the Ypres Salient battlefields and was fought over throughout the war. An important transport hub on the Menin Road, from Ypres to frontline trenches, Hellfire Corner was in a particularly exposed area, remaining under constant observation and within easy range of German guns, earning its grim nickname as 'the most dangerous corner on Earth'.

Fourth Battle of Ypres, 7–29 April 1918

Also known as the Battle of the Lys, during which Steenwerck was heavily bombed, it was part of the German Spring Offensive, in which their aim was to capture Ypres and drive the Allies back toward the English Channel ports.

Second Battle of the Marne, 15–18 July 1918

Allied tanks again proved their worth, stopping the German army by smashing its right flank, sending their divisions into retreat.

Battle of Amiens, 8 August–11 November 1918

The Battle of Amiens marked the beginning of The Hundred Days, dating from 8 August to 11 November, a line of Western Front offensives that successfully led to the collapse of the German army, helping to end the war.

Third Battle of Picardy, 3 September 1918

Part of the Hundred Days Offensive and considered to be one of the greatest achievements of the war, Allied forces advanced more than 11 kilometres (7 miles) on the first day. Troops included General Henry Rawlinson's British Fourth Army, with nine of nineteen divisions supplied by General John Monash's Australian Corps and Lieutenant-General Currie's Canadian Corps.

Battle of Péronne, 31 August–2 September 1918

Germans attacked and heavily shelled the French town of Péronne. Outnumbered Australians were pushed back off the summit of Mont St. Quentin, with much hand-to-hand combat. Relief battalions and reinforcements retook Péronne at the cost of 3000 casualties.

Battle of St. Quentin Canal, 29 September–23 October 1918

The Battle of St. Quentin Canal involved British, Australian and American forces operating as part of the British Fourth Army under General Sir Henry Rawlinson, with sections of the British Third Army also supporting the attack further north.

Battle of Montbrehain, 5 October 1918

Early in the morning on 5 October 1918, the 6th Brigade A.I.F. succeeded in occupying Montbrehain village, capturing over 400 German prisoners, at the loss of 430 Australian casualties. This would be the last battle to involve Australian infantry on the Western Front.

Final Battle of Mons, 11 November 1918

Fought on World War I's final day, Canadian Corps recaptured Mons in Belgium, a town that had been held by the Germans since the initial Battle of Mons in August 1914. A Canadian soldier, Private George Price, was shot by a sniper at 10.58 am, two minutes before the armistice began.

He was the final soldier to die on that day.

ACKNOWLEDGEMENTS

Australian War Memorial, Canberra.

City of Canada Bay Heritage Society, Concord NSW.

The Monash family for permission to reprint extracts of Monash diaries and letters.

The Suranyi family for permission to reprint extracts of Jim Armitage's diary.

Trove, State Library of NSW, Sydney. Numerous references.

Phillipa Poole for permission to reprint Jean Curlewis' letters.

The McNicoll family for permission to reprint *Epitaph to a Soldier*.

Sydney Grammar school – Honour Board information.

Newcastle Herald for permission to reprint extracts of Joanne McCarthy's article.

Sophie Hamley, Libby Turner, Annie Zhang, Jacquie Brown, Madison Garratt of Hachette.

My agent, Selwa Anthony, for her wonderful support during the past few years.

ABOUT THE AUTHOR

Patricia Skehan is a founding executive member of Concord Heritage, now City of Canada Bay Heritage Society. She guest-speaks for organisations including Rotary, Probus and VIEW clubs and historical societies, and lectures for U3A. She has presented heritage talks on FM radio and has been published nationally. Patricia conducts tours at Yaralla and Rivendell estates in Concord West. Since 1999, Patricia has travelled across NSW to give over 1000 heritage talks on 16 different subjects. She travelled to Britain in 2001 and 2005, researching the Thomas Walker family's royal connections at the University of Cambridge.

In 2013, Ethel Turner's granddaughter asked Patricia to transcribe letters from Jean Curlewis to her famous mother, written while a volunteer nursing aide during the 1919 Spanish Flu epidemic. Sourcing rare archives from Royal Prince Alfred Hospital, the Red Cross, Sydney University, Trove newspaper collections and museum sources, she found clues about Anzac secrets when given the seemingly unrelated diary of a young WWI soldier.

Patricia was guest speaker at the Cenotaph in Sydney on Armistice Day 2020; her talk on the impact of the Spanish flu epidemic was televised nationally.

Born on Armistice Day, 1946, Patricia is married to a retired police sergeant. They live on the Central Coast.

ENDNOTES

1. Marsden, William. (1922, 23 December). What is Time? *Newcastle Morning Herald*, 5. nla/140011798.
2. Armitage, James. WWI diary. Reprinted with permission from the Suranyi family.
3. Ibid.
4. Campbell, Norman. (1936, 26 January). General Monash. *The Sydney Morning Herald*, 13. nla/17137438.
5. The Walrus. (1929, 25 April). Disobeyed orders. *The Herald, Melbourne*, 1. nla/244450061.
6. London Representative. (1919, 20 June). General Monash's staff. *The Sun*, 4. nla/221449603.
7. Ibid.
8. Ibid.
9. Hunn, Stewart. (1919, 20 June). Lost diaries. *The Sun*, 4. nla/221449603.
10. Uncredited. (1919, 27 June). The Aussie as a Spy. *The Richmond River Herald*, 8. nla/132523410.
11. Bell, Edward. (1918, 19 September). Cobbers. *The Sun*, 5. nla/15908152.
12. Uncredited. (1916, 1 July). Ducked my head. *Don Dorrigo Gazette*, 3. nla/172002997.
13. Dawson, Doctor Joseph. (1915, 30 December). The rendezvous of empire. *The Register*, 6. nla/59981508.
14. Ibid.
15. Special Correspondent at the Front of the Australian Press Association. (1917, 17 October). Mud! Flanders, a morass. *The Argus*, 9. nla/1656795.

16 Stacy, Harold S. (1924, 17 December). Distinguished surgeon. *Newcastle Morning Herald*, 8. nla/137773087.
17 Monash, John. (1935, 2 January). An Australian soldier's letters. *Sydney Mail*, 36. nla/166110849.
18 Campbell, Norman. (1935, 5 March). General Monash. Some sidelights. *Daily Mercury*, 8. nla/173070200.
19 Monash, John. (1934, 6 December). 'Anzac' name disappears. *The Herald*, 7. nla/243083353.
20 Hansen, Stewart. (1916, 22 April). Abolishing Anzac name. *Williamstown Advertiser*, 2. nla/87750939.
21 Uncredited. (1916, 17 July). Anzac, a name sacrosanct. *Casterton News*, 4. nla/74486308.
22 V.F.M. (1922, 17 August). Destiny. *Evening News*, 4. nla/118859174.
23 Uncredited. (1917, 18 December). 2nd Casualty Clearing Station. *Daily Mercury*, 3. nla/173909402.
24 Digger. (1919, 5 February). Local and General. *Zeehan Herald*, 2. nla/84293866.
25 Parsons, Harold. (1917, 4 August). A soldier's letter. *Oakleigh and Caulfield Times*, 1. nla/88808152.
26 Downing, Wilbert. (1919, 26 July). The massacre at Fleurbaix. *Geelong Advertiser*, 9. nla/165750121.
27 Ibid.
28 Johnson, Norman. (1917, 24 November). Still alive. *The Capricornian*, 21. nla/69806181.
29 Downing, Wilbert. (1919, 26 July). The massacre at Fleurbaix, *Geelong Advertiser*, 9. nla/165750121.
30 Uncredited. (1917, 18 December). MacKay Nurse in France. *Daily Mercury*, 3. nla/173909402.
31 Ibid.
32 Uncredited. (1918, 2 February). A Queensland nurse's experiences. *Queensland Times*, 8. nla/119924831.
33 Murdoch, Keith. (1917, 4 September). Brilliant feats of airmen. *The Daily Mail*, 5. nla/215258835.
34 Uncredited (1931, 18 April). Death of Harold 'Pompey' Elliott. *Smith's Weekly*, 1. nla/234990370.
35 Gibbs, Philip. (1927, 5 December). Wounded souls. *The Telegraph*, 5. nla/180797919.

36 Powell, Alexander. (1915, 12 March). German atrocities. *Creswick Advertiser*, 1. nla/119521075.
37 Ibid.
38 Longmore, Cyril. (1921, 26 August). 44th Battalion. *The Australian*, 2. nla/210691641.
39 Ibid.
40 Longmore, Cyril. (1937, 30 September). Armentieres sector. *Western Mail*, 11. nla/38696994.
41 Ibid.
42 Monash, John. (1934, 1 December). I hate the business of war. *The Sun*, 8. nla/230162074.
43 Monash, John. (1934, 1 December). Monash War Letters. *Courier Mail*, 14. nla/35620391.
44 Monash, John. (1934, 1 December). Through the war with Monash. *The Herald*, 7. nla/243089500.
45 Ibid.
46 Monash, John. (1934, 29 December). Monash letter. *The Newcastle Sun*, 9. nla/166294800.
47 Williams, H.J. (1933, 23 October). *Sydney Mail*, 13. nla/165962221.
48 Uncredited. (1930, 25 September). A doubtful issue. *Western Mail*, 2. nla/38515220.
49 Johns, Thomas. (1918, 5 January). Impressions of France. *Bunbury Herald*, 3. nla/87169438.
50 Armitage, James. WW1 diary. Reprinted with permission from the Suranyi family.
51 Walker, Dallas Bradlaugh. (1918, 5 June). Soldier's letter. *MacLeay Chronicle*, 5. nla/174421708.
52 Parry, Walter. (1917, 2 March). Soldiers' letters. *The Geraldton Express*, 4. nla/214197945.
53 Pip, O. (1930, 11 January). Soldier of fate. *Smith's Weekly*, 20. nla/234424754.
54 Cogwheel. (1933, 18 March). Round and round. *Smith's Weekly*, 12. nla/235071299.
55 Toxites. (1936, 9 January). A digger's story. *Western Mail*, 2. nla/37772635.
56 North, Charlie. (1926, 16 March). By order. *The Inverell Times*, 7. nla/186061972.

57 Pat. (1935, 5 October). Steenwerck's popularity. *Smith's Weekly*, 16. nla/234618183.
58 Uncredited. (1918, 11 September). France bans alcoholic drinks. *Northern Star*, 7. nla/92944195.
59 J.G. (1935, 13 April). Madame Cognac. A remembrance. *Smith's Weekly*, 16. nla/234618496.
60 I.B. (1936, 23 July). Heavy bombardment. *Tweed Daily*, 7. nla/192426411.
61 Gibbs, Philip. (1918, 29 October). German retreat. *Kyneton Guardian*, 4. nla/129615224.
62 Williamson, John. (1939, 22 June). Hellfire Corner. *Western Mail*, 51. nla/38401433.
63 Ibid.
64 Morton, Henry. (1927, 4 November). Ypres revisited. *The Scone Advocate*, 3. nla/157648659.
65 Uncredited. (1923, 19 September). Polygon Wood. *The Sydney Morning Herald*, 8. nla/16094254.
66 Uncredited. (1919, 22 September). A Great Anniversary. *The Sydney Morning Herald*, 8. nla/15850245.
67 Brownie. (1936, 18 July). German chivalry. *Smith's Weekly*, 16. nla/235832119.
68 Stutley, Sydney James. (1917, 9 November). On the Road to Tipperary. *Australian Christian Commonwealth Magazine*, 13. nla/214065181.
69 Ibid.
70 Chesterton, Gilbert Keith. (1930, 30 August). One thing and another. *The West Australian*, 4. nla/33340342.
71 Longmore, Cyril. (1921, 7 October). 44th Battalion. *The Australian*, 2. nla/210693780.
72 Bencubbin. (1935, 29 August). To wear or not to wear. *Western Mail*, 55. nla/38940477.
73 B.B. Mount Magnet. (1933, 5 January). Nobby. *Western Mail*, 2. nla/37694128.
74 Longmore, Cyril. (1937, 21 October). Guy's Luck. *Western Mail*, 11. nla/38695248.
75 Murdoch, Keith. (1918, 12 December). 2nd A.C.C.S. Steenwerck. *The Herald*, 3. nla/242658052.

76 Murdoch, Keith. (1915, September). Letter to Andrew Fisher. *Australian War Memorial*. nla.ms-ms2823-2-1-s1-t.
77 Murdoch, Keith. (1918, 12 December). A Haven of Rest. *The Herald*, 3. nla/242658052.
78 Parker, Albert. (1918, 18 January). Letters from the Front. *West Wimmera Mail*, 4. nla/129404822.
79 Birdwood, William. (1919, 6 March). Mangrove's Brave Lads. *The Gosford Times*, 8. nla/167216072.
80 Parker, Albert. (1918, 11 January). Gone to His Reward. *Horsham Times*, 4. nla/725920868.
81 Clark, P. Ken. (1918, 2 March). On Anzac Ridge. *Mildura Cultivator*, 10. nla/74808021.
82 Uncredited. (1917, 6 July). Major-General Holmes. *The Sydney Morning Herald*, 7. nla/15752192.
83 United Service. (1917, 9 July). Col. Heritage's Tribute. *Daily Herald*, 5. nla/124854886.
84 Shearer, John Hugh.(1918, 2 April). Messines. *Brisbane Courier*, 7. nla/20219406.
85 Uncredited. (1918, 9 February). Front Line Theatricals. *Daily Telegraph*, 6. nla/239247186.
86 Sun Representative. (1917, 30 December). After the Battle, *The Sun*. nla/221403749.
87 Uncredited, (1917, 18 December). Field cinema shows in France. *The Register*, Adelaide 8. nla/58865134.
88 Carlisle, Rannall. (1918, 24 April). Anzac Coves performance. *Darling Downs Gazette*, 3. nla/171761041.
89 Troly-Curtin, Marthe. (1918, 22 June). The Art of the Anzacs. *The Argus*, 4. nla/1667725.
90 Uncredited. (1920, 9 April). Amusements. *Illawarra Mercury*, 2. nla/136374746.
91 Uncredited. (1923, 19 May). Bits and Bubbles. *The Daily Telegraph*, 22. nla/245814713.
92 M.G.S. (1916, 20 November). Yarns about soldiers, the Scotsman. *Daily Telegraph*, 7. nla/152740024.
93 M.G.S. (1917, 8 February). Nursing sister's report. *Cobram Courier*, 7. nla/130079749.

94   Armitage, James. WWI diary. Reprinted with permission from the Suranyi family.
95   Ibid.
96   Gibbs, Philip. (1918, 3 April). Old inns story. *The Daily Standard*, 6. nla/178834258.
97   Ibid.
98   Adamson, Bartlett. (1924, 20 December). Mademoiselle. *Smith's Weekly*, 20. nla/234433645.
99   Adamson, Bartlett. (1927, 13 November). Mademoiselle from Armentieres song. *Smith's Weekly*, 6. nla/235899001.
100 'Old Sweat'. (1937, 15 April). Songs from the war. *Listening Post*, 38. nla/257014798.
101 Adamson, Bartlett. (1933, 9 February). Snowy and the nurses. *Western Mail*, 2. nla/37696578.
102 Mattocks, Frank. (1917, 3 March). Cobbers. *Maitland Weekly Mercury*, 9. nla/128029979.
103 Ibid.
104 Ibid.
105 A.H.B. (1917, 19 December). Looking for a billet. *Daily News*, 9. nla/81816223.
106 Ibid.
107 Donovan, Herbert. (1919, 22 August). Imbibing Australian. *Weekly Judge*, 6. nla/257878813.
108 Shilling, Alan. (1918, 2 May). No mail for you. *South Western Times*, 3. nla/210426369.
109 Muir, Augustus. (1916, 19 February). Between two worlds. *The Evening Star*, 3. nla/209279400.
110 Ibid.
111 Ibid.
112 Ibid.
113 Gibbs, Philip. (1916, 23 December). Carols and cannons. *The Advertiser*, 5. nla/5547054.
114 Ibid.
115 Bodger, William. (1917, 23 April). Soldier's Christmas box. *Warrnambool Standard*, 2. nla/73927047.
116 St Clair, John. (1922, 25 December). Double Christmas. *The Register*, 11. nla/63750442.

117 Uncredited. (1920, 24 January). The 'Aussie' Corps. *Daily Telegraph*, 8. nla/239662581.
118 Ibid.
119 Ibid.
120 Jobson, Alexander. (1918, 9 June). Haig and Plumer. *The Sun*, 17. nla/221951506.
121 Ibid.
122 Uncredited. (1918, 8 March). From the war. *The Sydney Morning Herald*, 8. nla/15774066.
123 United Press Correspondent. (1918, 11 April). Ten Mile Battlefront. *Brisbane Courier*, 7. nla/20220973.
124 Uncredited. (1918, 13 April). Reuter's telegrams. *The Sun*, 1. nla/221935614.
125 Uncredited. (1918, 17 July). A Friend in France. *West Coast Recorder*, 3. nla/261152025.
126 Uncredited. (1918, 13 April). Definite crisis reached. War News, Reuter's. *The Sun*, 12. nla/221935614.
127 Ibid.
128 Ibid.
129 Ibid.
130 Ibid.
131 Uncredited. (1918, 12 April). The Way of the War. *The Daily News*, 4. nla/81764159.
132 War Office. (1918, 12 April). Casualty Clearing Stations. *The Sydney Morning Herald*, 7. nla/15782665.
133 Monash, John. (1934, 22 December). Through the War with Monash. *Daily News Weekend Magazine*, 19. nla/86022946.
134 Haig, Douglas. (1918, 13 April). A Definite Crisis. *The Sun*, 1. nla/221935614.
135 Jobson, Alexander. (1918, 20 April). The War. *West Echo*, 4. nla/188627893.
136 Haig, Douglas. (1918, 23 April). Enemy attacks beaten back. *The Scone Advocate*, 6. nla/156914859.
137 Jobson, Alexander. (1918, 21 June). Haig and Plumer. *The Inverell Times*, 3. nla/183604712.
138 Haig, Douglas. (1918, 15 April). To the last man. *The Sydney Morning Herald*, 7. nla/15772446.

139 Uncredited. (1918, 4 January.) Germany's Last Advance. *Barrier Miner*, 9. nla/45467413.
140 Ibid.
141 Armitage, James. WWI diary. Reprinted with permission from the Suranyi family.
142 Ibid.
143 Thurston, John. (1916, 4 November). Sausage Valley. *North-Eastern Advertiser*, 3. nla/51281410.
144 Armstrong, Millicent. (1918, 17 August). Amputated limbs. *Daily Mail*, 7. nla/215430991.
145 Uncredited. (1917, 18 December). Mackay Nurse in Queensland. *Daily Mercury*, 3. nla/173909402.
146 Handley, Perry. (1918, 17 October). Letter from France. *Northern Star*, 4. nla/92905518.
147 Armitage, James. WWI diary. Reprinted with permission from the Suranyi family.
148 Ibid.
149 Ibid.
150 Ibid.
151 Ibid.
152 McCarthy, Joanne. (1998, April). Silent Memories: That's not boredom. *Newcastle Herald*.
153 Armitage, James. WWI diary. Reprinted with permission from the Suranyi family.
154 Wallace, Allan Stuart. (1918, 29 November). Down the Roo de Kanga. *The Telegraph*, 7. nla/179040852.
155 Armitage, James. WWI diary. Reprinted with permission from the Suranyi family.
156 Ibid.
157 Neville, Dalton. (1922, 5 February). World's Super-Raider. *The Sun*, 13. nla/225214292.
158 Ibid.
159 Green, Herbert. (1919, 14 June). A Meditation at Zero Hour. *The Methodist*, 3. nla/155264766.
160 Monash, John. (1920, 4 February). Australian Victories in France. *Sydney Mail*. nla/159029036.
161 Uncredited. (1944, 8 August). Historic Zero Hour Order. *Daily Mercury*. nla/170345033.

162 Monash, John. (1920, 7 February). Australian Victories in France. *Townsville Daily Bulletin*, 5. nla/62755223.
163 Hampton, Meleah. (2020, 5 August). 8 August 1918: The Black Day of the German Army. *Australian War Memorial*. https://www.awm.gov.au/articles/blog/battle-amiens
164 O'Donnell, Thomas. (1922, 8 August). Australia's Greatest Feat of Arms. *The Advocate*, 4. nla/66726453.
165 McConnel, Kenneth. (1936, 13 June). Zero Hour on the Hamel Road. *Glen Innes Examiner*, 3. nla/178296125.
166 McConnel, Kenneth. (1936, 13 June). A Military Solomon. *Glen Innes Examiner*, 3. nla/178296125.
167 Ibid.
168 Whitcombe, Joseph. (1917, 5 January). Letters from Soldiers. *Ultima and Chillingollah Star*, 3. nla/130642251.
169 Paris Correspondent. (1915, 16 January). Pig in French Lines. *The Telegraph*, 9. nla/176151784.
170 McConnel, Kenneth. (1936, 13 June). Tales of Men and Horses. *Glen Innes Examiner*, 3. nla/178296125.
171 Armitage, James. WWI diary. Reprinted with permission from the Suranyi family.
172 Ibid.
173 McNicoll, David. (1944, 17 January). Epitaph for a Soldier. *Pt. Pirie Recorder*, 3. nla/96262184.
174 Armitage, James. WWI diary. Reprinted with permission from the Suranyi family.
175 Ibid.
176 Ibid.
177 Ibid.
178 Monash, John. (1934, 29 December). Letters from England. *The Newcastle Sun*, 8. nla/230155955.
179 Bell, Margaret. (1915, 2 December). Silence. *The Catholic Press*, 5. nla/115206070.
180 Ibid.
181 Bell, Margaret (1916, 10 February). In the Breadline. *The Catholic Press*, 4. nla/105162842.
182 Bell, Margaret, (1917, 3 March). A pitiful story. *The Journal Adelaide*, 1. nla/204691601.

183 Bell, Margaret, (1917, 7 February). Eventide in Flanders. *The Register Adelaide*, 9. nla/59901963.
184 Bell, Margaret (1917, 25 January) The Englishwoman. *Freeman's Journal*, 3. nla/116800482.
185 Bell, Margaret, (1918, 27 July). The nuns. *Bendigo Advisor*, 4. nla/90433958.
186 Bell, Margaret, (1919, 8 February). Silence. *The Journal Adelaide*, 14. nla/213255881.
187 The Digger. (1922, 16 April). Hidden Treasure. *The Sun*, 3. nla/223948773.
188 Ibid.
189 Armitage, James. WWI diary. Reprinted with permission from the Suranyi family.
190 Ibid.
191 3 Bar. (1932, 11 November). The devil's pyrotechnics. *The Telegraph*, 11. nla/179536335.
192 Uncredited. (1919, 19 June). Returned Officers. *The Sydney Morning Herald*, 7. nla/15842869.
193 Armitage, James. WWI diary. Reprinted with permission from the Suranyi family.
194 Ibid.
195 Uncredited. (1918, 2 November). War Horses: How they are trained. *Daily Mercury*, 6. nla/177697301.
196 Cocks, Nicholas John. (1926, 1 May). Eternity. *Queensland Figaro*, 5. nla/84897007.
197 Armitage, James. WWI diary. Reprinted with permission from the Suranyi family.
198 Cocks, Nicholas John. (1926, 1 May). Eternity. *Queensland Figaro*, 5. nla/84897007.
199 Morris, Lucy. (1923, 21 April). Always there are poppies. *The Daily Mail*, 9. nla/22056252.
200 Ibid.
201 Special Correspondent. (1921, 13 October). Vive Melbourne. *The Herald*, 16. nla/242640268.
202 Uncredited. (1922, 3 November). In Flanders Fields. *Armidale Express*, 4. nla/192029205.
203 Curlewis, Jean. (1919, April). Letters to her mother.

204 Ibid.
205 Davenport, Percival. (1918, 20 June). A Refugee's Sorrows. *Singleton Argus*, 2. nla/80713652.
206 Plouvier, Jeanne. (1918, 22 June). Safe But Heartbroken. *The Sydney Morning Herald*, 14. nla/15790403.
207 Uncredited. (1928, 28 February). Madame Louise Plouvier medal. *Catholic Advocate*, 26. nla/258696044.
208 Uncredited. (1918, 13 December). The Chateau. *The Urana Independent*, 6. nla/116177896.
209 Griffin, Gerald. (1916, 7 January). Time and Eternity. *Southern Cross*, 4. nla/166418601.
210 Monash, John. (1930, 25 April). Anzac Memorial Service. *Northern Territory Times*, 4. nla/4528550.
211 McCarthy, Joanne. (1999, April.) Silent Memories: That's not boredom. *Newcastle Herald*.

If you would like to find out more about Hachette Australia, our authors, upcoming events and new releases you can visit our website or our social media channels:

hachette.com.au
HachetteAustralia
HachetteAus